NON-TRADITIONAL SECURITY ISSUES IN NORTH KOREA

HAWAI'I STUDIES ON KOREA

WAYNE PATTERSON
The Ilse: First-Generation Korean Immigrants, 1903–1973

LINDA S. LEWIS
Laying Claim to the Memory of May: A Look Back at the 1980 Kwangju Uprising

MICHAEL FINCH
Min Yŏng-gwan: A Political Biography

MICHAEL J. SETH
Education Fever: Society, Politics, and the Pursuit of Schooling in South Korea

CHAN E. PARK
Voices from the Straw Mat: Toward and Ethnography of Korean Story Singing

ANDREI N. LANKOV
Crisis in North Korea: The Failure of De-Stalinization, 1956

HAHN MOON-SUK
And So Flows History

TIMOTHY R. TANGHERLINI AND SALLIE YEA, EDS.
Sitings: Critical Approaches to Korean Geography

ALEXANDER VOVIN
Koreo-Japonica: A Re-evaluation of a Common Genetic Origin

YUNG-HEE KIM
Questioning Minds: Short Stories of Modern Korean Women Writers

TATIANA GABROUSSENKO
Soldiers on the Cultural Front: Developments in the Early History of North Korean Literature and Literary Policy

KYUNG-AE PARK, ED.
Non-Traditional Security Issues in North Korea

HAWAIʻI STUDIES ON KOREA

Non-Traditional Security Issues in North Korea

KYUNG-AE PARK

University of Hawaiʻi Press, Honolulu
and
Center for Korean Studies, University of Hawaiʻi

Printed in the United States of America

15 14 13 12 11 10 6 5 4 3 2 1

Library of Congress Cataloging-in-Publication Data

Non-traditional security issues in North Korea / [edited by] Kyung-Ae Park.
pages cm. — (Hawai'i studies on Korea)
Many chapters are based on papers presented at the International Conference on Non-Traditional Security Issues in North Korea, held in Seoul, July 13–14, 2010.
Includes bibliographical references and index.
ISBN 978-0-8248-3739-6 (cloth : alk. paper)
1. Human security—Korea (North)—Congresses. 2. Korea (North)—Economic policy—Congresses. 3. Korea (North)—Social policy—Congresses. I. Park, Kyung-Ae, editor of compilation. II. University of Hawaii at Manoa. Center for Korean Studies. III. International Conference on Non-Traditional Security Issues in North Korea (2010 : Seoul, Korea). IV. Series: Hawaii studies on Korea.
JC599.K7N66 2013
355'.03305193—dc23
2012043129

The Center for Korean Studies was established in 1972 to coordinate and develop resources for the study of Korea at the University of Hawai'i. Reflecting the diversity of the academic disciplines represented by affiliated members of the university faculty, the Center seeks especially to promote interdisciplinary and intercultural studies. Hawai'i Studies on Korea, published jointly by the Center and the University of Hawai'i Press, offers a forum for research in the social sciences and humanities pertaining to Korea and its people.

University of Hawai'i Press books are printed on acid-free paper and meet the guidelines for permanence and durability of the Council on Library Resources.

Designed by Publishers' Design and Production Services, Inc.

Printed by Sheridan Books, Inc.

CONTENTS

PREFACE

The concept of security has undergone a significant change since the 1980s. Amid growing criticism of the realist security discourse, the concept has been increasingly enlarged to include agendas beyond the military dimension of interstate relations. Definitions of security and insecurity have been broadened to encompass the greater number of possible threats of the modern era and extended to include the larger number of agents in a globalized world. And yet despite the growing trend toward a more comprehensive concept of security, the vast majority of North Korean studies have continued to focus narrowly on the nuclear and missile issues and the traditional, state-centric security relations surrounding Pyongyang. This book is an effort to shift the focus of research and attention on North Korean security from traditional security issues to the largely unexplored area of non-traditional security issues.

This volume examines various non-traditional security issues in the Democratic People's Republic of Korea and the international community's efforts to promote a non-traditional, security–centered approach in dealing with North Korean security and insecurity. It brings together the work of leading North Korea experts, all of whom are longtime analysts of North Korea and experts on the issues at hand. Many of the contributors have enhanced this volume greatly with firsthand experience gained in visiting North Korea on multiple occasions. This carefully crafted collection of multinational perspectives sheds light on the most critical issues facing North Korea and threats to its non-traditional security. To my knowledge, no book-length study on North Korea's non-traditional security has been published; hence, the book is expected to make a significant contribution to the body of literature on the security of North Korea.

The volume begins with an examination of the complex and multifaceted connections between traditional and non-traditional security in the North Korean context, which serves to situate many of the volume's subsequent issues in a larger theoretical framework. Within this framework, the volume delves into some of the most pressing non-traditional security threats that North Korea faces today. Chapter 2 examines energy security, looking specifically at Pyongyang's "energy insecurity predicament." It analyzes how energy problems affect Pyongyang's economic sectors, often in complex and indirect ways, and addresses a number of challenges that the international community faces in designing measures to improve North Korea's energy security. Chapter 3 explicates the particular challenges facing the women of North Korea, focusing particularly on their economic and societal security. It explores the highly gendered impacts of threats to North Korean non-traditional security, such as forced migration, human trafficking, and sexual violence. Chapter 4 explores how transnational organized crime is securitized in the context of North Korea, analyzing many of the issues surrounding North Korea's reputation as a criminal state. It seeks to separate the facts about North Korean criminal behavior from the political biases that so often bring this type of assertion to the fore, thus providing an accurate picture of the issues at stake. The first part of the volume concludes with two perspectives on food security in North Korea. Chapter 5 looks at the internal dimensions of North Korean food security and insecurity, covering key elements of the agricultural sector, its relationship to industry, and the role of government policy in shaping the behavior of cooperative farms and farmworkers. It also proposes a scenario in which North Korea is able to achieve self-sufficiency in food production. Chapter 6 clarifies the complex nature of the external dimension of North Korean food security and insecurity in the famine and current postfamine eras. It examines the prospects for an improved food security through inflows of food, fertilizer, and fuel from outside.

Part 2 focuses directly on the various ways of potentially promoting the non-traditional security of North Korea. Chapter 7 looks at the post–Cold War concept of the "responsibility to protect" (RtoP) and its applicability to the North Korean context. It shows how the narrowly defined concept of RtoP excludes a range of human-security problems facing the North Korean people. Chapter 8 analyzes North Korean refugee issues through an international legal perspective, which seeks legal and political solutions to the plight of defectors from the country. It discusses the legal measures available to refugees under international laws related to human rights, humanitarian issues, and refugee protection. Chapter 9 examines the role of nongovernmental organizations (NGOs) in enhancing the non-traditional security of the North Korean people. It evaluates NGOs' contributions and scope of activities with special reference to the challenges that U.S. NGOs face in navigating their respective relationships with both the American and North Korean governments. The volume concludes by bringing the traditional versus non-traditional security debate back to the fore in consideration of the preceding, substantive issue-area examinations. As a whole, the book presents a significant body of work on an array of increasingly important non-traditional security threats as they apply to North Korea.

Earlier versions of many of the chapters in this volume were presented at the "International Conference on 'Non-Traditional Security Issues in North Korea,'" co-organized by the Centre for Korean Research at the University of British Columbia, the Institute for Far Eastern Studies at Kyungnam University, and the Friedrich Naumann Foundation for Liberty, Korea Office. I would like to acknowledge the financial support the Academy of Korean Studies provided for this conference. Thanks are due not only to the contributors whose work appears in this volume but also to all other conference participants for their contributions. I also express my deep gratitude to my research assistant Nick Anderson for his valuable assistance throughout the entire project, from conception to completion. I must finally thank all my colleagues who provided their constructive comments and advice, without which this volume would not have been possible.

Kyung-Ae Park

PART

I

Issues of Non-Traditional Security in North Korea

CHAPTER 1

Rethinking National and Human Security in North Korea via Non-Traditional Security Issues

JAE-JUNG SUH

Most discussion of North Korea (the Democratic People's Republic of Korea) focuses on traditional security issues. The Korean People's Army remains the target of obsessive analysis, for it is one of the most serious sources of threat to the peace and security of the neighboring countries. Its Special Forces receive special attention since they are deemed especially capable of wreaking havoc on South Korea's defense. Its weapons of mass destruction and missiles top news headlines and the lists of national security concerns in many capitals worldwide. Movements of tanks, airplanes, and ships are scrutinized for any clues to the military's tactics, strategy, or objectives. Reporters, scholars, and policy makers routinely produce reams of analyses of the North's military, defense budget, war-fighting capability, weapons systems, exercises, and so on. We are intensely focused on traditional security issues.

Though these issues matter a great deal to outsiders who can potentially suffer disastrous consequences, there is a host of non-traditional security (NTS) issues that have more immediate and graver impacts on the people in North Korea. And I argue, as do other contributors to this volume, that outsiders would do well to pay closer attention to these issues, for they can in turn impinge upon the North's security policies, with consequences for people outside the country.[1] Supplies of cooking fuel and foodstuffs, for example, are more pressing and more immediate issues for most in the North than weapons of mass destruction assembled in a remote military facility. But if Pyongyang chooses, in the face of high costs of petroleum and an unreliable supply of foreign natural gas, to develop a light-water reactor as a means to provide domestically produced energy, its choice raises nuclear safety issues that can potentially impact not only people in the immediate area adjacent to the reactor but also many more outside the country. Its choice is also accompanied by a traditional security concern: the fuel for the reactor can be enriched to weapons grade and used to manufacture and proliferate nuclear fission bombs.

How then do we study the NTS issues that leave their mark on traditional security issues? I submit human security may serve as a valuable concept that links national security to NTS.[2] Charles Tilly offers a promising place to start exploring their relationship, if his famous dictum—states make war and war makes the states[3]—is modified. War makes states only under the condition that the competitive pressures of war facilitate a state's efficiency enhancement; but war also breaks, or at least weakens, states to the extent that it drains resources and skews their allocation. War may improve the social positions and general welfare of traditionally disenfranchised groups such as minority groups and women, whereas war may also displace, maim, and of course kill a disproportionally large segment of marginal groups. Domestic cohesion and vigor may enhance the state's capacity and thus its incentive to wage war, but domestic instability and decay may also lead to a weakening of the state's ability to restrain certain societal elements from starting war. The relationship between national security and human security is complex. It represents a master switch that determines the nature of the effect that war making has on state making and the effect that state making has on war making. The complex nature of the relationship has not been fully appreciated, much less understood.

It would be helpful, as a first step in analyzing the relationship, to recognize that there is recursive causality between national insecurity and human insecurity. On the one hand, national insecurity may lead to human insecurity through a number of pathways. National insecurity can divert resources from human development. It can drain energy. It can create a permissive political circumstance where national security is privileged over human rights. Furthermore, it is likely to produce and perpetuate Manichean discourses that create what Agamben has called the state of exception, making the exceptional use of internal as well as external violence *by* the state a permanent feature *of* the state.[4] Fear on a national level percolates down to fear on an individual level.

On the other hand, human insecurity can exacerbate national security in a number of ways. Fear on an individual level, for example caused by violence by other individuals or even the state, may lead a group of victims to take refuge in a neighboring country, impacting its human security condition. Worse, those refugees may regroup, recruit, and rejuvenate to strengthen their capacity to undermine the security of those who forced them to flee.[5] Also, want on an individual level such as a lack of food or energy—especially if it is spread unevenly across the nation—may undermine national cohesion and weaken national strength, increasing national insecurity. Fear on an individual level may percolate up to fear on a national level.

Once the vicious cycle between national insecurity and human insecurity is recognized, therefore, it becomes at least plausible that one way to address human insecurity is to help the target state ameliorate its national security concerns. To seek freedom from fear is to provide for national security. Freedom from fear is integral to national security and vice versa, although one does not necessarily guarantee the other. One of the challenges for scholars and practitioners alike is to better understand the vicious cycle between national insecurity and human insecurity so as to explore the possibility of creating a virtuous cycle between human security and national security. Analyzing fear in North Korea on an individual and a national level, this chapter articulates the vicious cycle between national insecurity and human insecurity in order to better understand the recursive causality, the vicious cycle, between the two insecurities and to explore the possibility of transforming the vicious cycle into a virtuous cycle between human security and national security.

This chapter first explores the relationships between national security and human security and argues that there are four distinct types: secure state, safe society; secure state, unsafe society; insecure state, safe society; and insecure state, unsafe society. The second section focuses on one of the distinct types, insecure state, unsafe individual, in analyzing causal pathways that connect these two insecurities. I argue that a focus on NTS issues reveals at least some of these causal pathways. The chapter concludes by speculating about the possibility of transforming these causal pathways so that the insecure state and the insecure individual may escape the "state of nature" into the secure state, secure individual ensemble.

NATIONAL SECURITY AND HUMAN SECURITY

Do the new concepts of human security and NTS issues help develop, or detract from developing, a better understanding of North Korea and particularly its national security concerns? South Korea and the United States are concerned about the North primarily because it might wield its million-strong military equipped with conventional and nonconventional weapons systems to wreak havoc on the South and its allies. Although compassionate individuals have humanitarian concerns about the sufferings of the North Koreans and support humanitarian assistance to alleviate them, the governments of South Korea and the United States have their survival as their raison d'état and first and foremost responsibility. One might argue that it is only appropriate for them to focus on national security issues that might be threatened, and peace and stability undermined, by the North. Is it then that we are being negligent, or at least sidetracked, when we turn our attention to human security and NTS in North Korea?

My answer is an emphatic no. It is precisely because the prevailing theories and notions of national security fail to offer an adequate explanation of the national security threats posed by the North that we must turn our attention to human security and NTS issues. It is precisely because our exclusive focus on national security blinds us to effective causes of national insecurity that are rooted in human insecurity and NTS issues. It is only when we adequately understand the causes of North Korea's national insecurity that we will be better able to handle the threats posed by the North to our national security. And we can begin to understand the North's national insecurity when we see the causal pathways between its national insecurity and human insecurity that are embedded mostly in NTS issue areas.

How does an exclusive focus on national security blind us to the causes of national security threats? National security concerns, by necessity hierarchically ordered to give priority to issues that bear directly upon the survival or death of the state as a sovereign owner of the means of violence, can negatively impinge on the security of the general public and as a result backfire on national security itself. Because the top tier of the hierarchy is usually reserved for such concerns as what the military can do to protect the borders, how it can deter and defeat potential adversaries, and how political and military leadership can be preserved, concerns about the safety, welfare, and way of life of the people are relegated to a lower tier. Such relegation is not only unfortunate for the people who are likely to bear the brunt of war, especially in the modern age of industrial, total war, strategic bombing, and network-centric warfare, but can also undermine sovereign capacity and legitimacy from within, creating blowback on the national security that the hierarchy is designed to secure first.

It is well established that a strong state does not necessarily guarantee human security at an individual or societal level for two main reasons.[6] First, the state's strength in protecting its sovereign independence does not necessarily translate into an ability to deliver freedom from fear, because the military is too coarse a tool with which to mediate conflicting domestic groups or serve as a peacekeeping force. Soldiers are not usually as well trained to keep peace, much less to mediate, as they are to fight to defeat an adversary. Furthermore, if the state is party to the conflict, the military may even become a cause of human insecurity within the country, in which case the stronger military will simply be able to do more harm. The state may divert resources from civilian to military sectors in order to raise and maintain the military for national security purposes. Not only may a secure state fail to provide individuals with peace, but it can also in fact undermine peace and security within the country. The state's failure then tarnishes or diminishes, in the eyes of the general public, the legitimacy of the state's monopoly of the legitimate means of violence.

The second reason lies in the fact that the tools necessary for national security are different from, if not competitive with, those needed to free the general public from want. Soldiers and weapons systems are less adept at digging potatoes than at digging trenches, or growing wheat than greasing wheels. Worse still, soldiers take away the food that could otherwise be used to feed the general public, and weapons systems consume the resources that could otherwise be used to produce consumer goods. Not only is the military engaged in a zero-sum competition with nonmilitary sectors for scarce resources, popularly known as the guns-and-butter trade-off, but also it can mobilize its means of violence to forcefully extract resources from the public in what can be called state extortion. In short, the secure state can be a cause of human insecurity.

However, it is as well established that a secure state can make positive contributions to the general welfare of its population. The fundamental raison d'état is the provision of safety to its people: individuals come together under a great leviathan in order to escape the state of nature where life is solitary, poor, nasty, brutish, and short, as Hobbes noted.[7] The sovereign guarantees that even the weakest can expect to live without fearing the undue loss of life or property. A secure state is better able than an insecure one to provide social order, on the basis of which economies grow, individuals develop, and communities and societies prosper.[8] A secure state that has the capability to plan and execute a coherent economic strategy, furthermore, can even help grow the economy at a faster rate than can an insecure and incapable state, as the developmental state literature demonstrates.[9] All these characteristics of a secure state contribute to freeing its population from fear and want and thus enhance their human security. A secure state can be a positive force for a safe society.

If a secure state can lead to either a safe or unsafe individual, what makes the difference between the secure state, safe society and the secure state, unsafe society? I postulate that NTS issues serve as the causal pathways that distinguish one from the other. The degree to which a secure state helps provide food to its population, for example, is a good measure of whether the state will increase human security. Another causal pathway can be seen in the ways in which a state adopts security measures that systematically exclude a group on the basis of gender or ethnicity from its rightful benefits and singles it out as the primary bearer of the costs of those security measures.

A similar argument can be made about an insecure state: it can lead to either a safe or an unsafe society, depending on the causal pathways

TABLE 1.1 Four ideal types of national and human security

		National security	
		High	*Low*
Human security	*High*	Secure state, safe society	Insecure state, safe society
	Low	Secure state, unsafe society	Insecure state, unsafe society

of NTS issues. An insecure state can cause its population to feel unsafe if it is unable to protect the population from outside threats or if its inability to monopolize the legitimate means of violence allows individuals or groups to arm and threaten or harm others within the country. But even if a state is incapable of securing its borders against other states, its inability may be irrelevant to the people who are secure within their communities. The state's inability may even increase the security of a community that is at odds with the state. In short, the insecure state's relationship to human security is indeterminate.

In sum, I submit that there is no theoretical reason why national security and human security will be systematically correlated. Nor is there a priori reason why insecurity is directly related at the national and human levels. A secure state may be correlated with a safe or an unsafe society, and an insecure state with a safe or an unsafe society. The relationship between national security and human security thus can be categorized into the four ideal types shown in table 1.1.

I postulate that the indeterminate relationship between national security and human security can be usefully narrowed by focusing on NTS issues. The ways in which NTS issues can serve as the intervening variable that turns the secure state into either a safe society or an unsafe one are the subject of the following section.

NATIONAL AND HUMAN INSECURITY VIA NTS ISSUES

Of the four ideal types of national and human security, this section focuses on the insecure state, unsafe society as the type that illustrates the security challenges with which North Korea is faced. The country may project the image of a strong, secure state: a one-million strong military, nuclear weapons and missiles, and the military-first politics of Kim Jong Il—combined with risky provocations and harsh rhetoric such as turning Seoul into a "sea of fire"—create the image that the North is secure and perhaps even strong. But such a projected image—which well serves Pyongyang's purpose of deterrence while giving it leverage in diplomatic negotiations—does not stand up to the weight of facts. North Korea allocated 15.8 percent (68.4 billion North Korean won) of its 2007 national budget to defense.[10] Although the reliability of information released by Pyongyang is subject to dispute, it is estimated to be spending as much as a quarter of its gross national product on defense, with up to 20 percent of men ages seventeen to fifty-four in the regular armed forces.[11] Yet its 2008 gross domestic product (GDP) is comparable to South Korea's defense spending inasmuch as the size of its economy pales in comparison with that of South Korea.[12] In other words, the North cannot match the South in military spending unless Pyongyang allocates 100 percent of its productive activities to the military. The large size of its army, the high percentage of its defense in the government budget, and its tests of nuclear weapons are therefore all evidence of its weakness rather than its strength, because Pyongyang is turning to these measures in its desperate, and ultimately unsuccessful, effort to keep up with the South's superior military.[13] North Korea is an insecure state.

North Korea also manifests many signs of human insecurity. In the mid-1990s its population suffered from a severe shortage of food, and many—estimates still range from twenty-two thousand to over two million—died from it.[14] Although its food supply has since improved as the general economic conditions have improved over the years, there are groups of individuals—particularly women, the elderly, and orphans—who remain vulnerable to food shortages. Energy, whose supply took a nosedive in the 1990s, is scarce overall and unevenly distributed, a situation where the energy supply per capita borders on a minimal level for survival, and some areas fare far worse than others because of their geopolitical locations. People who leave North Korea for job opportunities, for example in China or South Korea, also are faced with multiple challenges, which undermine their human security. North Koreans are insecure.

Thus, if North Korea fits the ideal type of an insecure state, insecure individuals, how do we explain it? Is there a causal pathway that connects these two types of insecurity and that can explain why an insecure state may undermine human security or why human insecurity within a country may cause national insecurity? I argue that there is indeed a recursive causality between the two. Whereas there are many ways for the insecure state to exacerbate human insecurity and vice versa, my focus here is on how this might happen through threats to NTS issues such as the environment, public health, food, and energy. Following the United Nations Development Programme's contribution to the discussion of human security that identifies seven dimensions of human security—economic security, food security, health security, environmental security, personal security, community security, and political security—I concentrate on energy and food security to illustrate my argument about national security, human security, and NTS issues.[15] I also compare South and North Korea as a way to highlight the dilemma in any solution to these security issues.

Insecurity and Energy

South Korea and North Korea have adopted opposite approaches to providing energy to power their societies, with the former privileging energy security, and the latter energy sovereignty.[16] The South has integrated itself with the international energy market in order to secure a reliable and affordable supply of energy from overseas and has used part of the energy to produce goods for export. Its reliance on the international market for its energy security works so long as the cost of energy imports can be covered by the earnings from the exports, a strategy that is vulnerable to exogenous shocks, such as the oil shocks of the 1970s. The North has gone the opposite route of minimizing its reliance on the international market and maximizing domestic energy production as a way to maximize energy sovereignty. Its strategy can shield it from the vagaries of the international market, but its capacity for energy production is correlated directly to its internal economic vibrancy, a correlation whose upward mobility is constrained by the country's natural endowment and whose downward spiral can be triggered by a relatively minor slowdown anywhere in the chain of the integrated economy.

South Korea, recognizing that it has few adequate domestic energy sources to power its economy, has embraced the world market to build energy provision on the basis of imported materials and technologies. After decades of its energy import strategy, South Korea produces a relatively high 422.4 billion kilowatt-hours (kWh)[17] and has also built a national power grid and petroleum pipelines that maximize the economic efficiency of the energy so produced. According to U.S. Department of Energy statistics, it stands as the eleventh largest in terms of global total primary energy consumption.[18] But its needs are met by imports. It now imports almost all the petroleum, natural gas, and coal it consumes, and although it generates all the consumed electricity in country, its power plants rely on imported feedstocks, with renewable sources providing less than 2 percent. Because 96.4 percent of its energy supply depends on imports,[19] its energy sources and grids remain highly vulnerable to exogenous shocks such as market fluctuations and security threats. The South's energy security is contingent on the affordable, safe, and secure provision of energy imports, which is largely out of its own control.

The South's strategy of trading the sovereign control over energy for energy security without sovereign control is not without consequences for human security. Such a strategy exposes the individual to the many sources of volatility in the international market. Since South Korea is a price taker, the price it pays is subject to the caprices of the suppliers or larger consumers, and price hikes, which have nothing to do with the South's actions, can incur high costs on the individual whose life is now heavily dependent on energy consumption. The individual is also vulnerable to a disruption anywhere in the long supply chain that cannot be completely shielded from small-scale attacks. For example, an act of piracy against a tanker or a terrorist attack on a pipeline, no matter how far the attack may be from Korea, can have an immediate consequence on the individual's way of life.

Regarding North Korea, although it had, during the Cold War period, relied on the former Soviet Union and China to import critically needed resources, such as petroleum, at concessional rates, since the end of the Cold War it has highlighted energy sovereignty in its strategy by privileging domestic energy sources and minimizing its reliance on trade. Even at the height of the Cold War in the 1970s and 1980s,

Pyongyang's oil imports were far less than those of the South: North Korea imported 6.19 and 15.393 million barrels of crude oil in 1970 and 1980, respectively, whereas South Korea imported 69.15 and 182.861 million barrels, respectively, for the same years.[20] South Korea's crude oil imports have generally increased over the past three decades, reaching 864.872 million barrels by 2008, whereas North Korea reduced its imports to 3.878 million barrels in 2008.[21] In recent years, it has by necessity reduced its petroleum imports and instead increased its domestic energy production. In 2008, it was able to generate 255.0 billion kWh of electricity.[22] Its emphasis on energy sovereignty has led to an energy production and a power grid that are fragmented and decentralized. All these measures may maximize the North's energy sovereignty, but they minimize its energy efficiency at the national level, for the production cost per unit of energy is higher and the energy produced is not used at its optimal level. The more serious problem may be the structural constraints on the total amount of energy that the North can produce under its topographical and natural constraints, although it has sought to maximize its natural endowment by building small and medium-size hydroelectric generators throughout mountainous regions and even to surpass natural constraints by redirecting the flow of rivers to create new hydropower plants.

The most serious problem perhaps is the potential for a disastrous downward spiral inherent in an energy-sovereignty strategy that tightly integrates energy production with other sectors of the economy. This potential was demonstrated in the mid-1990s when floods damaged hydroelectricity production while increasing the demand for electricity by coal mines needing to pump water out from underground tunnels. The decrease of electricity production directly reduced the mines' production capacity, which in turn led to a drop in thermal-electricity generation, with wide repercussions throughout the economy. The reduction in electricity forced a brownout in manufacturing sectors, a slowing down of transportation systems, and a breakdown of agricultural production. The outcome was the near collapse of the entire economy.

The North has pursued an energy strategy that privileges sovereignty because of its concerns about national security, but its choice of energy sovereignty, ironically, undermines its national security. The sense of insecurity at the national level has, in other words, led

Pyongyang to adopt energy policies that ultimately contribute to the underproduction and inefficient use of energy. It relies on coal-fired generators that are less efficient than modern petroleum or gas-burning generators because it can depend only on its domestic supply of coal but not on petroleum or natural gas. It does not have a fully integrated national grid, much less a smart one, for it fears a national grid could be crippled by a single outside attack. Likewise it has not actively pursued connection with foreign national electricity supplies because it worries that an outsider's energy provision could become a weapon against it. All these choices have been driven by concerns about national security but have resulted in two counterproductive outcomes for its national security.

First, given that energy is critical to the functioning of industry and transportation, which in turn are responsible for the production of fertilizers, pesticides, and farming equipment, its underprovision has negatively affected the agricultural sector, undermining one critical dimension of human security: freedom from want. National insecurity has led to human insecurity. Human insecurity directly weakens national power. It also tarnishes the legitimacy of the regime.

Second, when Pyongyang started to seriously explore nuclear power as a way to address human as well as national insecurity, its desperate move directly challenged the national security of South Korea and other countries that have a stake in the region.[23] Its nuclear programs, even if they were limited to energy production, would nonetheless raise concerns about safety that go beyond its borders. The North's human insecurity led to a policy that may alleviate its internal problems at the cost of undermining the national security and safety of the surrounding countries. This provokes the affected countries to take, according to the security dilemma logic, countervailing measures, which in the end undermine the North's security.

Energy security and sovereignty represent the two distinct types of policy response to a country's needs, and neither is free of cost. Seoul's choice of energy security has deepened its dependence on the international market, making it susceptible to price fluctuations over which it has no control. Its choice facilitates, if not compels, a high consumption of energy, which contributes to the global problem of greenhouse-gas emissions. But Pyongyang's strategy of energy sovereignty has created complications for its provision of energy, resulting in the underprovision of energy. Its strategy has also led to its independent exploration of nuclear energy, which not only undermines the national security of its neighbors but also challenges the international nonproliferation regime.

Insecurity and Food

On food also South and North Korea have adopted opposite approaches. The South's choice is characterized by its emphasis on food security, whereas the North's strategy is characterized by an obsession with food sovereignty. Their choices are all the more peculiar because they have chosen against their natural endowments: the South has chosen to secure its food supplies in the international market although it is endowed with larger fields and a more hospitable climate for rice farming, whereas the North, with less arable land and a less-favorable climate, has taken the route of growing the food it needs. Their choices, as such, well illustrate the dilemmas of security and sovereignty in that each has ended up in an unsustainable food situation in its own unique way.

South Korea, as an ally of the United States, found itself on the side of a capitalist economy that facilitated its adoption of an export-led development strategy within which its comparative advantage privileged labor-intensive industry over agriculture. It has continually decreased its reliance on domestic production of agricultural goods, which have a lower comparative advantage in the international market, and now imports about 73.8 percent of its food from overseas.[24] Agriculture makes up less than 3 percent of its GDP and employs 7.1 percent of the total population.[25] Given the comparative advantages that South Korea's industrial products such as semiconductors, cell phones, and cars have in international markets, their exports bring in more than enough foreign capital to pay for food imports. This ensures food security for the Koreans in the South so long as the international market favors this kind of arrangement. But it also renders the South vulnerable to the whims of the international market that are beyond its control, as recent price hikes of food illustrate. South Korea's food security is susceptible to such exogenous shocks as a drought in Australia, a flood in Canada, a cold spell in Russia, a spike in the ethanol production in the United States, or population growth in India.

North Korea, in contrast, has emphasized sovereignty in its food policies. Though its ability to produce food is limited by geographical and climatic factors, it has chosen this course because of its deeply held anxiety of being subject to outside influences. Its choice has also almost been forced upon it by its geopolitical position: it is cut off from the South—its traditional source of food—and has suffered from Japanese colonial rule, war with the United States, and betrayal by China and the Soviet Union at one time or another. As a result of its policy choices, agricultural production in North Korea is around 21 percent of its GDP, yet an estimated 33 percent of its total population is still undernourished.[26]

The North's choice of food strategy reflects its profound sense of insecurity in the face of larger, more affluent, and militarily stronger neighbors. Given this disparity, its dependence on any one, or a combination, of them would make it not only sensitive but also vulnerable to the use or the threat of the use of their influence, potentially compromising Pyongyang's sovereign ability to provide for security. The insecure state has therefore embraced food sovereignty with zeal as a way to maximize its independence and security.

However, its choice of food self-sufficiency has proven disastrous for human security. Whereas the strategy succeeded in boosting agricultural productivity in the early decades, it began to show its limits in the 1980s when the growth rate of rice production slowed. When hit by the combination of the natural disasters of the 1990s and the collapse of the Soviet bloc that cut off petroleum and other inputs essential for agricultural production, the limits of food sovereignty exploded into massive starvation and famine.[27]

The resulting food insecurity in turn weakened the North's national security. The average height and weight of the North Korean population has fallen far below those of the South. The shorter, lighter, and weaker individual is less well suited to serve in the military, and it is possible that many in North Korea may not meet the physical requirements of the military. The stunted growth suffered by many infants and young children in the 1990s may leave long-term physical and mental effects, which will prove a drain on the North's national resources. The food insecurity has also diverted those who are in the military from engaging in military activities toward working on farms and in state infrastructure. Soldiers are known to be used for picking mushrooms in the mountains, catching crabs and fish in the sea, raising goats and rabbits, and digging potatoes in addition to planting and harvesting rice. Although such activities contribute to agricultural production, they detract the soldiers from their immediate task of providing for national security.

The North's food insecurity, furthermore, exacerbates security concerns among its neighboring countries. When the country was going through the worst of its food shortages in the late 1990s, not only did many of its population die of hunger but also many others left the country in pursuit of food, destabilizing communities in neighboring countries. It is of course those who leave the North who are exposed to the greatest direct challenges to their human security, but the host countries that receive them also have their difficulties. South Korea—which has about twenty thousand North Korean refugees residing there—has yet to figure out the best way to socially and economically integrate them, a problem that confronts China as well.[28] Seoul and Beijing are also concerned about a scenario in which a large number of North Koreans might suddenly cross the borders into their territories, which could strain their economies and social fabrics while creating national security problems. The South Korean and U.S. militaries, and China's as well, reportedly have contingency plans to deal with a sudden, large influx of North Koreans, although it is all but impossible to ascertain the existence of such plans.[29] The North's food insecurity, in short, can undermine the national security of its neighbors as well as its own.

I have argued that the North's national insecurity may lead to its human insecurity via such NTS issues as a lack of energy and food. A similar argument can be made about the other NTS issues—the environment, gender, and migration—that this volume addresses: policies that Pyongyang adopts in response to its perceived national insecurity can limit or diminish the provision of environmental sustainability or gender equality, and their underprovision weakens human security at the individual level. The resulting human insecurity in turn saps the North's national power and the regime's legitimacy. Not only does human insecurity in the end undermine the national insecurity that those policies seek to allay but it also creates problems for human and national security in neighboring nations.

CONCLUSION: TRANSFORMING AN INSECURITY DILEMMA INTO A SECURITY COMMUNITY

If there is a vicious cycle between national insecurity and human insecurity, as I have argued, is there a way to break it or even transform it into a virtuous cycle where national and human security improve each other? This volume pulls together thinking on how various NTS issues affect national and human security in North Korea and how these issues can be addressed in the context of an ongoing traditional security dilemma.

Pyongyang has in recent years sought to break the vicious cycle by resorting to what it calls *songun jeongchi* (military-first politics), which uses the military, the best organized and most ideologically committed, as a shock force for economic recovery.[30] In military-first politics, the military is mobilized as a corps of engineers to work on infrastructure projects and to construct power plants. The military "delivers services and goods to the people" in addition to providing security.[31] Soldiers are engaged in every aspect of farming, from tilling the earth to sowing seeds and harvesting crops. The military is also held up as a model that embodies the commitment to *juche* (self-reliance). Pyongyang seems to have successfully implemented the policy to stabilize society and to turn the economy around, although it remains to be seen if it can sustain the recovery.

Pyongyang has chosen to respond to the crisis of its sovereignty strategy by strengthening what was left of the strategy: the most ideologically committed and best disciplined—the military. Although its response has produced positive outcomes, especially when it was mediated by an emphasis on new technologies such as computer numerical control, it is not clear how much it can avoid the structural constraints of the sovereignty strategy that resulted in such disastrous outcomes in the 1990s. What is clear is that it will likely feel compelled to privilege a sovereignty strategy that gives priority to growing food and producing energy on its own so long as it feels insecure at the national level.

The chapters in this volume analyze various NTS issues in North Korea with a view toward addressing the tough nexus between national insecurity and human insecurity. I envision two possible paths out of the vicious insecurity dilemma. First, given the vicious cycle between national insecurity and human insecurity and Pyongyang's fixation on sovereignty as a way to address its national insecurity, one way to address the North's insecurity might be to start by allaying its national security concerns. Providing security assurances and creating institutional structures of peace may be an effective way to improve human security if it can be done in a way that increases energy and food security for the North Koreans. Second, given that the North's human insecurity undermines its own national security and ultimately that of neighboring countries, one way to increase their national security would be to help the North Koreans improve their living conditions. There is, of course, no guarantee that either path will succeed. One could also argue that a more effective strategy would be to create conditions under which Pyongyang can improve the country's human security even while holding on to its core sovereignty strategy.

This chapter only draws an intellectual framework that situates the debate in a larger theoretical context. It is hoped that the framework at least helps answer the initial question of why we bother with NTS issues. It is the chapters in this volume themselves that make substantive contributions to the debate by closely analyzing the ways in which NTS issues engage national and human security and by exploring causal pathways by which helping North Korea improve on these issues may lead to the allaying of national and human insecurity within and outside the country.

NOTES

I gratefully acknowledge the research assistance provided by Kah-ul Kim. This research was supported by the World Class University program through the National Research Foundation of Korea funded by the Ministry of Education, Science and Technology of the Republic of Korea (grant no. R32–20077).

1. For a discussion of NTS, see, for example, Mely Caballero-Anthony, Ralf Emmers, and Amitav Acharya, eds., *Non-traditional Security in Asia: Dilemmas in Securitisation* (Aldershot, UK: Ashgate, 2006).
2. The concept of human security was formally suggested first in a United Nations Development Programme report in 1994, UNDP, *Human Development Report 1994* (New York: Oxford University Press, 1994). For a

critical and historical discussion, see S. Neil MacFarlane and Yuen Foong Khong, *Human Security and the UN: A Critical History* (Bloomington: Indiana University Press, 2006).

3. Charles Tilly, "War Making and State Making as Organized Crime," in *Bringing the State Back In*, ed. Peter B. Evans, Dietrich Rueschemeyer, and Theda Skocpol, 169–192 (New York: Cambridge University Press, 1985).
4. Giorgio Agamben, *State of Exception* (Chicago: University of Chicago Press, 2005).
5. See, for example, Stephen John Stedman and Fred Tanner, *Refugee Manipulation: War, Politics, and the Abuse of Human Suffering* (Washington, DC: Brookings Institution, 2003), chap. 1.
6. UNDP, *Human Development Report 1994*; Mary Kaldor, *Human Security* (Cambridge: Polity, 2007).
7. Thomas Hobbes, "The State of Nature and the State of War," in *Conflict after the Cold War*, ed. Richard K. Betts, 47–50 (New York: Longman, 2002).
8. Douglass Cecil North, John Joseph Wallis, and Barry R. Weingast, *Violence and Social Orders: A Conceptual Framework for Interpreting Recorded Human History* (Cambridge: Cambridge University Press, 2009).
9. Alice H. Amsden, *Asia's Next Giant: South Korea and Late Industrialization* (New York: Oxford University Press, 1989); Meredith Woo-Cumings, ed., *The Developmental State* (Ithaca: Cornell University Press, 1999).
10. Ministry of Unification, *2007 nyeondo Bukhan gyeongje jonghabpyeongga* (2007 Review of North Korean Economy) (Seoul: Republic of Korea, Ministry of Unification, December 2007), 10.
11. Laicie Olson, "U.S. vs. Global Defense Spending," Center for Arms Control and Non-Proliferation, May 21, 2010, http://www.armscontrolcenter.org/policy/securityspending/articles/US_vs_Global/ (accessed June 23, 2010).
12. According to the latest survey by the Organisation for Economic Co-operation and Development (OECD), South Korea's economy is approximately thirty-eight times larger than that of North Korea and eighteen times larger on a per capita basis: North and South Korea's GDP in 2008 was estimated to be $24.7 billion and $928.7 billion, respectively. *OECD Economic Survey of Korea 2010*, vol. 2010/12, June 2010, http://www.oecd.org/document/24/0,3343,en_2649_33733_45393816_1_1_1_1,00.html (accessed June 23, 2010).
13. David C. Kang, "International Relations Theory and the Second Korean War," *International Studies Quarterly* 47, no. 3 (2003): 301–324; Jae-Jung Suh, "The Imbalance of Power, the Balance of Asymmetric Terror: Mutual

Assured Destruction (MAD) in Korea," in *The Future of US-Korean Relations: The Imbalance of Power*, ed. John Feffer, 64–80 (London: Routledge, 2006).

14. The low estimate is provided by Park Kyŏngsuk, "Bukhanui ingu: 1990 nyeondae kyeongjenan/kikungwa ingubyeondongui gwangye" (The Population of North Korea: The Effects of Economic Crises/Famines in the 1990s on Population Dynamics) (paper presented at the Institute for Peace and Unification Studies, Seoul National University, February 5, 2010). A "range of 600,000 to 1 million deaths" is the estimate from Stephan Haggard and Marcus Noland, *Famine in North Korea: Markets, Aid, and Reform* (New York: Columbia University Press, 2007), 11. An average North Korean death rate of 4.3 percent for 1995–1997 is the estimate in W. Courtland Robinson, Myung Ken Lee, Kenneth Hill, and Gilbert M. Burnham, "Mortality in North Korean Migrant Households: A Retrospective Study," *Lancet* 354, no. 9175: 291–295. A figure of 2.5 million deaths, extrapolated to the larger population, is the estimate found in Andrew S. Natsios, "Special Report: The Politics of Famine in North Korea" (Washington, DC: United States Institute of Peace, 1999), 8.
15. UNDP, *Human Development Report 1994*.
16. On the subject of energy and insecurity, see also chap. 2, this volume.
17. Bank of Korea, *Baljeonryang, Nambukhan jooyojipyo bigyo (chongryang)* (Electricity Output, Comparison of North and South Korean Major Indicators [Total]) (Seoul: Bank of Korea, Economic Statistics System, 2008), http://ecos.bok.or.kr/EIndex.jsp.
18. U.S. Energy Information Administration, "Korea, South: Energy Profile," http://www.eia.gov/cfapps/ipdbproject/iedindex3.cfm?tid=44&pid=44&aid=2&cid=all,&syid=2005&eyid=2009&unit=QBTU (accessed June 28, 2012).
19. Korea Energy Management Corporation, "Enŏji suibŭijondo" (Overseas Energy Dependence), 2008, http://www.kemco.or.kr/data/e_static/energy_chart/energy_static_view_main.asp (accessed June 23, 2010).
20. Korean Statistical Information Service, Statistics Korea, North Korea Statistics Portal, "Wonyoo doibryang mit jeongyunoongreok" (Crude Oil Import and Refining Capacity), http://kosis.kr/bukhan/bukhanStats/bukhanStats_01List.jsp?subId=101_101BUKHANB01_AA19# (accessed June 23, 2010).
21. Ibid.
22. Bank of Korea, *Baljeonryang*.
23. The North's nuclear programs are dual-purpose, although many in the West see them only as weapons programs.

24. Controversially, a substantial amount of the imported food is used as livestock feed, making South Korea's food imports for human caloric consumption around 49.2 percent. However, South Korea is unable to produce all the necessary livestock feed domestically for meat production and consumption, which also contributes to a nation's food security. Thus, including food imports for the purpose of livestock feed, South Korea's degree of food self-sufficiency is only 26.2 percent. Chun Hye-kyung, "Oisik saneobeeul noksaeksaneobeuro" (Turning the Eat-Out Industry into a Green Industry), *Weolgan siktang*, January 26, 2010; "Sikryangjageumnyul, heosooga manta" (There Are Many False Numbers in Food Self-Sufficiency Rates), interview with Lee Taeho, *Hwangyeong ilbo*, February 25, 2010.
25. Korean Statistical Information Service, *2009 nyeon nongeob mit eoeobjosa kyeolgwa* (2009 Report on Agriculture and Fishery) (March 9, 2010), http://kosis.kr/index/index.jsp; Ministry for Food, Agriculture, Forestry and Fisheries, *Nongrimeob saengsanaek mit saengsanjisoo* (Agriculture and Forestry Production and Indicators) (2009), http://www.mifaff.go.kr/main.jsp; Bank of Korea, *Gyeongje hwaldongbyeol GDP mit GNI* (GDP and GNI per Sector) (Korean Statistical Information Service, 2009), http://ecos.bok.or.kr/EIndex.jsp.
26. World Food Programme, "DPRK Facts & Figures," http://www.wfp.org/countries/korea-democratic-peoples-republic-dprk (accessed June 24, 2010).
27. Chong-Ae Yu, "The Rise and Demise of Industrial Agriculture in North Korea," *Journal of Korean Studies* 12, no. 1 (2007): 75–109; Stephan Haggard and Marcus Noland, *Hunger and Human Rights: The Politics of Famine in North Korea* (Washington, DC: U.S. Committee for Human Rights in North Korea 2005), 14.
28. Byung-Ho Chung, ed., *Welkeom too Koria—Bukchoseon saradeuleui Namhansari* (Welcome to Korea—North Korean People's South Korean Life) (Seoul: Hanyang University Press, 2006); Jih-Un Kim and Dong-Jin Jang, "Aliens among Brothers? The Status and Perception of North Korean Refugees in South Korea," *Asian Perspective* 31, no. 2 (2007): 5–22.
29. There have been reports that the U.S. and South Korean militaries have an operational plan to deal with an influx of North Korean refugees. See, for example, Jung Sung-ki, "U.S. to Remove N. Korean WMDs in Contingency," *Defense News*, November 5, 2009, 30.
30. Han S. Park, *Military-First Politics (Songun): Understanding Kim Jong-il's North Korea*, KEI Academic Paper Series 2, no. 7 (September 2007).
31. Ibid.

CHAPTER 2

North Korea's Energy Security

Challenges and Assistance Approaches

DAVID VON HIPPEL
AND PETER HAYES

Energy-sector needs and requirements for energy security together constitute a critical dimension of the North Korean nuclear weapons challenge. Energy-sector issues—specifically, the difficulties of the Democratic People's Republic of Korea (DPRK) in obtaining energy supplies and maintaining aging energy-supply infrastructure—have been a driver of its nuclear weapons policies. On the other side of the coin, addressing energy-sector needs in the DPRK has played, and will continue to play, a key role in working toward a solution of the DPRK nuclear weapons dilemma. Assuming—though it is hardly a given—that the current (as of this writing) crisis involving the sinking of the *Cheonan*, a naval ship belonging to the Republic of Korea (ROK), in the Korea West Sea is resolved without resorting to extensive armed conflict, the Six-Party Talks or a similar regional/international forum on the nuclear weapons program of the DPRK can be expected to eventually resume. At that point, as in past discussions on "denuclearization" of the DPRK, resolving the DPRK's energy-sector problems and ensuring, or at least making substantial steps toward, its energy security will be a critical component of the transformation of the DPRK economy to one that is compatible with peaceful relations with other nations, is not dependent on weapons exports or illicit activities to earn hard currency, and is self-sustaining.

The effective denuclearization of North Korea will require provision of energy assistance by the international community in a phased package that is carefully coordinated with milestones in the denuclearization process. These energy assistance options must be based on a realistic assessment of the needs and capabilities of the DPRK, noting economic and humanitarian conditions as well as political priorities in the country. In order to understand the DPRK's energy needs and capacity to use energy-sector assistance of different types, it is necessary to understand the DPRK's energy security situation and its impacts on its broader economy and society. In this chapter, we provide a summary of the DPRK's "energy insecurity" predicament, starting with a brief history of the DPRK's energy problems and continuing with a discussion of the impacts of a lack of energy security—broadly defined—on the DPRK economy and society. We note a number of key challenges in addressing DPRK energy-security issues and suggest assistance approaches that would help to start the process of improving the DPRK's energy security while addressing other key DPRK problems and international concerns. We conclude with a summary of what we see as the key lessons that the international community should take to heart in working with the DPRK to address its energy-security needs while improving the overall security of the region as a whole by dismantling the DPRK's nuclear weapons program.

HISTORY OF "ENERGY INSECURITY" IN THE DPRK

We provide here a brief introduction to the recent trends in and current status of the DPRK energy sector that have contributed to the lack of energy security and to the impacts and implications of this energy-security deficit—which we collectively call energy insecurity. Please see our more comprehensive reports on the topic for further background on the DPRK energy sector.[1]

The economic, if not social and political, landscape in the DPRK changed markedly during the 1990s. Although only very limited and fragmented data have been available from inside the DPRK itself, information from outside observers of the country indicates that the North

Korean economy was at best stagnating, and most probably in considerable decline, through the mid-1990s. This economic decline has been both a result and a cause of substantial changes in energy demand and supply in North Korea since 1990. Though anecdotal evidence suggests that the economy in some parts of the DPRK, particularly near Pyongyang, may have improved somewhat, albeit in selected sectors and in an up-and-down fashion, between about 2003 and today, it is not clear that the energy-supply situation has changed substantially for the better nationwide since 2000, even to this day, though some local improvements have occurred.

Among the key energy-sector changes on the supply side in the DPRK in the early 1990s was a vast drop in imports of fuels, mainly oil, from the Soviet Union and (after 1990) Russia. The DPRK has no, or at best very little, domestic crude-oil production,[2] so is reliant on imports. Though China continues to supply a largely steady five hundred thousand metric tons or so of crude oil per year to the remaining one of the DPRK's two major refineries that still operates, oil-import restrictions have reduced the availability of refined products in the DPRK. These restrictions arose primarily from North Korea's inability to pay for oil imports with hard currency. Though domestically produced coal has traditionally been, and remains, the DPRK's main source of energy to fuel household heating and cooking, industry, and power plants, the lack of petroleum fuels, particularly for the transport sector, has contributed to the DPRK's economic malaise since 1990. Also contributing to the decline in the country's economic fortunes has been the inability to obtain key spare parts for both energy infrastructure and factories, including factories built with foreign (often Soviet) technical assistance and technology in the 1970s (or earlier).

The other key changes (or continuing processes) in the energy sector since the mid-1990s include the following:

- Continuing degradation of *electricity-generation infrastructure* due to lack of spare parts, maintenance not performed, or use of aggressive (high-sulfur) fuels—including, reportedly, the heavy fuel oil supplied by the Korean Peninsula Energy Development Organization (KEDO) under the terms of the 1994 Agreed Framework—in boilers designed for low-sulfur coal.

- Continuing degradation of key *electricity transmission and distribution* infrastructure, resulting in much *reduced availability and quality of electricity* in most parts of the country away from Pyongyang, and, in the past few years or so, significant problems in Pyongyang as well.
- Continuing *degradation of industrial facilities* in general and damage to industrial electric motors from poor-quality electricity. Lack of markets (since the breakup of the USSR) for DPRK industrial goods has reduced fuel demand in those factories that actually remain operable. In our visits to the DPRK, we have observed factories being dismantled for scrap and others that appeared to be largely idle (though we visited only a few areas).
- Evidence of significant international trade in magnesite (or magnesia—a valuable mineral used for lining furnaces) and, more recently, in coal and iron ore (trade with China) and other minerals.
- Continuing difficulties with *transport of all goods, especially coal,* and reduced availability of passenger transport.
- Difficulties in *coal production* related to lack of electricity as well as mine flooding (in the Anju and other regions) and lack of production and safety equipment.
- Some *economic revival* has been noted periodically since 2000, but mostly, it seems, associated with foreign aid, small markets and restaurants, small export-oriented industrial facilities, trade in raw materials with China, or in other areas of the economy that are generally not energy intensive.

Figure 2.1 compares estimated final energy demand by sector (*top*) and by fuel (*bottom*) for the years 1990, 1996, 2000, 2005, and 2008.[3] In addition to the marked decrease in overall energy consumption between 1990 and 2000, there are two notable features of these comparisons. The first is that, compared with 1990, the residential sector in recent years has been using a larger share of the overall energy budget, whereas the industrial-sector share has shrunk to one-third of the total. This change is the combined result of continued reduction in fuel demand in the industrial sector, relatively constant (if not expanded) use of wood and other biomass fuels in the residential sector, and reductions in the use of other residential fuels (notably coal and electricity) that are

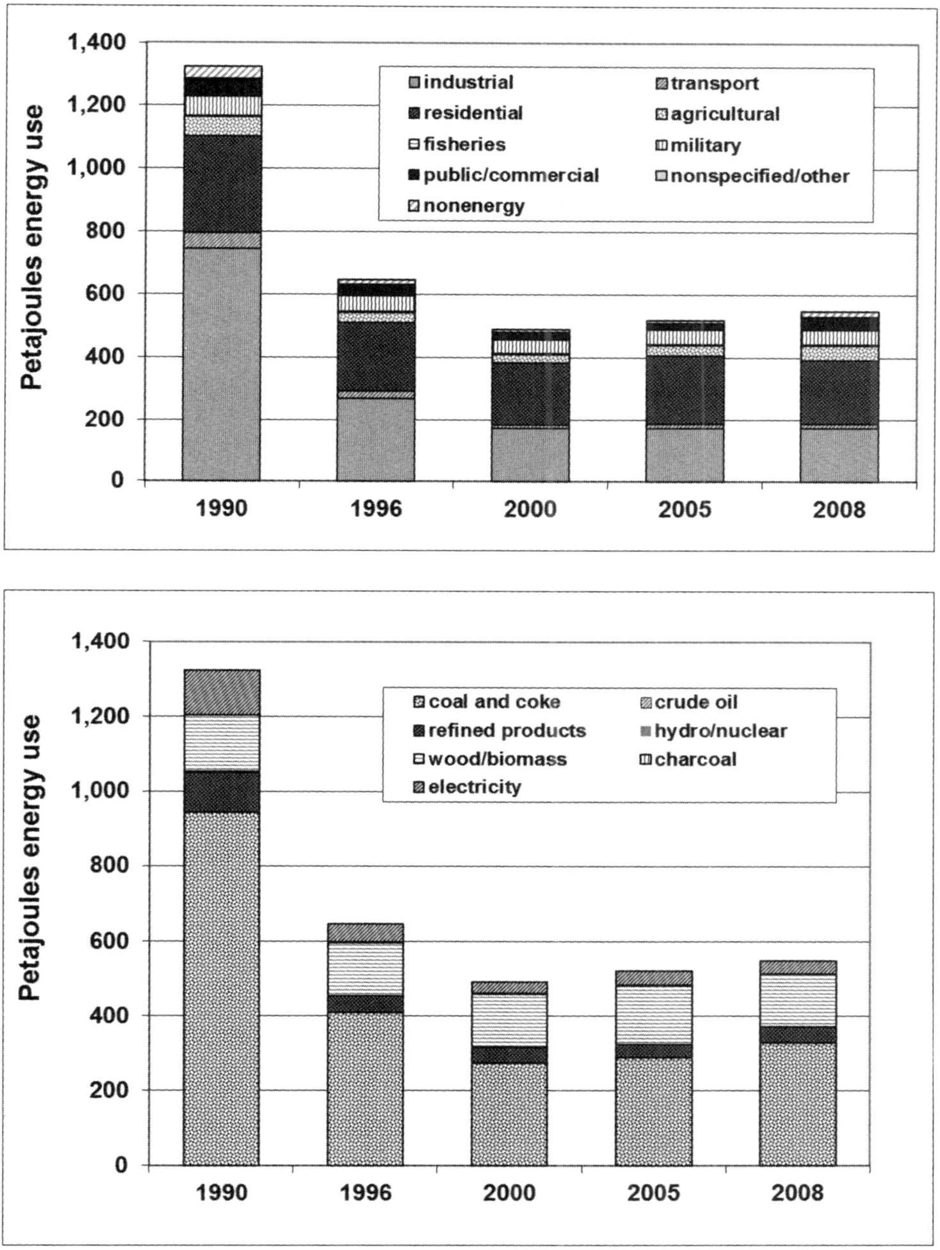

FIGURE 2.1. Estimated energy demand by sector and fuel in the DPRK, 1990, 1996, 2000, 2005, and 2008.

not as severe as the reductions experienced in the industrial sector. Second, and for similar reasons, the importance of wood/biomass fuels to the energy budget as a whole is estimated to have increased dramatically over the course of the 1990s, persisting through the first decade of the twenty-first century, while the importance of commercial fuels has decreased. Increased use of wood and other stresses have resulted in significant deforestation and degradation of forest lands in the DPRK.

Lack of fuels in many sectors of the DPRK economy has caused demand for energy services to go unmet. When and if supply constraints are removed, there is likely to be a surge in energy (probably particularly electricity) use, as residents, industries, and other consumers of fuels increase their use of energy services toward desired levels, though the magnitude of such a surge will depend on the DPRK's developing the economy to pay for fuel supplies.

The DPRK electricity sector is often a focus of interest, for both the impact that the sector has on the economy of the DPRK and on the daily lives of its citizens, and because the status of the electricity sector had (and may again have) important political implications related to the former KEDO Light Water Reactor (LWR) Project and to electricity grid interconnection options.[4] Analysis of the current status of the DPRK electricity sector suggests that the thermal power generation system in the DPRK has been eroding significantly. In virtually all the large power stations, only selected boilers and turbines are operating, and those that are still in use operate mostly at low efficiency and low capacity factors[5] due to maintenance problems and lack of fuel. As a consequence of the difficulties with thermal power plants, hydroelectric plants have shouldered the burden of power generation in the DPRK. Hydroelectric output is limited by maintenance problems and, equally important, the seasonal nature of river flows in the DPRK, but construction of hydroelectric plants of various sizes—small plants for local areas and plants up to a few hundred megawatts for regional grids—is a recent focus of DPRK energy policies.

The total estimated supply of electricity decreased substantially between 1990 (46 terawatt-hours, or TWh)[6] and 1996 (23 TWh) and fell still further (by our estimate) by 2000 (to 13 TWh) before increasing somewhat to an estimated 16.6 TWh in 2005. We are still completing an analysis of electricity generation in the DPRK in recent years but thus far have no reason to think that the output of the sector was significantly different nationwide in, for example, 2008 than in 2005.

IMPACTS OF ENERGY INSECURITY ON THE DPRK

Working with colleagues in Northeast Asia, Nautilus has adopted a definition of "energy security" that goes beyond the traditional fuel supply/fuel cost focus to include elements of energy supply, economics and economic impacts, environmental impacts and environmental security, technological security, social and political security, and military security.[7] In the case of the DPRK, the past two decades have seen a profound erosion of energy security in both the narrow and broad senses, with significant impacts on the DPRK's economy, society, and environment. A few examples of these impacts include the following:

- Lack of consistent supplies of coal and electricity for *industry* have idled many, perhaps most of the DPRK's industrial capacity, leaving the former workers at those largely state-owned facilities also idled, though they may nominally continue to hold their jobs. The relationship between energy supplies and the industrial sector in the DPRK is complicated, however, because when the Soviet Union was dissolved in 1990, the DPRK lost not only its major supplier of crude oil and parts for its (in many cases Soviet-built) power plants and factories but also the markets for the bulk of the goods that its factories were designed to produce. It is thus difficult to fully understand what fraction of the decline of the DPRK industrial sector is due to a lack of energy and which part is due to a lack of markets, though presumably with sufficient energy supplies, coupled with funds for investment in new capital equipment (and access to international markets to purchase equipment), DPRK factories would be able to retool to provide goods needed at home and in markets abroad.
- Lack of energy for *transport*, including gasoline and diesel fuel for trucks, buses, and cars, and electricity for trains and trams, exacerbated by energy-related problems with obtaining spare parts for

vehicles and transport systems, has decreased the amount of passenger and freight transport available. This in turn has affected a number of other sectors, including agriculture, and electricity generation, since, with the exception of a few large power plants that are located next to coal mines, the lack of energy for transportation systems keeps coal from being distributed to power and central-heating plants. In particular, the lack of transportation fuels means that in many areas, particularly away from cities, most North Koreans are obliged to walk, ride bicycles, or use animal carts to get where they are going and transport goods, or to hitch rides on (mostly military) trucks when they can. Apart from the burden to individuals, the lack of sufficient passenger transport in most areas means that time that people could be spending on productive activities is spent in getting from place to place. This mostly human-powered transport also uses calories in a country where food shortages have been frequent in recent years.

- In the *agriculture* sector the lack of commercial fuels—specifically electricity and diesel fuel—increases the requirement for human and (where available) animal labor to plow fields, cultivate, weed, harvest, and transport crops. This has, in part, resulted in the use of urban workers to help in agricultural activities. It is entirely possible (though we have not confirmed this) that lack of fuel for key end uses such as land preparation and planting have reduced crop yields, but a number of sources have indicated that lack of energy and equipment for proper and timely postharvest processing (threshing, drying, and cleaning of rice, for example) have caused crop losses on the order of 15 percent, with additional losses of up to 5 percent from crops harvested too early.[8] In addition, and as further evidence of the many ways in which energy shortages in one sector of the DPRK economy affect other sectors, lack of energy in the industrial sector has resulted in shortages of fertilizer, which have further depressed crop yields, and in shortages of spare parts for domestically produced agricultural equipment, further reducing the availability of motive power for agriculture. The lack of availability of electricity for water pumping for irrigation, including flooding of rice fields, was previously a serious problem but has become somewhat less of an issue in several growing areas of the DPRK as a result of the recent completion of major irrigation canals providing water by gravity flow. The first of these, the Kaechon–Taesong Lake irrigation canal, was completed in 2002 and provides water to one hundred thousand hectares of land along the western coast of the DPRK.[9] Another key factor inhibiting agricultural production in many areas is soil erosion caused by deforestation, which itself has been the result largely of the use of wood and other biomass in recent years in homes as substitutes for other fuels.

- *Residences* and even, in some areas, *military units* suffer from lack of commercial fuel, largely coal, for cooking and heating of living space. The result—again varying in severity by region—has been increased use of wood and other biomass fuels, which have in many areas been harvested beyond the levels of sustainable yields as well as on slopes, where the result has been significant erosion, often with potentially long-term effects on soil fertility. In cities, lack of fuel for central heating plants and/or lack of spare parts for those plants result in reduced or no provision of heat to apartment blocks, leaving those residences without heat or with small amounts of other fuels when available—kerosene, coal, or biomass, for example—to make up for the lack of heat from central heating plants. Lack of heat in winter combined with often inadequate diets makes residents more susceptible to disease and less productive when they are able to work. *Office buildings*, even in Pyongyang, are reported by visitors to be often barely heated during the winter, exacerbating productivity problems. Lack of electricity—outages range from occasional in places like Pyongyang to chronic in more isolated areas—means that residents must either do without light or use poor substitutes, such as lamps (in our experience, sometimes makeshift) burning diesel fuel or battery-powered lanterns. Lack of light makes it difficult or impossible for students to study and also affects other educational, social, and productive activities.

Beyond these direct or interrelated impacts—on the economy, the environment, and human health and well-being—of the lack of access to fuels, there are indirect, political impacts. Lack of domestic oil and shortages of other fuels, coupled with limited opportunities to earn the hard currencies needed to pay for imported fuel, are arguably one factor in the DPRK's use of sales or barter of weapons, as well as other, sometimes illicit, activities, to earn hard currency. Imports of significant amounts of crude oil to the DPRK from Libya and Iran in the early 1990s, for example, were thought to have been as a result of sales or barter of weapons, including missiles, to those countries. Shortages of energy are also part of why the DPRK uses the threat of military action to try to induce the international community to meet its demands. Lacking the fuels to run a modern economy, it has few other options.

We would also argue that the DPRK's lack of energy security has a keen impact on the DPRK's military security and thus that of its neighbors as well. It needs to be remembered that with about 5 percent of its populace in the armed forces and perhaps a quarter of its residents in the armed forces reserves, the military plays a huge role in the DPRK economy. As such, when the economy itself is short of fuel, the military is as well. Though military-related manufacturing probably gets preferential access to what fuels are available, it seems certain that it suffers from some of the same energy shortages that affect the broader economy as well as a similar lack of, for example, spare parts for industrial infrastructure.

Another military-security consideration affected by national energy security is related to fuel supply to the military in the event of a large-scale conflict on the Korean Peninsula. Several years ago, we carried out an admittedly rough calculation that suggested that it would take about three months of DPRK refinery output, at current levels, to resupply the gasoline and diesel fuel that the military would use in the first month of an active conflict. By the end of the first month of conflict, it would take about two months of total refinery production plus imports (assuming current levels of production and imports, which is hardly a given in a conflict scenario) of gasoline and diesel to operate the DPRK's remaining (i.e., those not yet destroyed in the conflict) military vehicles and armaments for one month. Though this calculation includes several simplifying assumptions, each with significant to considerable degrees of uncertainty, the essential finding is that the DPRK military would quickly—in a matter of weeks or certainly months—run short of fuel in any major armed conflict. This in turn implies that the DPRK must depend on strategies other than prolonged conflict to prevail. The "other strategies" that seem, given current circumstances, to be implied are either overwhelming first-strike capability in conventional or nuclear weapons or the use of its own "nuclear umbrella" to support deterrence of attack or coercive use of force by adversaries. This further underlines the need to address the DPRK's energy insecurity as a necessary, though not sufficient, condition for addressing the DPRK nuclear weapons issues that have had such a profound effect on military security in Northeast Asia.

CHALLENGES IN IMPROVING DPRK ENERGY SECURITY

Improving the DPRK's energy security is clearly a requirement of improving the security situation on the Korean Peninsula and in the region as a whole. Measures designed to improve the DPRK's energy security, however, including measures undertaken with assistance from groups in other nations, will and do face an array of challenges that must be fully appreciated and reflected in assistance plans. These challenges range from technical challenges related to DPRK infrastructure to institutional challenges related to the structure of the energy sector in the DPRK, to challenges related to lack of human capacity. A sampling (but hardly a complete list) of key challenges that assistance activities must address is provided below.

Problems with the DPRK economy's *physical infrastructure*, and most notably its energy infrastructure, pose a challenge to getting energy assistance under way. Much of the energy-using infrastructure in the DPRK is reportedly antiquated and poorly maintained, including heating systems (including district heating systems) in residential and other buildings. Industrial, power supply, and other facilities are likewise aging and based on outdated technology and often (particularly in recent years) are operated at less-than-optimal capacities (from an energy-efficiency point of view). The North Korean electricity system, though it is nominally a nationwide transmission and distribution grid, is in effect a patchwork of a few regional and some local grids, centered around major and smaller power plants. Most of the large thermal (almost all coal fired) power plants are only partially in operation due to damage of various kinds to one or more generating units and/or to transformers, substations, or other parts of the transmission and distribution system. This means that even if large amounts of fuel for power plants or supplies of electricity from outside the country[10] were suddenly to be available to the DPRK, distribution of that energy would be problematic.

The combination of erosion in its energy system and industrial infrastructure and similar erosion in its transport infrastructure in many areas and lack of investment capital means that the DPRK will not be able to reconstitute, or, perhaps more accurately, redevelop, its energy system and economy in general without outside help. Rebuilding power plants—most of which, remember, were built with major components imported from the USSR or elsewhere—could not be done, at least for many years, using materials "made from scratch" in the DPRK because the industrial infrastructure to make the required power-plant components either is no longer operating or, in fact, was never present in the DPRK. Similarly, decades of relative isolation have left the DPRK substantially without the capabilities in modern metallurgy, electronics, and other fields that would allow it to develop new industries. This means that the DPRK cannot redevelop its infrastructure sufficiently to develop a sustainable, peaceful economy without outside help.

There is a *suppressed and latent demand for energy services* in the DPRK economy. Lack of fuels in many sectors of the DPRK economy has apparently caused demand for energy services—lighting, heating, and transportation of people and goods among them—to go unmet. When and if supply constraints are removed, there is likely to be a surge in energy (probably particularly electricity) use, as residents, industries, and other consumers of fuels increase their use of energy services toward desired levels. This means that as energy infrastructure is established or rebuilt, it will need to accommodate or otherwise manage this surge in demand. In addition, key energy-sector measures such as energy-efficiency improvements—sorely needed in virtually all sectors of the DPRK economy—will not appear as effective as anticipated because a significant portion of the energy saved will be absorbed by previously latent demand.

The DPRK *substantially lacks markets for energy products*. Compounding the risk of a surge in the use of energy services is the virtual lack of energy-product markets in the DPRK. With a few small exceptions, most electricity is provided to residents and organizations for a flat monthly fee per connection, if it is priced at all. Other fuels are more typically allocated to end users rather than sold in markets. Although markets for some goods and services have started to develop, sometimes haltingly, in the DPRK in recent years, input factors for goods, including energy goods, are still not priced at market levels, which makes determining market prices that will cover costs of production difficult. Without fuel-pricing reforms, there will be few incentives for households and other energy users to adopt energy-efficiency measures or otherwise control their fuel consumption, and no guarantee that electricity generators, coal mines, and other fuel suppliers will recover through energy sales sufficient funds to cover their costs of production, let alone to reinvest in further supply expansions or other upgrades. The lack of a rational pricing system also deters outside lenders and investors from supporting energy-sector improvements because there is no guarantee that, for example, electricity generators will be able to recover their costs, including costs of financing infrastructure investments, from consumers. Anecdotal indications are that some pricing reforms are under way in the DPRK economy, including, for example, some experiments with card-based metering systems in the Pyongyang area, but it is not yet clear (to us) to what extent pricing reforms have been broadly implemented in the energy sector.

A lack of *human capacity* in many fields in the DPRK will need to be overcome to implement most types of measures to improve the DPRK's energy security. DPRK citizens generally have a strong basic education in reading, writing, math, and science and are among the hardest working, most disciplined people on the planet. In working directly with North Koreans, we have found our colleagues to have good fundamental engineering skills and to be quick and eager to learn. Decades of relative isolation, however, have made human capacity scarce in the DPRK in such fields as advanced science and engineering (particularly with respect to the use of modern tools and analytical methods), economics and finance, regulation, and policy development. Lack of expertise and understanding in these and related areas among DPRK engineers, technicians, and officials will therefore constrain, at least until capacity-building programs bear fruit, the rate at which measures to improve energy security can be implemented

An institutional lack of *capacity to usefully absorb aid*, including energy aid, is also an important challenge to be overcome as the DPRK energy system and economy are rebuilt. At present, the DPRK's political structure is set up such that a limited number of DPRK officials can come into contact with foreigners. These limits on interactions with the outside world currently constrain the number of projects that the DPRK can be involved with at any given time. In addition, the compartmentalization of the DPRK's dealings with foreigners means that it is often difficult for foreigners working on projects with the DPRK to contact and be allowed to work freely with the right people in the DPRK. For example, the political officers controlling a cooperation project may limit foreigners' access to the technical people in the DPRK with the knowledge and expertise who could help design a new energy system that would work with existing DPRK infrastructure. Even when the right people to work with can be identified and are made available, decisions on how to proceed may be made as much on political grounds as with regard to practical considerations, sometimes with suboptimal results in terms of project impacts. Finally, an existing culture where graft and patronage are commonplace means that it is highly likely that providing too much aid too soon—particularly in the form of very large projects with necessarily complex management structures—will result in inefficient use of resources and, at worst, failure of the projects altogether.

Taken together, these constraints on the capacity to absorb aid and the other, generic challenges to energy projects in the DPRK drive our advice to focus, especially in the first years of energy-sector assistance, on small, fast, cheap, and local energy projects with significant demonstration value. This aid approach is reflected in the list of areas for assistance and assistance-phasing suggestions provided below.

ASSISTANCE APPROACHES TO IMPROVE DPRK ENERGY SECURITY

Agreements reached in 2005 and 2007 under the Six-Party Talks framework addressing the DPRK's nuclear weapons programs included general consideration of options by which the international community could assist the DPRK in improving its energy security. In the short run, however, these agreements resulted primarily in the provision of heavy fuel oil, a fuel of limited utility (though also of limited military diversion potential) to the DPRK, plus some provision of requested materials for repairs to energy infrastructure. Although these actions provided a start on engagement with the DPRK on energy-security issues, much more is needed. Assistance options need to be informed by consideration of the DPRK's energy problems, economic needs, and constraints in making use of assistance, as well as the resources that the DPRK would bring to assistance programs.

Key economic resources for the DPRK include a large, well-trained, disciplined, and eager workforce, an effective system for disseminating technologies, the ability to rapidly mount massive public works projects (or, in fact, any project, large or small, requiring hands and shovels) by mobilizing military and other labor, and extensive reserves of minerals. What the DPRK lacks is modern tools and manufacturing methods, adequate supplies of fuel, reliable transport and energy infrastructure, sufficient arable land to reliably feed its populace, and above all investment capital to enable the import and/or manufacture and development of tools, equipment, materials, and know-how to fill these key gaps. As a consequence, a coordinated program of assistance from the international community that builds upon these attributes will be needed. Providing key assistance in a timely manner will enhance security in Northeast Asia, accelerate (or, given recent events, help to reestablish) the process of North Korean rapprochement with its neighbors, and help to position countries and firms as major suppliers for the DPRK rebuilding process.

The nature of the DPRK's energy-sector problems, however, means that an approach that focuses on one or several massive projects—such as a single large power plant—will not work.[11] A multipronged approach on a number of fronts is required, with a large suite of coordinated, smaller, incremental projects addressing needs in a variety of areas. Below we identify priority areas where we see DPRK energy-sector assistance as both necessary and in the best interests of all parties. These energy-sector initiatives will assist the process of rapprochement with the DPRK, help the DPRK to get its economy and energy sector working in a sustainable (and peaceful) manner, and help pave the way for additional cooperative activities in the energy sector. In addition, all these interventions would put foreign engineers and other program staff in direct contact with their DPRK counterparts and with DPRK energy end users. In general, these initiatives can be thought of as projects that could be part of an overall program to provide incentives for and spur a DPRK denuclearization process (i.e., freezing of the DPRK's nuclear weapons program, followed eventually by dismantling of the program and, ultimately, removal of nuclear weapons and related materials from the Korean Peninsula). In some cases, however, these initiatives could be started unilaterally, though perhaps in limited ways, by foreign governmental or nongovernmental organizations working with DPRK counterparts.

- *Assistance for internal policy and legal reforms to stimulate and sustain energy-sector rebuilding in the DPRK.* This could include reform of energy-pricing practices, development of energy markets and the physical infrastructure to implement both, capacity building for careful energy planning to allow aid to be based on need and rational objectives, training for energy-sector actors, strengthening regulatory agencies and educational and research institutions in the DPRK, and involving the private sector in investments and technology transfer.
- *Work to open opportunities for private companies to work in the DPRK.* Grants or loans from foreign governments cannot begin to fill the needs for energy infrastructure in the DPRK, but the U.S., ROK, European, and other governments can help to facilitate the efforts of private companies (including independent power producers) from abroad in the DPRK energy sector. One key, in the medium and longer term, to facilitating the involvement of private companies is to, as just noted, provide assistance for policy and legal reforms in the DPRK needed to make it possible, or at least more straightforward, for private companies to work there.
- *Rebuilding of the electricity transmission and distribution (T&D) system.* The need for refurbishment or rebuilding of the DPRK T&D system has been touched upon earlier in this chapter as a key challenge. The most cost-effective approach for international and ROK assistance in this area will be to start by working with DPRK engineers to identify and prioritize a list of T&D-sector improvements

and investments and to provide limited funding for pilot installations in a limited area—perhaps in the area of a special economic zone or in a "demonstration" county.

- *Rehabilitation of power plants and other coal-using infrastructure.* An initial focus should be on improvements in small, medium, and district heating boilers for humanitarian end uses such as residential heating, as well as in small institutional settings such as schools and hospitals.
- *Rehabilitation of coal supply and coal transport systems.* Strengthening of the coal supply and transport systems must go hand in hand with boiler rehabilitation if the amount of useful energy available in the DPRK is to increase. Coal supply system rehabilitation will require provision of basic systems in mines for providing ventilation, light, and motive power for water pumping and extraction of coal, as well as improvements in mine safety. Coal may or may not be the fuel of the future for the DPRK, but it is the fuel of the present, and it is hard to conceive of an economic improvement in the DPRK, at least in the short to medium term, that does not substantially rely on coal.
- *Development of alternative sources of small-scale energy and implementation of energy-efficiency measures.* The North Koreans we have worked with have expressed a keen interest in renewable energy and energy-efficiency technologies.[12] This interest is completely consistent with both the overall DPRK philosophy of self-sufficiency (*juche*) and the practical necessities of providing power and energy services to local areas when national-level energy-supply systems are unreliable at best. Such projects should be fast, small, and cheap and should (especially initially) emphasize agricultural and humanitarian applications. Included here would be the provision of technical and institutional assistance in implementing energy-efficiency measures and cooperation in technology transfer for energy efficiency and renewable-energy applications. Focusing in particular on energy efficiency, regional cooperation would be useful in providing the DPRK with access to energy-efficient products, materials, and parts; pursuing sector-based implementation of energy-efficiency measures; and carrying out demonstration projects.

- *Rehabilitation of rural infrastructure.* The goal of a rural energy rehabilitation program would be to provide the modern energy inputs necessary to allow North Korean agriculture to recover a sustainable production level and meet the basic needs of the rural population.
- *Begin transition to gas use in the DPRK with liquefied petroleum gas (LPG) networks.* LPG is more expensive than natural gas, but the infrastructure to import LPG, relative to liquefied natural gas (LNG), is much easier, quicker, and less expensive to develop and allows imports in smaller quantities. LPG is also clean burning, has limited military-diversion potential, and setting up LPG networks can be a first step toward the use of natural gas in the DPRK—if done with a future transition to natural gas use in mind. Ultimately, natural-gas pipelines and LNG terminals, shared with neighboring countries, can serve as a step toward economic development coupled with regional energy and economic integration.

Many of these options, or elements of them, are included in the following recommended suites of assistance opportunities matched to phases of assistance that might be matched to progress in denuclearization discussions. More detailed descriptions of these options are provided in previous reports by the authors.[13]

In the *short term,* the key goal is for the parties to restart dialogue and to begin substantive negotiation on issues related to the DPRK weapons program. Energy-assistance options offered as inducements for the DPRK to join and continue in productive negotiations with the United States and other partners will need to be easy to deliver (with a lead time of a few months or less to mobilize), generally modest in cost and scope, and, ideally, have significant symbolic and confidence-building value to both the North Koreans and those on the other side of the table. Short-term assistance options include *provision of fuels* such as coal and heavy fuel oil for input to power generation and district heating facilities and possibly to mineral-export-oriented industrial plants; *provision of diesel engine–generator sets and agricultural equipment such as tractors, threshing and milling equipment, and pumps,* necessarily including diesel fuel, as well as parts and maintenance supplies, for the "gensets" and other equipment for probably several years; and *initial efforts at building human capacity in the DPRK* to move its energy system forward. Capacity-building efforts in the short term could include study tours of DPRK officials, engineers, and technicians to the United States and other countries on topics including energy efficiency, renewable energy, power-systems design, energy markets, and training by experts from elsewhere on similar topics for groups in the DPRK. Involvement of DPRK students in existing university-based short courses on energy-related topics in other countries is also a possibility. Setting up capacity-building efforts such as those above would involve at least limited interactions with officials from a wide range of ministries and from institutes operating under ministries, but the deepest and most effective interactions would be with the individual trainees—themselves academics, officials from ministries or related institutions, or engineers and technicians nominated for participation by officials.

In the *medium term*, the objective of talks will be to make progress on getting the DPRK to disable and dismantle, or re-disable, its nuclear fuel–cycle facilities for producing fissile material for weapons and to allow the international community to set up and run monitoring facilities to ensure that facilities remain dismantled and that nuclear materials remaining in the country stay secure. In this phase, which could last months or years, energy-assistance options would include ongoing aid in the form of fuel supply but would also shift to at least starting, perhaps on a local or county or provincial scale, to address infrastructure and human-capacity issues related to the DPRK's energy economy.

Refurbishing of selected major energy facilities in the medium term involves projects to rebuild, and in some cases replace, a few key individual large energy facilities. In many cases, these individual refurbishment efforts could effectively be first projects to demonstrate and work out technical, logistic, financing, and other details of infrastructure rebuilding on a broader scale in the longer term. For coal-fired plants for power generation and heating, such measures could include replacing and repairing boilers and steam systems, installing modern control and environmental-monitoring systems, better insulation of steam lines and boilers, improved or rebuilt heat exchangers, and better coal-preparation systems. Assistance with refurbishing one or a few larger (say, 50 to 400 MW) hydropower plants, including repairing dams to reduce leakage (and danger of failure), dredging reservoirs to improve or restore capacity, and replacing or repairing turbines and generators to restore and, in some cases, add capacity to hydro systems is also a possible class of energy facilities refurbishment to be carried out selectively in the medium term, as is assistance with rebuilding coal-supply infrastructure in one or a few key mines, including advice on the refurbishment of selected existing mines with long-term economic potential, providing mining equipment (including electricity supply, water pumps, air supply, and other crucial inputs), helping with evaluating new coal seams, and assisting with rebuilding coal-transport infrastructure.

Integrated energy supply, grid refurbishment, and economic development assistance constitutes another class of medium-term options, potentially including mini-hydro and biomass-fired plants for new or rebuilt mini-grids and modest-size coastal LPG terminals (delivery and distribution points for LPG) and gas-fired power generation, again with new or rebuilt mini-grids, to start the development of gas-distribution infrastructure and use for an export-oriented (nonweapons) factory complex, mine, or agricultural development (for example) at a local level, such as a DPRK county.

Additional capacity building and related pilot or demonstration projects, distinguished from short-term capacity building in that they involve a broadened scope, could include training for many more North Koreans through enterprise-level training, training within DPRK universities and institutes with the ultimate goal of international experts providing training of trainers for much broader knowledge dissemination, and training of DPRK undergraduate and graduate students, as well as specialized postgraduate training, in universities around the world. Training and pilot or demonstration applications would be needed to support all types of energy-sector activities in the DPRK but would ideally also include humanitarian applications of renewable and other energy systems in health care, education, and water-treatment facilities, guided by international experts but with considerable hands-on work by DPRK technicians.

Reforestation of areas degraded by the overuse of land for agriculture or wood harvesting for fuel in lieu of coal addresses another key energy-security need with impacts well beyond the energy sector. This medium- (and longer-) term activity will need to be coupled, in many cases, with provision of fuel supplies for local cooking and heating end uses in order to (help) ensure that reforested areas grow mature trees.

The ultimate goal of negotiations, once existing nuclear fuel–cycle facilities are dismantled, is to induce the DPRK to give up its nuclear weapons, including dismantling its existing nuclear warheads and handing over to the international community for proper disposal its existing plutonium inventory. In recognition that this agreement on the part of the DPRK means giving up a significant military—and thus, through its effect on the military budget, economic—asset, energy-sector assistance in the longer term will need to have considerable economic and symbolic value and be of a nature that demonstrably upgrades the capabilities of the DPRK's energy sector.

In the *longer term*, perhaps three or so years to ten or more years from now, the DPRK will expect a significant level of economic and energy-sector assistance as well as implicit (through integration into international activities) and explicit security guarantees in exchange for divesting itself of its nuclear weapons and fissile-material inventory. Some of the categories of long-term options include the following:

- Completion of one or both of the *Kumho light water nuclear reactors.* As unappealing as this option may be to some in the United States and elsewhere, it is an important issue of national pride to the DPRK, having been negotiated by Kim Il Sung as part of the 1994 Agreed Framework. The DPRK's recent announcement that it is moving forward with its own domestic program to build smaller (probably on the order of 50 to 400 MWe) LWR units is emblematic of the importance that the DPRK government places on nuclear-energy technology.[14] There are also a number of reasons, related to its own nuclear-energy sector and to the energy system in an eventual reunified Korea, why this option is also appealing to the ROK. Completion of the LWRs would probably, in fact, be a topic of discussion from the very early days of reconvened negotiations, though likely at the DPRK's insistence, not that of the other parties, and implementation phases—including, for example, training in adherence to International Atomic Energy Agency protocols and nonproliferation measures, assessment of the current status of reactor construction (including any degradation of work completed through

2003 due to exposure to the elements or vandalism), and planning for restarting of construction—would likely start in the medium term. The nuclear components of a revived Kumho project, however, would not be delivered for many years, that is, not until just before an on-line date that would probably, even with early and absolute agreement and cooperation from all involved, not be before 2018. Alternatively (or in addition to one LWR unit), a LWR-equivalent "package" of a variety of energy-sector-assistance options could be provided that offers the same net "value" to the DPRK as an LWR unit.[15]

- *Larger national and international infrastructure projects,* candidates for which include a smaller LNG receiving facility (shared between the ROK and DPRK), more extensive—relative to initiatives undertaken in the medium term—national electrical-grid reconstruction, assistance with building natural-gas grids (and marketing and metering systems) in conjunction with regional gas-trade initiatives bringing pipeline natural gas from the Russian Far East to the DPRK, and (for most of the pipeline volume) through the DPRK to the ROK, and more extensive assistance with coal-supply infrastructure, offering more extensive development and modernization of the largest key mines, completion of long-term refurbishment of major mines damaged by floods over the past fifteen years,[16] and provision of electricity supplies to mines in order to power safety and mechanized mining equipment. These large infrastructure projects will be of benefit to the DPRK economy and, in some cases, to the environment and will also help with integration of the DPRK into the regional and global economies.
- *Continued training, technology transfer, and other multifaceted assistance in energy efficiency and renewable energy.* This might extend the capacity-building and related activities in earlier phases of assistance to include establishing major degree programs at North Korean universities, for example, or facilitating (through such mechanisms as loan guarantees) investment by companies from outside the DPRK in production facilities for solar water heaters, solar photovoltaic panels, wind power, insulation materials, high-performance windows, and other devices with markets both inside the DPRK and beyond. This type of assistance builds the human

infrastructure for the DPRK to address its energy and economic problems in the longer term, including problems (such as climate-change mitigation) not unique to the DPRK. Building a renewable energy and energy-efficiency industry in the DPRK may help the whole region to move toward a low-carbon future, as well as being consistent with stated DPRK desires for the evolution of their own energy future.

CONCLUSION: KEY LESSONS FOR WORKING TO IMPROVE DPRK ENERGY SECURITY

The DPRK's energy insecurity has its roots in a complex combination of historical economic dependencies, resource endowment, policy choices by the North Korean regime, and international responses to those policy choices. The DPRK's lack of energy security is manifest in a considerable drop-off in energy supplies—of in particular imported crude oil and petroleum fuels and electricity, but also domestic coal—since 1990, the result not only of a simple deficit of fuels but also of interrelated difficulties in the industrial, transport, and energy sectors exacerbated by the DPRK's political isolation. The impacts of energy insecurity in the DPRK affect every sector and profoundly affect industrial output, the availability of transport services, agricultural production, military posture, and, in many different ways, human welfare.

Challenges for the international community in working with the DPRK to address its energy-security problems are many and range from lack of sound physical infrastructure to reliably distribute fuels to lack of institutional infrastructure—markets, meters, and regulatory authorities, for example—to make sure that fuels are distributed efficiently and to make it possible to attract investment, to lack of trained personnel in key areas needed to build a sustainable, peaceful modern economy.

Carefully considered energy assistance to the DPRK in a broad suite of areas is needed, and that assistance must be coordinated both with steps in addressing the DPRK's nuclear weapons issue and with economic assistance of various types. Though the DPRK's energy-sector needs are many and varied, possible energy-aid options for the DPRK require consideration from many points of view or risk unintended consequences when applied. In addition, assistance must also be internally coordinated and phased so that the types of energy aid offered work well together and that the DPRK's human and organizational capacities are developed so as to allow the people of the DPRK to use and benefit optimally from outside assistance and investment. For example, options that involve energy efficiency and renewable-energy initiatives are generally robust for application in the DPRK, fulfilling many different considerations with few downsides. One aspect of such options that should not be overlooked, however, is that they will require a good deal of organization and coordination per unit of cost—relative, say, to work on a single major power plant or provision of tankers of heavy fuel oil. This requirement has many benefits, in terms of capacity building and intercultural interactions, but will need good communications between the groups providing assistance and between those groups and their DPRK counterparts to be effectively implemented and administered.

Assistance in forms that help induce the DPRK to reengage in regional energy and economic cooperation projects—such as the Greater Tumen Initiative,[17] gas pipelines, or power-line interconnections—can help to complement grassroots-level engagement offered by smaller projects with national-level engagement opportunities. Considering the energy import and export needs and goals of regional players—such as the Russian Far East, China, and the ROK—will help planners understand how to best integrate the DPRK into the regional energy economy and avoid problems in doing so.

Larger-scale options that contribute to regional economic integration, as well as economic integration of the Koreas, may have significant benefits but will likely be candidates for longer-term application, set up by smaller, local projects and extensive human capacity building that can ultimately be linked together in a more substantial change.

Providing, or at least helping the DPRK toward, a sustainable solution to its long-term energy problems is a necessary, though not sufficient, condition for enduring success in getting the DPRK to give up its nuclear weapons, nuclear materials, and nuclear weapons programs. Conversely, failing to address the DPRK's underlying needs for energy services now unmet (or poorly met) will virtually guarantee that any solution to the nuclear weapons issue will be unsustainable.

NOTES

1. For details on the estimates provided in these figures and for related information, see David von Hippel and Peter Hayes, "Fueling DPRK Energy Futures and Energy Security: 2005 Energy Balance, Engagement Options, and Future Paths," Nautilus Institute Special Report, 2007, http://nautilus.org/wp-content/uploads/2011/12/07042DPRKEnergyBalance.pdf (accessed June 12, 2011). An update to this analysis is currently under way. Other related articles by the authors include David von Hippel and Peter Hayes, "Energy Security for North Korea," *Science* 316, no. 5829 (2007): 1288–1289; David von Hippel and Peter Hayes, "Growth in Energy Needs in Northeast Asia: Projections, Consequences, and Opportunities" (paper presented at the "2008 Northeast Asia Energy Outlook Seminar," Korea Economic Institute Policy Forum, Washington, DC, May 6, 2008), http://s3.amazonaws.com/zanran_storage/www.keia.org/ContentPages/44539229.pdf (accessed June 27, 2012).
2. There have been reports, however, of potential oil resources in onshore and offshore areas of the DPRK. The Anglo-Irish oil exploration company Aminex has been negotiating with the DPRK for over a decade for the rights to explore and develop oil resources off the coast of the DPRK. The signing of an agreement on production sharing between the DPRK and Aminex was recently announced (C. Oliver and K. Brown, "Anglo-Irish Group Seeks North Korean Oil," *Financial Times*, June 1, 2010, http://www.ft.com/cms/s/0/03026d26–6d05–11df-921a-00144feab49a.html [accessed June 12, 2011]). Whether or not this arrangement ultimately results in substantial crude-oil production, this news vividly underscores perhaps the prime requirement for outside organizations in working with the DPRK: patience.
3. The Nautilus Institute is updating its DPRK energy-sector analysis from a 2005 to a 2008 base year, so the values shown in figure 1 for 2008 should be considered preliminary. The slow growth of the DPRK economy, coupled with the ending of the heavy fuel oil imports under Phase 2 of the Six-Party Talks and our initial review of available data on, for example, China-DPRK energy trade, suggests, however, that the 2008 figures will, as shown, be likely to be sufficiently similar to 2005 figures for energy

supply and demand that the general conclusions of this chapter will not be affected. In particular, customs data on Chinese crude-oil and oil products exports to the DPRK in 2005 through 2009 show little year-to-year variation in quantities shipped.

4. For a more thorough discussion of this issue, see David von Hippel, Peter Hayes, Masami Nakata, Timothy Savage, and Chris Greacen, "Modernizing the US-DPRK Agreed Framework: The Energy Imperative," Nautilus Institute Report, February 16, 2001, http://oldsite.nautilus.org/DPRK briefingbook/agreedFramework/ModernizingAF.pdf (accessed June 27, 2012).
5. The "capacity factor" of a power plant refers to the equivalent fraction of time (for example, during a year) that the power plant is producing its full rated output.
6. One terawatt-hour is equal to 3,600 terajoules, 3.6 million gigajoules, or one billion kilowatt-hours. By way of comparison, the amount of electricity use in the South Korean region of Daegu alone was about 13 TWh in 2007 (Korea Energy Economics Institute [KEEI], *Yearbook of Energy Statistics, 2008* [Seoul, KEEI/Ministry of Knowledge Economy, 2008]), which was perhaps a little more, after accounting for losses in electricity transmission and distribution, than the whole of the DPRK used in 2005.
7. See, for example, David von Hippel, Tatsujiro Suzuki, James H. Williams, Timothy Savage, and Peter Hayes, "Energy Security and Sustainability in Northeast Asia," *Energy Policy* 39, no. 11 (November 2011): 6719–6730, http://dx.doi.org/10.1016/j.enpol.2009.07.001 (accessed June 12, 2011); David von Hippel, Timothy Savage, and Peter Hayes, "Introduction to the Asian Energy Security Project: Project Organization and Methodologies," *Energy Policy* 39, no. 11 (November 2011): 6712–6718, http://dx.doi.org/10.1016/j.enpol.2008.01.010 (accessed June 12, 2011). See also David von Hippel, Tatsujiro Suzuki, James H. Williams, Timothy Savage, and Peter Hayes, "Evaluating the Energy Security Impacts of Energy Policies," in *The Routledge Handbook of Energy Security*, ed. Benjamin K. Sovacool, 74–95 (Abingdon, UK: Routledge, 2011).
8. Hugh Bentley, "Trends in the DPRK Agricultural Sector and Implications for Energy Use" (paper presented at the "DPRK Energy Experts Working Group Meeting," San Francisco, June 26, 27, 2006), based in part on experiences during the United Nations Agricultural Rehabilitation and Environmental Protection Programme in the DPRK, 1998–1999; see also James H. Williams, David von Hippel, and Peter. Hayes, *Fuel and Famine: Rural Energy Crisis in the DPRK* (Berkeley: Nautilus Institute,

2000), published as a policy paper for the Institute on Global Conflict and Cooperation, University of California, San Diego; available at http://igcc.ucsd.edu/assets/001/501195.pdf (accessed June 12, 2011).

9. Randall Ireson, "Why North Korea Could Feed Itself," *38 North*, May 1, 2010, www.38north.org/?p=533 (accessed June 12, 2011).
10. For example, in 2005 the ROK government proposed sending 2 GW of power across the DMZ to make up (in part) for the suspended KEDO LWR concept and to revive denuclearization talks. In fact, it would have taken (and would take, if the offer were to be made today) many years of rehabilitation of the T&D grid and of end-use equipment to allow 2 GW of power coming in from the ROK to be used in the DPRK, and it would have taken on the order of two to three years to prepare the necessary infrastructure in the ROK to supply that much power to the North. See, for example, Peter Hayes, David von Hippel, Jungmin Kang, Tatsujiro Suzuki, Richard Tanter, and Scott Bruce, "South Korea's Power Play at the Six-Party Talks," *Japan Focus*, 33-2-05 (2005).
11. This argument should *not*, however, be interpreted to mean that the former KEDO LWR project must be totally abandoned (at least without the negotiated agreement of the DPRK). For all its many faults, the reactor project, when active, was one of the few avenues for constructive communication with the DPRK, and it remains a political priority for the DPRK and thus a past-and-future main point of negotiation in the Six-Party Talks.
12. See, for example, DPRK Delegation, "The Status of the Building Energy Sector in DPR Korea" (paper presented at the "Building Energy Efficiency Technology Training Workshop," Beijing, March 9, 2008).
13. For example, David von Hippel and Peter Hayes, "DPRK Energy Sector Development Priorities: Options and Preferences," *Energy Policy* 39, no. 11 (November 2011): 6781–6789, http://dx.doi.org/10.1016/j.enpol.2009.11.068 (accessed June 12, 2011); David von Hippel and Peter Hayes, "Fueling DPRK Energy Futures and Energy Security: 2005 Energy Balance, Engagement Options, and Future Paths," Nautilus Institute Report, June 2007; David von Hippel and Peter Hayes, "Energy Security for North Korea," *Science* 316, no. 5829 (June 1, 2007): 1288–1289; DOI: 10.1126/science.1142090; David von Hippel, Peter Hayes, James H. Williams, Chris Greacen, Mick Sagrillo, and Timothy Savage, "International Energy Assistance Needs and Options for the Democratic People's Republic of Korea (DPRK)," *Energy Policy* 36, no. 2 (February 2008): 541–552; David von Hippel and Peter Hayes, "DPRK Energy Sector Assistance to Accompany Progress in Denuclearization Discussions: Options

and Considerations" (paper produced as part of the project Improving Regional Security and Denuclearizing the Korean Peninsula: U.S. Policy Interests and Options, organized by Joel Wit, Weatherhead Institute for East Asia, Columbia University, and the U.S.-Korea Institute, School of Advanced International Studies, Johns Hopkins University, Washington, DC); available at http://www.nautilus.org/projects/dprk-policy/vonHippel.pdf (accessed June 12, 2011).

14. See, for example, David von Hippel and Peter Hayes, "Engaging the DPRK Enrichment and Small LWR Program: What Would It Take?" Nautilus Institute Special Report, December 23, 2010, http://www.nautilus.org/publications/essays/napsnet/reports/vonHippelHayesLWR.pdf (accessed June 12, 2011).
15. We estimate this value to be a total of about $600 million in discounted 2010 dollars, though this is of course a very rough estimate. See Peter Hayes and David von Hippel, "The Six-Party Talks, Energy Assistance, and Korea's Energy Security" (paper presented at the IPUS conference "The Future of North Korea and Global Cooperation," Seoul, March 13, 2009).
16. Some key DPRK coal mines located near the sea were flooded in the 1990s. Since then, the lack of sustained availability of electricity has kept these mines from being fully pumped out and restarted.
17. For example, the DPRK has recently withdrawn from its long-standing (since the early 1990s) participation in the Greater Tumen Initiative (formerly the Tumen River Area Development Programme), which is now a four-country (formerly five, with the DPRK) effort to sustainably codevelop energy, transport, tourism, trade, and environmental resources in the Tumen River area around the common borders of Russia, China, the DPRK, and Mongolia, with the ROK involved as well. See http://www.tumenprogramme.org/ (accessed June 12, 2011).

CHAPTER 3

Gender Security in North Korea

KYUNG-AE PARK

Amid growing criticism of the realist security discourse, the concept of security has undergone significant changes over the years. Many studies have argued that the principal unit of security analysis should not be confined to the state but should include society and the individual as well. In particular, the Copenhagen school and human-security scholars define security in terms of freedom from threats to the safety and welfare of society and the individual. They have widened the definition of security to include not only military but also political, economic, societal, and individual issues. The process of globalization has created new security threats, and scholars have identified non-traditional security (NTS) challenges that relate to threats to both inter- and intrastate security. Many new NTS issues, including terrorism, drug and human trafficking, migration, climate change, identity issues, piracy, disease, and poverty have been identified as new security threats. The Copenhagen school places particular emphasis upon the securitization of certain non-traditional economic, societal, and environmental concerns, a process in which these issues are framed as a security problem.[1] Through securitization, an issue is presented "as an existential threat, requiring emergency measures and justifying actions outside the normal bounds of political procedure."[2]

Although there has been an increasing trend toward expanding the security agenda, not many studies have examined how gender intersects NTS, especially in the case of North Korea. Gender mediates many NTS concerns, causing them to render different impacts on men and women. This chapter therefore embodies a gendered approach to the study of NTS in North Korea. It examines the major NTS issue of economic security in connection with women in North Korea and its effects on the gender aspects of other NTS and human-security issues such as forced migration, trafficking of women, and sexual violence.

Some studies that have examined the impact of economic crisis on women in developing countries have suggested that economic difficulties are a setback to gender equality. They argue that economic recessions affect women disproportionately in the labor market.[3] Women have consistently been the first to be laid off because they are not traditionally considered family breadwinners. Thus, most women have been forced into marginalized informal-sector employment at low wages or back into their traditional roles as housewives, which clearly threatens their economic security. Economic crisis has also been found to increase demands on women and accentuate the multiplicity of women's roles, forcing them to carry a disproportionate share of the burdens of hardship[4] and endangering their well-being in the social arena. In most cases, women have had to provide subsistence food for their families, and their income has become the mainstay of the family, as shown in the rise of female-headed households. However, these women's new role as income generators has imposed on them a double burden, since the new role does not necessarily reduce their domestic responsibilities. As many men become less able to fulfill their economic role, the burden of both economic and household tasks often falls to women. Furthermore, the cutbacks in welfare and state provisions in most countries have resulted in higher demands being placed on women to provide health care, education, and other domestic duties for their families previously provided for by the state. According to some studies, women have increasingly responded to economic difficulties by migrating in order to find employment. Economic crisis has caused a "feminization" of labor migration, and the many women serving as domestic servants, sex workers, and export processing factory workers have become a significant part of transnational labor networks.[5]

Although some studies have analyzed the gendered impacts of economic difficulties in various countries, few have examined the case of North Korea. With regard to the North Korean economic crisis, several studies have examined the famine of North Korea in the past decade and its effects in the economic and social arenas. They probe the emergence of a dual formal and informal market as the primary venue for the distribution of goods, on-again, off-again government raids on the market, a bottom-up process of economic reform, and the impact of these new phenomena on people's daily lives.[6] Another strand of recent studies on the North Korean famine have focused on the refugee issue, including human rights abuses faced by North Korean refugees, the political and economic conditions of the refugees in receiving countries (especially in China and South Korea), their resettlement process, and regional conflicts caused by their movement.[7] Though some of these studies on the famine address gender-related issues, the main concern of research has been markets and refugees, rather than gender.

Building on these studies, this chapter explores the gendered impacts of economic crisis in order to examine how the crisis has affected women's economic security in North Korea. It examines the changing pattern of women's economic participation, focusing on their exit from the official economic sector, engagement in private-market ventures, and exit from their homeland, and probes how these changes have posed a threat to women in the non-traditional economic security sector. It then analyzes the impact of women's economic security on their security in other NTS sectors and also on the human-security issues related to individual well-being. Finally, it looks into the challenges North Korean women are facing in their efforts to enhance their security in connection with NTS issues.

WOMEN'S TRADITIONAL ECONOMIC SECURITY

North Korean women experienced a series of profound changes in the post–socialist revolution era. During the state-building period, North Korean leaders were committed to changing traditional family, economic, and social systems by instituting new legal and social provisions. In an effort to promote equal rights between men and women, North Korea promulgated various laws, including the Law on Sex Equality, which emphasized equal rights in all spheres, aiming for the most progressive change in the traditional position of women. The policies and laws adopted in the regime-formation stage laid a basis for the emancipation of women from the feudalistic patriarchy of the family and social systems. From the beginning, the socialist regime strongly emphasized women's emancipation from traditional oppression as an integral part of state building, and various legal rights and guarantees were given to women, from above, almost overnight. However, granting equal rights in law was not enough to liberate women from patriarchy, although these sweeping legal changes had a profound impact on traditional patriarchal systems. In the authoritarian culture so prevalent in North Korea, the concept of equality was alien to both men and women.

Related to women's economic role, Pyongyang embraced the Marxist premise that women's participation in economic production outside the home leads to their full emancipation. Several policies aimed at achieving the goal of Engels' "liberation through labor" were instituted, and women were urged to participate vigorously in social production. The total collectivization of agriculture and industry, which eliminated private property and destroyed the material basis of traditional patriarchy, accelerated the mobilization of women outside the family for their productive labor. Intended to encourage women to participate fully in the economic sphere, the regime defined women's rights at work through the Labor Law. As a result, women's participation in the labor force greatly expanded and women began to play a particularly prominent role in agriculture, light industry, and education.

In order to mobilize women outside the family, the regime also pushed for socialization of housework by establishing nurseries, kindergartens, laundries, and an efficient food industry. By 1976, almost 100 percent of the 3.5 million children in North Korea could enter more than sixty thousand nurseries and kindergartens.[8] One Women's Union member praised the socialization of housework for the country: "Children are brought up at state expense. If there is pressing and ironing [to be done] it goes to the laundries. The foodstuffs industry has been developed, so food can be bought at any time. So what is there left to do in the family?"[9] The socialization of housework and child rearing greatly relieved working women of the double burden of work at home and outside employment. A number of legal provisions aimed at freeing women from the heavy burden of household chores encouraged them to take on a new economic role as "one wheel of a wagon" in the work of nation building.

Despite the legal provisions and institutional mechanisms for improving women's lot in the economy, however, North Korean women never achieved a level of economic security equal to that of men. Women continued to receive lower wages than men and remained concentrated in occupations with low wage levels and high wage differences between men and women.[10] Some scholars have argued that when women are incorporated into a labor market, they are absorbed into the so-called secondary market, whereas men are recruited into the primary market, thus creating a segregated labor market.[11] In North Korea, the male and female wage structure was never equitable, which resulted in unequal representation of women in various occupations. For example, in the industrial sector, women remained concentrated in light industry, occupying about 70 percent of total workers.[12] By 2001 they constituted 86 percent of all schoolteachers and 100 percent of nurses, whereas over 65 percent of all office workers were men.[13] Despite women's integration into the labor market, gender subordination remained largely persistent in North Korea, which continued to threaten women's economic security.

RECENT CHANGES IN WOMEN'S ECONOMIC SECURITY

Exit from the Labor Market

Many studies have characterized the female labor force as a "reserve army of labor" that is available to be drawn into the labor market when necessary and that withdraws to the private sphere when unemployment rises.[14] When deployed as part of a reserve army of labor, women suffer a destabilization of their employment status. In North Korea, with a decline in the national economy in the late 1980s, women tended to leave their jobs after marriage, and the state's efforts to recruit women in the labor market were scaled down. Married women's labor-force participation thus steadily declined, and it was reported that a majority of married women, about 70 percent, did not work outside the home at all.[15] Clearly, the female labor force exhibited more vulnerability to economic difficulties, which resulted in reduced economic opportunities, and married women became the first to suffer from layoffs.

As North Korea shifted its emphasis from heavy to light industry during the economic crisis, many women were mobilized into household production teams designed to promote sideline production. Some married women gave up their jobs voluntarily since they could generate some income by participating in sideline production teams while staying at home. This practice reduced the double burden of housework and economic employment. However, women's exit from the formal labor force increased their economic insecurity and dependency since they received no official wages. They were also ineligible for welfare benefits awarded to regular workers and thus were ultimately subordinate to the male heads of their households.

Participation in the Informal Economy

The chronic economic crisis in North Korea eventually led to a virtual malfunctioning of the economic sector and the state-controlled distribution system. The state economy began to fail in its responsibility to pay workers their regular wages, and the Public Distribution System (PDS) proved an unreliable source of food,[16] since only a small fraction of the population had access to it. In 2006, it was estimated that almost one-third of all agricultural output was produced by private farming.[17] This breakdown of the national economy facilitated private production and trading as viable venues of income generation, which, in turn, contributed to the spread of informal markets. These markets have grown over the years in gigantic proportions.

Farmers' markets that were opened for the trade of agricultural products grew rapidly throughout the country, taking over the function of a primary venue for the exchange of goods. The government at first tried to crack down on illegal markets, arguing that they were the breeding ground for "antisocialist activities" and capitalist evils, and forced people to pledge that they would not engage in such antisocialist activities. However, the authorities later had to acquiesce as the PDS came near to collapsing. As a result, farmers' markets were officially turned into general public markets, such as the Tongil Market in Pyongyang, which opened for business in March 2003. Nonetheless, the government again cracked down, in 2007, imposing tighter restrictions on market trading. In March 2009, markets were ordered to open for only five hours a day in the afternoon and were allowed to sell only farm products, excluding rice. No industrial goods or imported products were allowed to be traded. After the surprising currency reform[18] at the end of November 2009, the government accelerated the suspension of markets. It argued that the existing market management formed by the people hindered its way of socialism and constituted an act of corruption and distortion. Despite the crackdown, however, market activities continue behind the scenes, and the government reluctantly condones the market as a temporary measure. In fact, after acknowledging the failure of the currency reform, which caused confusion in the supply of currency and the distribution of goods, and thus causing soaring commodity prices and foreign-exchange rates, North Korea retracted its policy against the market: the Workers' Party issued an order in February 2010 that all markets were to be reopened until the state distribution system was running smoothly. Some observers estimate that there is twice as much money floating in unofficial markets as in the government's annual budget.

Such vast changes in the overall spectrum of the national economy led to a dramatic shift in the pattern of women's economic participation. In order to find an alternative means of feeding themselves and their families, women began to leave their workplaces and to engage in both legal and illegal private market ventures. Almost 70 percent of women who were not employed in the formal state sector became involved in trading activities.[19] In addition to these unemployed women, many women in the professional sector eventually left their jobs to engage in market ventures. Wives of party cadres also participated in private-trade activities, often achieving commercial success thanks to their connections with government authorities. A North Korean female defector observed, "Party cadres, police officials, security officials and their family members were prohibited from taking part in trade. However, they did so through other people, giving these people money and then sharing in the profits."[20] Women traders have come from diverse class backgrounds. The market has helped some privileged women accumulate wealth through commercial activities involving restaurants and trading companies and services, but for most other women, the market has provided merely a means to survive. Through various market activities, women assumed the duty of family breadwinner in lieu of men, who were still bound to the official economic sectors, often working without receiving their regular wages. Furthermore, men were reluctant to get involved in selling at markets, since in North Korea such business activity is regarded as a degrading and face-losing act. As a result, women became the driving force of the nonstate economic sector, representing a majority of market traders and owners of small and medium-size businesses.

Women's economic participation ranged from trading, vending, and peddling of food, household items, and domestic manufacturing and farm products to running home-based small-scale service businesses such as beauty shops, inns, sewing shops, and restaurants. In addition, some women were desperate enough to get involved in the smuggling of consumer commodities, including South Korean videos, natural resources, and antique items from and into China. This illicit activity led women into further conflict with the law as they were forced to bribe the authorities. North Korean market ventures began to be led by women, and women soon became the leading force in the bottom-up process of Pyongyang's marketization. Women's various market activities have helped them to gain economic livelihood and thus relieve their economic insecurity to some degree.

Exit from the Country

North Korean women began entering China in large numbers in the mid-1990s, when famine spread throughout the country. Cross-border traffic has grown over the years as the PDS system has become increasingly ineffective. Although it is difficult to obtain reliable information on the number of North Koreans living in China, partly because many of them stay in hiding and some move back and forth across the border, most observers cite a figure of 100,000 to 300,000. The estimate by the U.S. State Department is much lower at approximately 30,000 to 50,000,[21] and the 2008 Amnesty International Report cites a ballpark figure of close to 50,000.[22] For the overwhelming majority of North Korean refugees, the primary motivation for leaving their homeland is a desire to survive and to generally improve their living conditions. In various surveys, more than 80 percent of women cite hunger as the main reason for crossing the border.[23] Only a few list political reasons for leaving the country. More than three-quarters of the total refugees come from the North and South Hamgyong provinces, the two poorest provinces and the ones worst hit by the famine,[24] which are located in the northeastern region near the Chinese border. More people from these provinces have been driven to exit the country for their survival than those in other areas.

Nearly 80 percent of all North Korean refugees are women, and their numbers have grown dramatically over the years. Between 2002 and 2003, women constituted only 20 percent of all refugees, but by 2004 they were half of them.[25] Women also accounted for 67 percent of the 6,304 total North Korean refugees in South Korea in 2004, and their ratio continued to rise, to 69 and 78 percent in 2005 and 2008, respectively.[26] Although it is difficult to discern why the overwhelming majority of border crossers are women, this phenomenon appears to reflect the increasing role of women as breadwinners in their families. Another possible reason could be the higher value ascribed to women, which makes them an easy target for arranged marriages, forced labor, and even a source of entertainment in various sex industries. Furthermore, North Korean men, who are still tied to the place of their official employment, are considerably less mobile. Women's exit from the country is an unprecedented phenomenon and has significant implications for their economic security.

THE IMPACT OF WOMEN'S ECONOMIC SECURITY ON OTHER NTS AND HUMAN-SECURITY ISSUES

Increased Dual Burden

Women's changing economic roles in North Korean society have had far-reaching implications for their human security, namely their individual well-being. In most cases, women's workload both in and outside the home has increased significantly. Outside the home, they have to carry the burden of financially supporting their families. At the same time, the increased load of household chores, because of the state's escalating inability to deliver on its promise of socializing housework and child rearing, has doubled the amount of responsibility women need to shoulder inside the home. In fact, the 1998 Constitution of North Korea is notable for its deletion of the clause that the state shall "liberate women from heavy family chores," which had been clearly stipulated in the 1972 constitution. As the economy began to deteriorate, social service and child-care programs were the first to become affected, and thus the socialization of housework ceased to function. Accordingly, women had to fill the vacuum by taking on the excessive dual burden of both at-home and outside work.

In addition, the state targeted women to participate in social mobilization programs, mainly through the Women's Union, whose membership was mandatory for any nonworking women over the age of thirty. The Korean Democratic Women's Union was characterized as a "transmission belt" of the party, responsible for conducting ideological education for women to enhance their role in revolution. Women were strongly encouraged by the union to take an active part in economic and social production and construction in order to contribute to nation-building work through their own social labor. Women's labor was called for in various economic activities, such as in road construction and recycling of consumer products. With the deteriorating economy, demand for women's social labor has significantly increased. Furthermore, in recent years North Korean women have become expected to assume more responsibilities in the military. The government decided to press for the enlistment of women into the military because of the lower numbers of male recruits and their poor health conditions.[27] The male population currently facing conscription is much smaller than that of the past, since these men are the first generation born during the famine of the mid-1990s, when the birthrate began to fall sharply. According to the new official guideline of March 2008, women who wish to be entitled to promotions into executive positions must provide evidence that they have served in the military. In addition to their new economic roles, young North Korean women now have to carry the burden of military service.

Sex Trafficking and Sexual Violence

Since the food crisis, North Korea has witnessed a significant increase in NTS threats such as sexual violence against women and human trafficking for the commercial sex business, particularly in the border regions. The U.S. Department of State, in its annual Trafficking in Persons Report, has placed North Korea in the lowest tier for seven consecutive years since 2003, classifying it as a major source country of commercial sexual exploitation. The report describes North Korea as "a source country for men, women, and children trafficked for the purposes of forced labor and commercial sexual exploitation. The most common form of trafficking involves North Korean women and girls who cross the border into China voluntarily. . . . Once in China, they are picked up by traffickers, and sold as brides to Chinese nationals, usually of Korean ethnicity . . . or forced into prostitution."[28] A substantial majority of North Korean women in China end up as victims of trafficking.

North Korean women most often fall prey to three distinctive patterns of trafficking: abduction, allurement, and volunteering. In most circumstances, women are abducted by either North Korean or Chinese men and sold into a forced marriage, slave labor, or prostitution. One important pull factor stimulating trafficking of women to China is the gender imbalance caused by China's one-child policy and parents' general preference for male offspring. Also fueling this gender gap in China's rural areas is the continued economic boom and modernization of cities, which sees more and more women leaving their native countryside in search of employment in the better-paid urban industrial sector. In the rural Yanbian area, for example, the gender ratio between males and females among the unmarried age group is a staggering 14 to 1, suggesting a high demand for women.[29] China's State Council also estimates that thirty-eight million bachelors in its rural provinces have difficulty finding a spouse.[30] Desperate to find a marital partner, Chinese bachelors resort to entering the North Korean bride market, thus aggravating the issue of women's trafficking. More than half of female refugees are estimated to be living with local Chinese spouses, and some of these women are not only married to Chinese men but also have their North Korean spouses and children back home. By entering into a second marriage in China, they are trying to alleviate their North Korean family's poverty.

In other cases, intermediaries lure women into crossing the border by promising them employment in China as waitresses or factory workers. Intermediary agents typically receive a commission. Many women who fall into such traps soon become victims of sexual violence in their new workplaces, such as hotels, karaoke bars, restaurants, and massage parlors. Women who ultimately manage to find regular employment often do not receive any wages, however, and continue working merely for room and board. Even the few lucky women who receive wages are paid very little because of their illegal status in China. The most fortunate women are those who manage to secure better-paying jobs for themselves in South Korean businesses or as housemaids for South Korean families residing in China.

Unfortunately, some women are so desperate that they opt for voluntarily entering into the commercial sex trade by selling themselves into virtual sex slavery. Defectors have testified that North Korean women were actively looking for professional guides who could facilitate their entering into the North Korean bride market in China.[31] Other women who had lived in China for some time and had acquired basic survival skills volunteered to go selectively into live-in arrangements with local Chinese or South Korean men.[32] By accepting live-in propositions from men, they could feel more financially secure than if they continued working at low wages in restaurants and bars. In addition, the arrangements with Chinese of Korean descent or South Korean men could reduce their risk of getting arrested by the police for staying illegally in China.

Sex trafficking makes North Korean women in China an even more vulnerable group. Because of their illegal status in China, where they are considered illegal migrants rather than refugees, victims of trafficking live under constant fear of being deported back to North Korea. Once repatriated, they face forced labor or imprisonment. A North Korean woman who gives birth to a child in China faces a further risk of not being able to protect her child's basic rights, even if she has the child with a Chinese man. Children born to North Korean refugees are considered stateless in China and are therefore denied access to education and other basic rights.

According to defectors' reports, even sexual violence in North Korea itself has become more widespread. In the past, workplace-related sexual harassment was the main form of violence against women, common in cases when female employees were awarded party memberships or promotions and were in return expected to repay their male superiors by granting sexual favors. Although this form of sexual assault has decreased, a new form of so-called chance assault has recently emerged.[33] When women are not able to pay fines for minor offenses against the law while conducting illicit economic activities, or when forcibly deported from China back to North Korea, security agents at marketplaces, on trains, or at the border often demand sexual favors during the investigation. Furthermore, even though prostitution is illegal in North Korea, women sometimes choose to enter the commercial sex trade as another means of meeting their basic survival needs. Female college students were recently reported as prostituting themselves with foreigners and soldiers to feed themselves.[34] As a result, with the decline in the food distribution system, prostitution has become not only more pervasive but also more widely accepted by the general public as a survival strategy.

Sexual violence also often leads to unwanted pregnancies, thus affecting women's general health conditions. Fearing punishment, women with premarital or extramarital pregnancies may seek opportunities for illegal abortions. Because of the rapidly falling birthrate, women have been strongly encouraged to have more children and, accordingly, abortion is prohibited in North Korea. However, the testimony of a defector suggests that some hospitals have recently started to carry out abortions with the tacit approval of the authorities.[35] This change could indicate that the problem of unwanted premarital or extramarital pregnancies has become pervasive. Nonetheless, women who do not have access to such hospitals or do not have the requisite knowledge tend to undergo illegal procedures, which can often seriously affect their health. Also, when pregnant female refugees are repatriated, the authorities may order an abortion to avoid an interracial child, which North Korean society sees as undesirable. According to defectors, repatriated women made pregnant by non–North Korean men are subject to severe punishment and harsh treatment.

Family Breakdowns

Many North Korean women face another threat to their well-being at the individual level: family breakdowns. They experience separation from their families and possible marriage failures owing to their frequent absences from home while searching for food, trading in distant places, or peddling across the country. During the late 1990s, many married couples were forced to separate by the food crisis. Almost 86 percent of defectors in China reported that they had family members who had gone missing during the famine.[36] Famine also caused an increase in family breakdowns resulting in higher divorce rates because of women's selling of sex for survival both in and out of North Korea. It was found that almost 20 percent of women defectors who reached South Korea after 1994 had left their husbands behind, a substantial increase from the 6.9 percent prior to 1994.[37] Family breakdowns in turn contribute to an increase in trafficking of teenage girls whose parents can no longer provide for them.

In addition, female defectors' testimonies reveal that economic hardships have only aggravated domestic violence against women, and wife battering has become more prevalent in recent years. As women become financially independent and more resourceful, their husbands' economic roles shrink and they become increasingly frustrated. Men experience a certain loss of identity when their traditional role of primary breadwinner transfers to women. Suffering from a loss of what they perceive as their "manhood" and feeling as if they are living "in limbo," they are more inclined toward substance abuse. Under such circumstances, domestic violence can often turn into a serious problem for women, especially since getting a divorce for anything other than political reasons can be difficult in North Korea. Many women reported that they fled North Korea simply to escape their husbands' physical, mental, and verbal abuse.[38] Leaving the abusive relationship and their husbands behind was the only solution for many female defectors who have settled in South Korea with their children.

Thus, the economic insecurity of North Korean women has brought about a number of negative effects on women's daily lives, creating new security threats. Forced to engage in mostly unskilled labor for survival, women must now face numerous threats, including an increased workload, sexual trafficking and violence, and family breakdowns, which are major concerns of NTS and human security.

CHALLENGES TO ENHANCING WOMEN'S NTS AND HUMAN SECURITY

It is difficult to assess the long-term prospects for women's NTS and human security in North Korea. Yet it is clear that women's new economic roles could bear both positive and negative consequences. On a positive note, women tend to have a stronger voice in household matters and are becoming more conscious of their rights. As women are acquiring more economic abilities, they are beginning to question the sexual division of labor at home. They are starting to demand that their husbands share in domestic chores and to resist their orders at home. Interviews with female defectors attest that women have become more influential and assertive in the family.[39] As a result, more men now help with housework and child care, suggesting that traditional patriarchal structures in the family are beginning to weaken, which can help women to form new identities. Recently, several derogatory terms referring to financially incapable husbands have emerged, such as "daytime lightbulbs," referring to their uselessness.

Not surprisingly, young North Korean women are becoming reluctant to get married and start supporting a dependent husband or children, especially when the state has failed to deliver socialized housework and child care. Female defectors in South Korea attest that many North Korean women no longer regard marriage as mandatory, viewing single life as more desirable. This change in women's attitudes toward marriage, along with the drop in birthrates because of the food crisis, has contributed to a sharp reduction in the number of children in nurseries and schools.[40]

Although women's greater voice and increased self-consciousness in family matters may not immediately result in a systematic improvement in the socioeconomic aspect of their NTS and human security, they could encourage women in the long run to critically assess their current status and strengthen efforts to overcome their insecurities. Women's new role as providers of daily family necessities might create more space for challenging prevailing gender insecurities. It is true that North Korean women's improved position in the family was not brought about by their desire for economic security and independence or by a growing awareness of their independent rights. Rather, it is a by-product of their responsibilities in connection with supporting their families, which, because of the famine, are in turn the product of women's need to assume previously male-dominated duties. Nevertheless, women's roles as primary breadwinners might lead to a cultivation of their self-consciousness and awakening of their right to resist any threats to their livelihood and well-being. This could then render a positive long-term effect on women's security and their identity.

Still, women's recent participation in private economic activities shows no grounds for optimism as to the possibility of advancement of gender security in the near term. Even in many capitalistic developing economies, including South Korea, it has been observed that women's vigorous participation in the market economy has not been accompanied by a corresponding enhancement of their socioeconomic status.[41] In North Korea, women's increased economic participation in the private market may initially allow them to better articulate their security interests and demands on the government through some form of collective action. In fact, a report on an extremely rare women's protest in Chongjin in March 2008, in which thousands of women staged a spontaneous protest across several markets in the city against age restrictions on women traders, supports this notion. According to a witness, there were "no organizers or leaders, but the number swelled into thousands in a very short time."[42] At the end of 2007, North Korea stipulated that women under the age of fifty were not allowed to engage in trading in the open market, thus being forced back to their workplaces. However, when authorities began to enforce the age-restriction rule, young women found their own way of carrying on in their business activities by forming partnerships with older women. What followed was a government crackdown. Soon after the Chongjin women's protest, a local government office responsible for market management withdrew the age-restriction regulation. However, the decision was subsequently reversed with an order from a central government office, and the age ban was reenforced.

In the event of other, future forms of women's resistance, the movement would likely react to grievances in a sporadic, spontaneous, and chaotic way, as demonstrated in the Chongjin case. We should not completely discount the potential threat of unorganized protests, since they could still invite differing views among the ruling elites as to the origins of such resistance and could eventually result in fragmentation of the North Korean leadership's solidarity, especially amid the uncertainty of the post–Kim Jong Il era. However, such unorganized and sporadic resistance can hardly trigger changes in women's security and power. The Chongjin women's resistance never translated into a strengthening of their influence over central government authorities in their effort to enhance their security. According to resource mobilization theory, poor people with grievances but no resources to fight for their rights are unable to initiate organized protest. Only those who have "economic basis, social standing, organizational network and political connections" possess the "capability to press their claims in the political arena" and can instigate some collective action.[43] Women fighting for the daily survival of their families are not likely to give participation in an organized mass rebellion priority, and thus they cannot be seen as capable of forming a resourceful critical mass. Since they do not have the power to present themselves as such a critical mass, women will not be able to raise their voices and increase their visibility. Under such circumstances, women cannot achieve improvement in reducing the NTS threats posed to them.

Another hurdle to North Korean women's security is that many women are exiting from the formal labor market, and even from the country itself. Their exit from the formal labor force has resulted in a rapid decrease in female representation in the professional and skilled employment sector, while their participation in unskilled trading activities for basic survival has increased overall. This pattern of economic activities does not, however, prove conducive for enhancing women's economic security in North Korean society. Rather, it could mean that female occupational segregation in the labor market will instead intensify.

Furthermore, as examined earlier, between Albert Hirschman's two types of reactions to discontent (i.e., a voice or an exit),[44] many North Korean women have been forced to choose the latter. Women's mass exit from the country could pose a serious threat to the state, and the state may react to the loss by taking measures to improve its performance in the area of gender-based security issues. However, as Hirschman has argued, mass exit can also reduce social protest. The exit can function as an outlet for dissatisfied groups and thus alleviate a number of economic and political problems for the state. When women have the exit option, their voice is likely to remain limited. In a country like North Korea, interest aggregation and articulation through established institutions is a difficult goal to achieve. However, as mentioned, women have emerged as a formidable force in protesting and are openly expressing frustration and anger with respect to market regulations.[45] They have initiated complaints about government policies related to their economic security and have contributed to turning the markets into a locus of protest. Although they currently lack organizational resources to be a critical mass, North Korean women will certainly lose their collective voice by exiting the country. If this happens, the new economic influence obtained through their roles as family breadwinners will not evolve further into any social and political power. Women's detachment from the country serves to dissipate their collective voice and hamper efforts to improve their security in North Korean society.

Moreover, in spite of their enhanced voice in the family, women still appear to accept, without much resistance, the common belief that men are the head of the household and that women should be in charge of family matters, including both managing home finances and earning a livelihood outside the home. Many female defectors surprisingly accepted the notion that supporting their husbands as master of the family was the best way of keeping the family at peace.[46] Although women have taken up a major role in supporting their families and replaced the male dominance in this sphere, their patriarchal perception of the male-dominant family structure appears to remain very much alive. Clearly, the transformation of women's attitudes toward gender division of labor at home and the changing perception of their rights have not yet led to a collapse of the patriarchal relations between spouses. This conflict is apparent in statements by female defectors that they were either solely responsible for household chores or at best shared them with their husbands, even though they were the main breadwinners.[47] They further affirmed that most decision-making authority in the family continued to belong to men, although men would, from time to time, consult with their spouses. This patriarchal perception is not conducive to diminishing women's NTS and human-security threats.

CONCLUSION

The North Korean economic crisis is indeed gendered, having had different impacts on men and women. It has changed the pattern of women's economic participation, pulling women out of the formal labor market and driving them into the informal private economic sector. It has also forced a number of women to leave their homeland in order to provide support for both their own and their families' livelihoods. Women's economic insecurity in turn has negatively affected other sectors of their NTS and human security in many ways, resulting in new threats, such as an increase in their workloads, sex trafficking and sexual violence, and the stress of family breakdowns. At the same time, however, the new economic roles women have assumed in the wake of the economic crisis have given women stronger voices in family decision-making matters and allowed them to develop, to some degree, a sense of self-consciousness and awareness of their own rights.

Nevertheless, women's new economic activities do not imply that the likelihood for advancement of their NTS and human security is very high. Women's exit from the country does not allow them to voice their opinions in matters related to existing gender insecurities. Moreover, North Korean women cannot be considered capable of forming a critical mass, since they lack economic, social, political, and organizational resources to collectively voice their security discontent. Furthermore, the neo-Confucian tradition of male superiority still so firmly entrenched in North Korean society is a major barrier that remains to be overcome.

NOTES

A different version of this chapter has been published as "Economic Crisis, Women's Changing Economic Roles, and their Implications for Women's Status in North Korea," *Pacific Review* 24, no. 2 (May 2011): 159–177.

1. Ralf Emmers, *Non-traditional Security in the Asia-Pacific: The Dynamics of Securitisation* (Singapore: Eastern Universities Press, 2004), 4. On securitization, see also Mely Caballero-Anthony and Ralf Emmers, "Understanding the Dynamics of Securitizing Non-traditional Security," in *Non-traditional Security in Asia: Dilemmas in Securitisation*, ed. Mely Caballero-Anthony, Ralf Emmers, and Amitav Acharya, 1–12 (Aldershot, UK: Ashgate, 2006). The primary book of the Copenhagen school is Barry Buzan, Ole Wæver, and Jaap de Wilde, *Security: A New Framework for Analysis* (Boulder: Rienner, 1998). On human security, see David Dickens, ed., *The Human Face of Security: Asia-Pacific Perspectives* (Canberra: Strategic and Defence Studies Centre, Australian National University, 2002); Moufida Goucha and John Crowley, *Rethinking Human Security* (Malden, MA: Wiley-Blackwell, 2008).
2. Buzan, Wæver, and de Wilde, *Security*, 24.
3. See, for example, Lourdes Benería, "Shifting the Risk: New Employment Patterns, Informalization, and Women's Work," *International Journal of Politics, Culture and Society* 15, no. 1 (September 2001): 27–53.
4. Lourdes Benería and Shelly Feldman, *Unequal Burden: Economic Crises, Persistent Poverty, and Women's Work* (Boulder: Westview Press, 1992); Kathryn Pitkin and Ritha Bedoya, "Women's Multiple Roles in Economic Crisis: Constraints and Adaptation," *Latin American Perspectives* 24, no. 4 (July 1997): 34–49.
5. Rhacel Salazar Parreñas, *Servants of Globalization: Women, Migration, and Domestic Work* (Stanford: Stanford University Press, 2001); Jean L. Pyle, "Sex, Maids, and Export Processing: Risks and Reasons for Gendered Global Production Networks," *International Journal of Politics, Culture and Society* 15, no. 1 (September 2001): 55–76.
6. For an analysis of famine and its economic and social effects, see Stephan Haggard and Marcus Noland, *Famine in North Korea: Markets, Aid, and Reform* (New York: Columbia University Press, 2007); Hazel Smith, *Hungry for Peace: International Security, Humanitarian Assistance, and Social Change in North Korea* (Washington, DC: United States Institute of Peace, 2005); Sonia Ryang, *North Korea: Toward a Better Understanding* (Lanham, MD: Lexington Books, 2009); Andrei Lankov, *North of the*

DMZ: Essays on Daily Life in North Korea (Jefferson, NC: McFarland, 2007); Ralph Hassig and Kong Dan Oh, *The Hidden People of North Korea: Everyday Life in the Hermit Kingdom* (Lanham, MD: Rowman & Littlefield, 2009); Barbara Demick, *Nothing to Envy: Ordinary Lives in North Korea* (New York: Spiegel and Grau, 2009).

7. See Stephan Haggard and Marcus Noland, *The North Korean Refugee Crisis: Human Rights and International Response* (Washington, DC: U.S. Committee for Human Rights in North Korea, 2006); U.S. Library of Congress, Congressional Research Service, *North Korean Refugees in China and Human Rights Issues: International Response and U.S. Policy Options*, by Rhoda Margesson, Emma Chanlett-Avery, and Andorra Bruno, RL34189, September 26, 2007; Hazel Smith, "North Koreans in China: Sorting Fact from Fiction," in *Crossing National Borders: Human Migration Issues in Northeast Asia*, ed. Tsuneo Akaha and Anna Vassilieva, 165–190 (Tokyo: United Nations University Press, 2005); Andrei Lankov, "Bitter Taste of Paradise: North Korean Refugees in South Korea," *Journal of East Asian Studies* 6, no. 1 (2006): 105–138; Byung-Ho Chung, "Between Defector and Migrant: Identities and Strategies of North Koreans in South Korea," *Korean Studies* 32 (2008): 1–27; Ihn Hyuck Kim, "Bukhan inkwon kwa talbukja munje" (Human Rights and the Problem of North Korean Refugees), *Tongil junryak* 5, no. 2 (December 2005): 69–112; Jooshin Jung, ed., *Hyundai talbukja moonjeeui ihae* (Understanding of Contemporary North Korean Refugee Problems) (Seoul: Prima Books, 2009); Suyeol Oh and Jusam Kim, "Talbuk sataerul dulrossan Dongbuka giyeokeui galdeungkwa hyupruk" (Conflicts and Cooperation on North Korean Refugee Issues in Northeast Asia), *Tongil junryak* 6, no. 1 (August 2006): 107–132.
8. Kim Il Sung, "On Further Developing the Nursing and Upbringing of Children" (speech delivered at the sixth session of the Fifth Supreme People's Assembly, Pyongyang, April 29, 1976).
9. Jon Halliday, "Women in North Korea: An Interview with the Korean Democratic Women's Union," *Bulletin of Concerned Asian Scholars* 17, no. 3 (1985): 53.
10. For more analysis, see Kyung-Ae Park, "Women and Revolution in North Korea," *Pacific Affairs* 65, no. 4 (Winter 1992–1993): 527–545.
11. David M. Gordon, Richard Edwards, and Michael Reich, *Segmented Work, Divided Workers: The Historical Transformation of Labor in the United States* (New York: Cambridge University Press, 1982).
12. *Bukhan junseo* (Compendium of North Korea) (Seoul: Institute of Far Eastern Affairs, 1983), 220.

13. Soo-am Kim, Keum-soon Lee, and Soon-hee Lim, *White Paper on Human Rights in North Korea, 2007* (Seoul: Korea Institute of National Unification, 2007), 225.
14. Heleieth I. B. Saffioti, *Women in Class Society* (New York: Monthly Review Press, 1980); Veronica Beechey, *Unequal Work* (London: Verso, 1987), 66; Marilyn Power, "From Home Production to Wage Labour: Women as a RAL," *Review of Radical Political Economics* 15, no. 1 (Spring 1983): 71–91.
15. "About 70 Percent of Women Quit Their Jobs after Marriage," *Hanguk ilbo*, May 7, 1991.
16. In October 2005, the PDS was reinstated by the government, and private rice trading was banned. However, as the PDS continued to malfunction, the grain market eventually reemerged.
17. Good Friends: Research Institute for North Korean Society, *North Korea Today*, no. 44 (2006): 1.
18. The reform set the exchange rate between the old and new currencies at 100:1 and imposed a ceiling on the amount of the old currency that could be exchanged. It was designed to revive state control over the economy by curbing the growing decentralized market and restructuring the resource-distribution system.
19. Myungsook Choi, "90 nyundai eiwho Josun yeosongdeul-eui gajungaeseoui samae kwanhaeyeo" (North Korean Women's Family Life after the 1990s), in *Life of Women in North and South Korea and Korean-Chinese Women* (Seoul: Korean Women's Institute, Ewha Womans University, 1999), 10.
20. Andrei Lankov and Kim Seok-hyang, "North Korean Market Vendors: The Rise of Grassroots Capitalists in a Post-Stalinist Society," *Pacific Affairs* 81, no. 1 (Spring 2008): 70.
21. U.S. Library of Congress, Congressional Research Service, *North Korean Refugees in China and Human Rights Issues*, 4.
22. Amnesty International, *Amnesty International Report 2008: State of the World's Human Rights*, 180, http://archive.amnesty.org/report2008/eng/Homepage.html (accessed April 20, 2011). According to Amnesty International, one hundred fifty to three hundred North Koreans who crossed the border were repatriated each week. See Amnesty International, *Amnesty International Report 2007: State of the World's Human Rights*, 159, http://archive.amnesty.org/report2007/ (accessed April 20, 2011).
23. See, for example, Sookjae Moon et al., "Bukhan yeosongdul-eui talbuk dongkia-wa sangwhal siltae" (Motivations for Defection of North Korean Women and the Status of Their Daily Lives), *Daehan gajonghakwheoji* 38, no. 5 (2000): 145.

24. On agricultural capacity and economic welfare of North Korean provinces, see Hazel Smith, "North Korea: Market Opportunity, Poverty and the Provinces," *New Political Economy* 14, no. 2 (June 2009): 231–256.
25. U.S. Library of Congress, Congressional Research Service, *North Korean Refugees in China and Human Rights Issues*, 4.
26. Republic of Korea, Ministry of Unification, *North Korean Refugee Statistics*, February 15, 2005; Republic of Korea, Ministry of Unification, *Statistics on Saeteomin*, 2009, http://www.unikorea.go.kr.
27. Institute for Far Eastern Studies, "Recruiting Difficulties Lead DPRK to Discard Conscription Standards," *North Korea Brief*, no. 08–5–29, May 29, 2008. In 2003, Pyongyang enacted a law, System of Military Service for All Citizens, that requires men to participate in a ten-year military service and women in a seven-year service, in supporting roles.
28. U.S. Department of State, *Trafficking in Persons Report 2008*, http://www.state.gov/g/tip/rls/tiprpt/2008 (accessed April 20, 2011).
29. Byung-Ho Chung, "Living Dangerously in Two Worlds: The Risks and Tactics of North Korean Refugee Children in China," *Korea Journal* 43, no. 3 (Autumn 2003): 198.
30. Sung Jin Lee, "Tragedy Is Inherited for Refugees," *Daily NK*, May 23, 2009.
31. Keumsooon Lee, *The Border-Crossing North Koreans: Current Situations and Future Prospects* (Seoul: Korea Institute for National Unification), 29.
32. Ibid., 34.
33. Lee and Lim, *White Paper on Human Rights in North Korea, 2007*, 231.
34. Sunhee Im, *Siklyangnan-kwa Bukhan yeoseongeui yeokhal-mit euisik byeonhwa* (Food Crisis and Changes in the Role and Consciousness of North Korean Women) (Seoul: Korea Institute for National Unification, 2004), 62.
35. Korea Institute for National Unification, *White Paper on Human Rights in North Korea, 2003* (Seoul: Korea Institute for National Unification, 2003), 174.
36. Joeun Beotdeul, "Bukhan jumin-eui Bukhan sawhoe gyungje-e daehan insik mit taedo josa," (A Survey of the Perception and Attitudes of North Koreans toward Their Society and Economy) (Seoul: Joeun beotdeul, 2000), 32–33.
37. Hyun-Sun Park, "Hyundai Bukhan-eui gajok jedo-ei gwanhan yeonku" (Research on the Contemporary Family System in North Korea) (Ph.D. diss., Ewha Womans University, 1999), quoted in Kyungja Jung and Bronwen Dalton, "Rhetoric Versus Reality for the Women of North Korea: Mothers of the Revolution," *Asian Survey* 46, no. 5 (September/October 2006): 755.

38. See Citizens' Alliance for North Korean Human Rights, *Class and Gender Discrimination in North Korea: Alternative Report*, July 2005, 20; Korea Institute for National Unification, *White Paper on Human Rights in North Korea, 2003*, 172.
39. Kim, Lee, and Lim, *White Paper on Human Rights in North Korea, 2007*, 228.
40. Mi-Kyung Lee, "Talbuk yeosong-kwaeui simcheung munjob-eul tonghaseo bon geongjenan eiwho Bukhan yeosung-eui giwee byunwha junmang" (The Prospects for Changes in North Korean Women's Status after the Economic Hardship: Interviews with Women Defectors), *Gajok-kwa munwha* 18, no. 1 (2006): 51.
41. For the South Korean case, see Kyung-Ae Park, "Women Workers in South Korea: The Impact of Export-Led Industrialization," *Asian Survey* 35, no. 8 (August 1995): 740–756.
42. "Women Revolt in North Korea, Authorities Back Down," *World Tribune*, April 3, 2008.
43. Rod Aya, "Popular Intervention in Revolutionary Situations," in *Statemaking and Social Movements*, ed. Charles Bright and Susan Harding (Ann Arbor: University of Michigan Press, 1984), 330–331.
44. Albert Hirschman, "Exit, Voice, and the State," *World Politics* 31, no. 1 (October 1978): 90.
45. Since the Chongjin incident, several other protests staged by women have been reported, especially after the currency reform. See "Women Power Gathers against North Korean Currency Shock," *Chosun ilbo*, December 7, 2009.
46. Kim, Lee, and Lim, *White Paper on Human Rights in North Korea, 2007*, 228.
47. Mi-Kyung Lee, "Talbuk yeosong-kwaeui simcheung munjob-eul tonghaseo bon geongjenan," 45.

*This work was supported by the National Research Foundation of Korea Grant funded by the Korean Government [NRF-2011-330-B00020].

CHAPTER 4

Securitizing Transnational Organized Crime and North Korea's Non-Traditional Security

DAVID C. KANG

In September 2005, the U.S. Treasury Department sanctioned a small bank in Macao named Banco Delta Asia (BDA), accusing it of laundering money for the Democratic People's Republic of Korea (DPRK). The repercussions were immediate and widespread: the bank itself was frozen out of global credit markets as other banks worried about the reputational effect of working with BDA. North Korea protested long and loud, arguing that no evidence of any crime had been provided. The general international community nodded in agreement that, once again, North Korea had been caught engaged in rogue activities as befits its reputation. Many U.S. government officials at the time saw such actions as an essential component in both curbing North Korea's illegal activities and applying pressure on the regime. Yet eighteen months later, the BDA case was quietly resolved, and much of North Korean money in BDA bank accounts was transferred to different banks at North Korean request. Although there are still questions and concerns about North Korean illicit activities, the days of taking on the "Sopranos' state" appear to be waning. Nonetheless, the weaker the North Korean regime becomes and the more it appears to lose control over internal conditions in North Korea, the more observers suspect the regime will explore and continue illicit activities in order to both prop up the regime and for personal aggrandizement among various elites.

As a result, questions of measuring North Korean illicit activities can quickly become politicized: under- or overestimation of the amount of illicit activity is believed to reflect prior political biases of the author reporting them. However, despite the difficulty in assessing the information, it is probably most reasonable to first attempt to measure as accurately as possible the levels and type of North Korean illicit activities before drawing any conclusions about the larger implications of the findings.

Indeed, whether or not the North Korean government is systematically engaged in illicit counterfeiting and drug trafficking, it is still one of the most reprehensible and repressive regimes on the planet. North Korean leader Kim Jong Il was a brutal dictator who impoverished a nation in order to sustain a massive military machine, and current provocative North Korean behavior over nuclear and missile programs is so far outside international norms that its defenders argue only over the best way to change or eliminate the regime, not over the basic facts of its provocations. Kim presided over horrifying human rights abuses and concentration camps. Because of its bungled economic policies, as many as one million North Koreans may have died from starvation during the famine of the late 1990s.

In this atmosphere, it is quite possible to hear rumors of North Korean illicit activities and accept them at face value. This leads to three important questions, one descriptive, and two practical: First, how much money does North Korea counterfeit, what is the evidence for money laundering and drug running, and in what other types of illicit activities and transnational organized crime does the DPRK engage? Second, what are the politics that lie behind various governments' approaches to North Korean illicit activities? Finally, what types of response is possible by other governments around the region?

IS NORTH KOREA INVOLVED IN TRANSNATIONAL ORGANIZED CRIME?

It has long been rumored that North Korea is engaged in counterfeiting, money laundering, drug smuggling, and other illegal activities. These rumors include using the various North Korean embassies as way stations, diplomats and quasi-governmental organizations being involved in illicit activities, and other rumors of North Korean official and private individual involvement. However, measuring these activities with any degree of accuracy is enormously difficult. Not only are such activities normally hidden from sight, but also the DPRK has no interest in letting this information become public. Nonetheless, there has been in the public domain a fair amount of research on this topic, and it is possible to provide at least an outline of what is available. Two key issues involve how large North Korea's share of worldwide counterfeiting and drug trafficking is and how large a share of North Korea's economy such illegal activity constitutes. In both cases, a close reading of the empirical evidence leads to the conclusion—somewhat counterintuitively—that the proportion of North Korean illegal activity is fairly low.

How Much Money Does North Korea Counterfeit?

David Asher, a former official in the Bush administration, estimated in 2005 that "the criminal sector may account for as much as 35–40% of DPRK exports and a much larger percentage of its total cash earnings," which would amount to over $400 million.[1] Balbina Hwang estimated in 2003 that "[annual] income from illegal drugs ran between $500 million and $1 billion."[2] Other sources give amounts smaller by a factor of almost ten: according to a February 1999 Congressional Research Service (CRS) report, "conservative estimates" indicate that North Korea's criminal activity "generated about $86 million in 1997—$71 million from drugs and $15 million from counterfeiting." U.S. congressman Ed Royce's office has also estimated total annual revenue from illicit activities at "$500 million in illicit activities . . . revenue generated from counterfeiting $15–25 million per year," although the sources all tend to be the same and rely particularly on a CRS report from 1999 (updated in 2006 and 2007).[3] The 2007 CRS report itself estimates counterfeiting income at $15 million in 1997; but of seven specific incidents mentioned in the CRS report from 1998 to 2004, five are based on media reports, and two lack any sources at all.

However, other scholars, and the U.S. Secret Service, have arrived at much lower estimates of the amounts of illicit North Korean activity.

In testimony before the U.S. Senate in 2006, Michael Merritt of the U.S. Secret Service reported that since 1989, the United States had seized about $50 million of North Korean counterfeited currency, for a rate of $2.8 million annually. Stephan Haggard and Marcus Noland have estimated a similarly small amount of income from counterfeiting, at $1.25 million per year, and they concluded that estimates of income from counterfeiting "indeed may have been exaggerated from the start. . . . In considering estimates of totals, it is important to be cautious. Many estimates make reference to prior periods, or peak levels of the given activity . . . moreover, past estimates do not consider the likely effect of closer scrutiny of North Korean economic activity that has occurred since the onset of the crisis in October 2002."[4]

To put North Korean counterfeiting in a comparative context, the Secret Service estimates that "the amount [of North Korean counterfeit currency] seized is comparatively low in contrast to other known counterfeits. . . . Investigation into counterfeit currency in Colombia yielded seizures in excess of $380 million."[5] For further comparison, between October 2007 and August 2008, $103 million in counterfeit U.S. currency was seized worldwide, and in the first four months of 2009 alone, $43 million in counterfeit U.S. currency was seized in Lima, Peru.[6]

Furthermore, *Time* magazine reported in 2007 that

> a 2006 State Department estimate puts the amount of counterfeit currency in circulation at $45 million to $48 million. Estimate is the key word. Of all the illicit businesses from which North Korea profits, counterfeiting is the one about which outsiders know the least. U.S. officials say they don't believe the North Koreans produced the equipment to print such high-quality counterfeit bills. If that's the case, where did they get it from? No U.S. agency interviewed for this story, including Treasury, State and the Secret Service, could say. U.S. sources also say they do not know where in North Korea the notes are produced.[7]

In March 2006, the Russian ambassador to South Korea, Gleb Ivashentsov asked the U.S. government to provide specific details and evidence of North Korean counterfeiting, because his country had no substantial evidence to support these claims, saying, "The side that raises the suspicions should present evidence. . . . Russia has not received any

TABLE 4.1 Counterfeit U.S. currency, fiscal years 1999–2005 (millions of U.S. dollars)

	Passed			*Seized*		
	Domestic	*Foreign*	*Total*	*Domestic*	*Foreign*	*Total*
1999	39.2	1.4	40.6	13.7	126.6	140.3
2000	39.7	1.4	41.1	209.0	190.8	211.7
2001	47.5	1.5	49.0	12.6	54.0	66.6
2002	42.9	1.4	44.3	9.7	120.4	130.1
2003	36.6	1.5	38.1	10.7	52.2	62.9
2004	43.6	1.2	44.7	10.3	33.6	43.9
2005	56.2	4.8	61.0	14.7	37.9	52.6

Source: U.S. Department of the Treasury, "Treasury, Federal Reserve and Secret Service Issue Report on High Use, Low Counterfeiting of U.S. Currency Abroad," HP-154, October 25, 2006, 48, http://www.federalreserve.gov/newsevents/press/other/20061025a.htm.

Note: "Seized" refers to counterfeit currency that was detected before being circulated, and "passed" indicates currency that was determined to be counterfeit after entering circulation. Only passed currency represents a loss to the public, whereas seized counterfeits represent an averted threat.

concrete evidence. There is rumor-level talk on the issue."[8] Perhaps most interestingly, the U.S. Treasury, Federal Reserve, and Secret Service completed a ten-year study of counterfeiting in 2006, concluding that about $61 million in counterfeit currency was passed worldwide, of which $56.2 million was passed in the United States (see table 4.1).[9] By most measures, then, if North Korea is counterfeiting money, the amounts are quite low, and there is very little knowledge about how North Korea produces supernotes of the quality to pass undetected throughout the global banking system.

Banco Delta Asia

Perhaps the most vivid example of North Korean illicit activities was the U.S. charges between 2005 and 2007 that North Korea laundered money through BDA. There are few factual details available to the public, because the U.S. Treasury Department has not released many details on the issue. However, there has been some detailed research that comes to some skeptical conclusions done by the China Matters blog, as well as by John McGlynn in *Japan Focus*.[10] They question many of the claims surrounding the BDA case. The Treasury Department's finding of September 20, 2005, argues that BDA "provided financial services for over 20 years to multiple North Korean government agencies and front companies that are engaged in illicit activities, and continues to develop these relationships."[11] Unfortunately, there is little concrete evidence contained in the finding, which consists mostly of listing suspected transactions.

A key factor appears to be the 1994 transfer of $250,000 in counterfeit notes into BDA by North Koreans. Stanley Au, BDA's principal shareholder, later testified:

> After the Bank reported this incident to the Macao police, I was contacted by agents of the United States government. Mr. Fung Tat Ping and I subsequently met with them and they asked a number of questions about the circumstances under which the counterfeit notes came into the Bank's possession. I cordially answered the questions and asked if their preference was that we should desist from doing business with North Korean entities. They said that they would like us to continue to deal with them, as it was better that we conducted this business rather than another financial entity that may not be so cooperative with the United States. . . . In the next couple of years, the Bank was periodically contacted by other U.S. government agents and we cooperated in their inquiries. Since those meetings, I believed that the U.S. government knew of my willingness to cooperate with regard to the Bank's North Korean business and, indeed, to end that business if this would help prevent unlawful conduct. I have not been contacted by the U.S. government since the mid-1990's and had no reason to suspect that its views on this matter had changed.[12]

Confronted with the lack of recent evidence of money laundering at BDA, Deputy Assistant Treasury Secretary Daniel Glaser said in 2006, "Now you might ask, why am I giving this example [of attempted North Korean money laundering in 1994]? This is 1994—so this is 12 years old now. Don't I have a better example? Don't I have something else that I could show you to demonstrate some sort of problem over the last 12 years?"[13] Unfortunately, he did not provide clear answers to his rhetorical questions.

The 2007 Treasury final rule lists a number of "suspected . . . failure[s] to take reasonable measures," and other nonspecific criticisms, but does mention one specific sum of suspected laundering, arguing that "one North Korean-linked entity deposited the equivalent of over U.S.$50 million."[14] To gain some perspective, even if the entire deposited amount were laundered money, this is a relatively small figure: ABN AMRO (a Dutch bank) laundered $3.2 billion between August 2002 and September 2003, and an Israeli bank was involved in transactions totaling $35.4 billion that "exhibited characteristics and patterns commonly associated with money laundering."[15] Thus, although BDA may have been involved in money laundering for North Korean agents, the scale is quite low, and the publicly available evidence is fairly scarce.

In What Other Illegal Activities Does North Korea Engage?

Although counterfeiting and money laundering have been the most visible of North Korean illicit activities, there are also many rumors that North Korea is engaged in drug running, prostitution, and other activities more typical of organized crime than of a sovereign government. Many of the estimates are probably exaggerated, and one reason they are overestimated has to do with differences between wholesale and retail prices. Even if the North Koreans are counterfeiting $100 bills, they are not getting $100 for each one; rather, they are distributed at some discount. Drugs are the same: farm gate versus street price differences are huge. Thus, no matter what the actual amount of illegal profits earned by North Korea, those profits are less than the retail-price value of those activities.

Perhaps the most vivid example is the interception in Australia in 2003 of the North Korean freighter *Pong Su*, found with 125 kilos of heroin aboard, evidently a distinctive brand from the Golden Triangle near Burma, Laos, and Cambodia, that is not from North Korea.[16] The *Pong Su* incident figures prominently in most accounts of North Korean drug trafficking. The crew itself claimed they had been hired by a Malaysian company to pick up secondhand BMWs in Melbourne, and although four Malaysians on board admitted to drug charges, the crew denied any knowledge of the drugs.[17] After three years in custody and 119 days of testimony, a jury of seven men and six women found them not guilty, the Australian government dropped the charges, and the Victorian Supreme Court acquitted the four North Korean officers who had been arrested and sent them home.[18]

Rumors of North Korean drug trafficking persist, of course, and the U.S. government's 2009 *International Narcotics Control Strategy Report* repeats the generic charges against North Korea: "There is substantial evidence that North Korean governmental entities and officials have been involved in the laundering of the proceeds of narcotics trafficking and other illicit activities and that they continue to be engaged in other illegal activities, including activities related to counterfeiting, through a number of front companies."[19] However, no specific details are provided. The 2007 report acknowledges that "there have not been any drug seizures or apprehensions of drug traffickers with a connection to the Democratic People's Republic of Korea (DPRK) since 2004," which presumably refers to the *Pong Su* incident.[20] Benjamin Sovacool has noted that "no confirmed seizures of drugs involving North Korean state officials have occurred since 2001," despite the fact that "the idea of a North Korean drug state has become widely entrenched in the media and academia."[21]

Using U.S. government estimates of North Korean acreage devoted to drug production, Haggard and Noland have concluded that "simple calculations of estimated acreage under cultivation, likely output, and wholesale prices lead us to believe that this estimate [of between $71 million and $200 million in annual North Korean drug revenues in the early years of the twenty-first century] should be treated as an upper bound. . . . If we take a generous estimate of $200 a kilo, this would yield a total farmgate value of opium production of only $6–9 million."[22] To put that number in perspective, opium production in the Golden Triangle is worth $120 million annually, whereas the opium farmers in Afghanistan are estimated to have earned in 2009 between $438 million and $1 billion (the street price of that heroin is dramatically higher, upward of $60 billion).[23] Sovacool has concluded that even if one accepts at face value a highly suspect set of data regarding North Korean drug trafficking, "North Korea accounts for less than .0005% of global heroin seizures, and .0089% of methamphetamine seizures every year."[24] Significantly, the *World Drug Report 2008* does not mention North Korea, either as a cultivator or trafficker of illicit drugs.[25]

In sum, North Korean entities are clearly guilty of suspicious behavior and consorting with undesirable types. Yet the publicly available evidence and attempts to measure the scale of illicit activities using macroeconomic data both appear to lead to a conclusion that the scale of North Korean counterfeiting or drug trafficking is quite small relative to entities operating in other countries, such as the drug cartels in Mexico or the Golden Triangle, or to other money launderers around the world. These amounts are also quite small relative to the size of the North Korean economy—estimated at between $20 billion and $40 billion. This does not absolve North Korea of anything, of course, but it does lead us to ask questions about how best to pursue action against such activities.

THE POLITICS OF FIGHTING TRANSNATIONAL ORGANIZED CRIME

There are two basic approaches to the questions of whether North Korea is involved in these crimes and how best to restrict them. The first approach sees activities by the DPRK as basically no different from those of other groups involved in drug running, money laundering, and counterfeiting, such as the Medellín drug cartel or Russian gangsters. This approach sees all this activity as essentially a law-enforcement problem and best dealt with by the various enforcement agencies both in the United States and around the world.

The reality is that North Korean activities such as money laundering and drug trafficking are almost impossible to treat as simple matters of law enforcement because the politicization of North Korea itself means that such activities will have a much larger public and policy impact than if the same actions were undertaken by citizens of a country with good standing in the international community. A figure of $50 million in money laundering from Singapore or Germany would not elicit the same attention as the same amount does from North Korea. Given the inevitable link between any North Korean behavior and its larger political-military stance in both the public's and leaders' minds these illicit activities are necessarily part of the larger security issue in dealing with North Korea.

However, the U.S. government claimed during the BDA action that there was no link between BDA and the political issue of North Korea. Christopher Hill, former assistant secretary in the U.S. State Department Bureau of East Asian and Pacific Affairs, said in July 2006, "North Korea has engaged in illicit activities for decades. . . . The United States will continue to take law enforcement actions to protect our currency and our citizens from illicit activities. . . . Contrary to North Korean assertions, these actions are not related to the Six-Party Talks."[26] However, if the amounts of North Korean illicit activity are so low, it would be a reasonable question to ask how much attention should be paid to curtailing North Korean activities and how much money and personnel should be directed to the far larger problems of drug importation from Southeast Asia and Latin America and money laundering and counterfeiting by far larger organizations around the world.

At the other extreme, some argue that such illicit activities constitute an act of war against the United States. David Asher has argued, "North Korea's serial violation of international laws and agreements begs the question whether it should be allowed normal protections granted to states under the United Nations treaties."[27] This second approach links North Korean activity in organized crime to the larger North Korean nuclear problem, the question of North Korean human rights, and ultimately the survival of the regime itself. This group sees curbing North Korean illicit activities as a primary means by which to pressure and weaken the ruling cabal in Pyongyang. After all, the benefits of those activities accrue primarily to the inner circle, and thus there is a way to have "targeted sanctions" on the regime while not harming the North Korean citizens. Finally, illicit activities are also a component of the proliferation problem: not only is it possible that North Korea is proliferating missiles and nuclear technology in order to finance the regime but also, perhaps just as important, procuring inputs for the missile and nuclear programs requires foreign exchange, which can be obtained through illegal activities. Thus, dealing with the illicit activities issue does have an indirect link to larger security questions.

The issues involved are both practical (can other governments significantly limit North Korean illegal behavior, and do such actions put discernible pressure on the leadership worth the effort?) and "moral" (why should other governments ignore this issue?). The larger theoretical question involves how governments cooperate to restrict illegal activities. Given North Korea's widely accepted status as "rogue" nation involved in flouting international norms and rules there is an almost inevitable link between any North Korean behavior and its larger political and military stance in the world. That is, it is unlikely that governments will treat North Korean illicit activities as simply law-enforcement issues, despite claims to the contrary. North Korean international behavior of any type is inherently politicized. For example, North Korean exports are curtailed under numerous UN and U.S. sanctions; consequently, engaging in economic exchange with North Korea is an inherently political act, and it is the same way with drugs and money laundering.

Ultimately, then, the question about North Korean illicit activities becomes a larger question about how best to deal with the regime. North Korea's second nuclear test, in 2009, its long-range missile tests, reputed sinking of the South Korean naval vessel *Cheonan* in March 2010, and continually provocative rhetoric have once again threatened stability in Northeast Asia. Again North Korea has engaged in bluster designed to project strength and resolve in the face of international disapproval. The North Korean nuclear issue has been the most important security issue in the region for almost two decades, and despite the death of North Korean leader Kim Jong Il and new leaders in both South Korea and the United States, the underlying issues remain depressingly the same: how to rein in North Korea's nuclear programs and entice North Korea to open its markets and borders to greater foreign interaction.[28] Probably the only way to curtail North Korean illicit activities is by curtailing its other political and economic actions.

In the United States, most observers from across the political spectrum agree on the goal: a denuclearized North Korea open to the world, pursuing economic and social reforms, and increasingly respectful of human rights. Disagreement occurs only over the tactics—what policies will best prod North Korea onto the path toward these outcomes. These debates over which strategy will best resolve the North Korean problem remain essentially the same as they were decades ago: is it best to engage North Korea and lure it into changing its actions and its relations with the outside world, or is it better to contain the problem and coerce North Korea into either changing or stopping its bad behavior?[29]

Yet underlying all these questions is an even more fundamental question, to which there is no clear answer: is the United States willing to coexist in a long-term relationship with North Korea and grant it equal status as a sovereign nation-state? This question is actually much more difficult to answer than any of the preceding questions, and indeed how one answers this question may condition the responses to the other questions. That is, the United States is certainly willing to normalize diplomatic relations with North Korea if it changes completely by abandoning nuclear weapons programs, opening up its economy, and respecting human rights. But this is also essentially pointing out that the United States is willing to live with regime change in North Korea. The real question is whether the United States can live with North Korea if it changes just enough to pose little threat to U.S. interests and allows for normal law enforcement to take precedence over illicit activities but remains essentially the same in character, outlook, and other policies. As Robert Litwak has pointed out, historically the United States has cared about other states' behavior. Recently, however, the United States has been concerned with their character.[30]

Sanctions are an option for putting pressure on the North Korean regime, and the Obama administration is following the Bush administration by punishing North Korea with sanctions after its 2009 nuclear and missile tests. Technically, actions against illicit activities are not exactly sanctions, even though the North Koreans saw them that way. The United States is currently cooperating with UN resolutions 1718 and 1874 (both of which apply various sanctions on the DPRK), and its own Proliferation Security Initiative is aimed at interdicting any transport or exports of North Korean weapons or nuclear technology and arms to other countries. Regarding illicit activities, they are already outlawed, and removing North Korea from the international banking system could have a debilitating effect on its economy. The question is whether that policy—which could help—would hurt more.

However, sanctions are also unlikely to achieve their stated goal of changing North Korean behavior. The problems are threefold. First, sanctions are likely to intensify the North Korean regime's illicit activities as leaders search for more income with which to fund the regime, buy internal support, and live in the manner to which the elites have become accustomed. Second, even the United States is unwilling to punish North Korean citizens by engaging in blanket economic sanctions against the North that would include basic foodstuffs and other materials. Thus, the sanctions have been "targeted" at the regime, focused on luxury goods and the like. But these will have a limited impact. Sanctions rarely force a country to change its ways; they remain more symbolic than practical for changing behavior.[31] Haggard and Noland have argued that "it is highly unlikely that the sanctions by themselves will have any immediate effect on North Korea's nuclear program or on the increasing threat of proliferation. Sanctions need to be coupled with a nuanced policy that includes a strongly stated preference for a negotiated solution as well as defensive measures, of which the sanctions are only one part."[32] As Rüdiger Frank concludes in his study of sanctions against North Korea, "In the long run, [sanctions] lose their impact and become a liability."[33]

The second difficulty with sanctions involves the coordination problem (discussed later in this chapter); neither Russia nor China is eager to push sanctions too hard on the North, and thus any sanctions the United States puts on the regime are likely to be cosmetic in nature. The only country that could realistically impose severe enough sanctions on North Korea is China. Were China to impose draconian sanctions on North Korea, it could have a devastating effect. The Chinese appear to be fairly angered at North Korea's latest moves, and the nuclear test in particular has been a real insult to Chinese diplomatic efforts. After the first North Korean nuclear test, in 2006, China called the test flagrant and brazen and voted with other UN Security Council members for resolution 1718, which imposed a series of sanctions on North Korea.[34] There has also been intense debate within China about the best way to deal with North Korea and even whether North Korea remains strategically important to China.

Nevertheless, Chinese economic and political influence is quite limited. As Adam Segal has noted, "The idea that the Chinese would turn their backs on the North Koreans is clearly wrong."[35] Although China has voted for the various UN sanctions (resolutions 1695, 1718, 1874), the Chinese also reduced the severity of those sanctions, including opposing the use of military action to enforce the sanctions. The Chinese (and Russians) also interpreted the sanctions in a way that rendered them essentially ineffective. Noland has estimated that Chinese exports, and even exports of luxury goods, have actually increased 140 percent since the imposition of sanctions.[36] Indeed, China is North Korea's main trading partner, and despite the economic sanctions imposed by UN resolutions 1718 and 1874, trade between the two countries continues to increase. Total trade in 2008 was 41.3 percent greater than trade in 2007 and amounted to between half and two-thirds of North Korea's total foreign trade (see figure 4.1).[37] In fact, Chinese trade now accounts for between 60 and 80 percent of North Korea's entire foreign trade.[38]

Thus, China retains considerable economic leverage over North Korea. However, it is unlikely that China would use such economic pressure, nor that such pressure would work. China has continued to build economic relations with North Korea over the past few years, and to a considerable degree Chinese economic policies toward North Korea have been designed to prevent instability through expanded economic assistance. That is, China faces the same problem that other countries

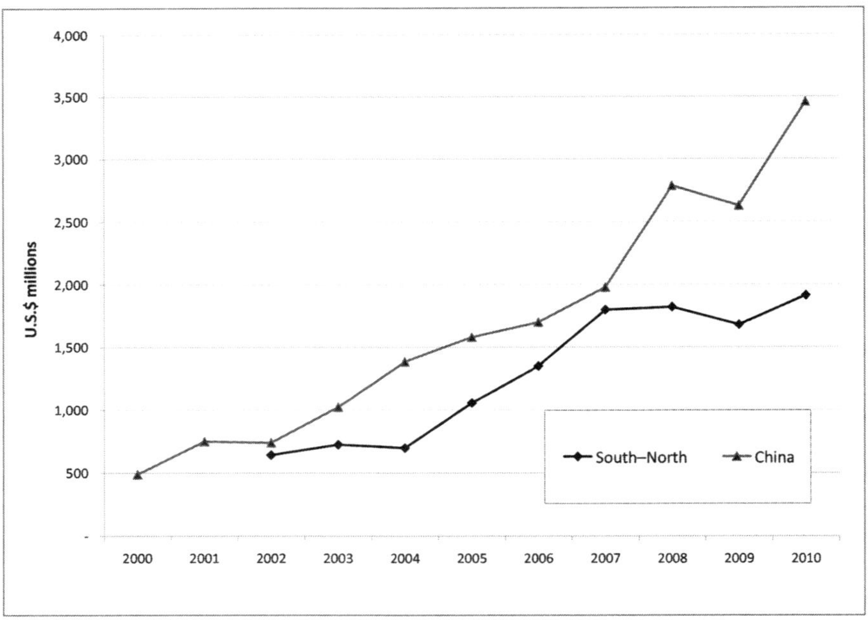

FIGURE 4.1. North Korean trade with China and South Korea, 2000–2010. (Source: Congressional Research Service)

do—how to pressure and persuade North Korea to take a more moderate stance without pushing so hard on North Korea that it collapses. In this way, North Korea's dependence on Chinese aid limits China's ability to pressure North Korea—North Korea is so vulnerable that China needs to be quite careful in its policies toward it. Thus, the prospects of China's putting any significant pressure on North Korea are slim.

Finally, some have argued that long-term financial sanctions could weaken the regime and slowly degrade North Korean capabilities. However, the problem with this approach is that it requires concerted effort on the part of the United States and needs to be done in a quiet manner. Any public knowledge of this degrading of North Korea's capabilities would provoke a North Korean response, leading to the same problems that accompany more overt pressure. That is, some believe that coercion will eventually cause the North to capitulate, and that "just a little more" pressure on the regime will force it to submit. Unfortunately, past history reveals that this appears unlikely. North Korea has little history of giving something for nothing; but the leadership in Pyongyang has a consistent policy of meeting external pressure with pressure of its own.[39] There is little reason to think that applying even more pressure will finally result in North Korea's meeting U.S. demands and a deescalation of tension.

The sad fact is that the range of policy options available to the United States and other countries involved in the Six-Party Talks is quite narrow. Few countries would consider military action to cause the regime to collapse given that Seoul is vulnerable to their conventional weapons and that war or regime collapse could potentially unleash uncontrolled nuclear weapons and draw all the surrounding countries into conflict with one another. At the same time, the United States, South Korea, and Japan are unwilling to normalize relations with North Korea and offer considerable economic or diplomatic incentives in the hope of luring Pyongyang into more moderate behavior. As a result, U.S. and regional governments are faced with the choices of rhetorical pressure, quiet diplomacy, and mild sanctions.

The United States has consistently stated that a range of political and economic relationships and initiatives is available to North Korea provided that it first resolves the nuclear problem. This basic policy has spanned the Clinton, Bush, and now Obama administrations.

For example, former secretary of state Condoleezza Rice has said that "the first step is to have, from the North Koreans, a clear indication to the rest of the world and a plan for the dismantling of those programs. Much is possible after that."[40] Stephen Bosworth, special U.S. representative for North Korea policy, said in 2009 that

> President Obama came into office committed to a willingness to talk directly to countries with which we have differences and to try to resolve those differences. This commitment to dialogue was communicated directly to North Korea in the President's first days in office. . . . It is North Korea that faces fundamental choices. . . . We will welcome the day when North Korea chooses to come out of its cave, and we will be prepared to receive them.[41]

Dealing with North Korea, then, will most likely require more than the coercive components of sanctions and potential military strikes. This will include engagement, inducements, and hard negotiating from the United States. The willingness by the United States and other countries to engage in consistent negotiations with North Korea has wavered, and talks have been sporadic at best. The mood for such negotiations is often described as "appeasement" or "blackmail," and thus U.S. administrations are hesitant to appear too soft on a regime such as North Korea's. As a result, the situation has incrementally deteriorated over the years.

As this process has dragged on for almost fifteen years, the beliefs of both sides may have changed. Although in the mid-1990s North Korea may have been willing to exchange nuclear weapons for normal diplomatic relations with the United States, leaders in Pyongyang may very well believe that events over the years have shown that the United States and South Korea will never choose to live with a North Korea. As for South Korea and the United States, though it was previously possible to imagine that North Korea might give up its nuclear weapons under certain conditions, many observers now believe that will never happen. Thus, the leadership in all three countries may now believe that no real solution is possible.

As a result, the real issue facing countries may not be "how to denuclearize North Korea" but rather how best to manage living with a nuclear North Korea, contain the problem and others such as money laundering and drug trafficking, and ultimately how to enhance peaceful political and economic change in the North. This is a much more difficult problem, especially given that putting too much pressure on North Korea could very well cause either a devastating war on the peninsula or a regime collapse and corresponding threat to stability throughout the region.

To some, economic and human rights issues are as important as nuclear weapons regarding the security of the peninsula. In many ways, the challenge of encouraging change in North Korean economic or social policies is seen as tied to the nuclear policy—solve the economic and human rights issues by solving the nuclear issue. The U.S. Congress passed a North Korean human rights bill in 2004, and there is a U.S. human rights commission. However, U.S. administrations have consistently ranked economic and human rights issues as a lower priority in its North Korea policy than solving the nuclear issue. Although this has led to criticism from some quarters, it reflects U.S. national security interests and has not changed substantially under the Obama administration.

South Korean president Lee Myung-bak has not backed away from emphasizing the plight of North Korean citizens, the vast majority of whom lead impoverished and miserable lives. This is a change from the previous two South Korean administrations, which were relatively silent on the issue. Japan's concerns about its abducted citizens are well known.[42] Nongovernmental organizations of various stripes have been working publicly or quietly to help North Korean refugees along the China border and in North Korea itself.[43]

North Korea's human rights abuses are also well known: there exist between one hundred thousand and two hundred thousand political prisoners, there are forced abortions, and an absence of basic political, economic, and social rights.[44] The agricultural sector remains unstable, and food production is barely sufficient in good years to provide subsistence for the population. Adequate access to medical services is almost completely absent, and the population continues to have an almost complete lack of basic political, economic, and social freedoms.

As with the nuclear issue, most agree on the goals regarding economic and human rights, yet few agree on the means. And, as with the nuclear issue, the debate about how best to change North Korean economic and human rights tends to fall into two general approaches of pressure or engagement. That is, the South Korean and Western approach to human rights is not monolithic, and the various groups and individuals that have human rights as their main agendas have a limited range of options in actually affecting conditions in North Korea. Some groups and individuals have worked quietly along the China–North Korea border or even within China, helping to alleviate the medical or agricultural problems of North Korean citizens. Other groups are more public, hoping to shame the North Korean leadership into reforming its ways. As with the nuclear issue, it is unlikely external pressure alone can force North Korea to change its behavior. An isolated regime concerned about its survival and control of the population places little value on international opinion or approval. As Katharine Moon has concluded, "Neither U.S. threats and hectoring, nor an attempt to impose a rights agenda on the six-party talks, holds much promise for improving human rights in North Korea."[45]

As to encouraging economic changes in North Korea, although a decade ago North Korea began to experiment with limited opening of its markets and small adjustments to the centrally planned economy, that process largely stalled with the second nuclear crisis that began in 2002. On July 1, 2002, North Korea significantly adjusted the Public Distribution System (PDS), a major element of the centrally planned economy. The country also adopted monetized economic transactions and changed the incentives for labor and companies.[46] It also adopted a number of policies and strategies designed to increase foreign investment and trade. However, although the reforms were centrally planned and administered, they were not comprehensive. As a result, there emerged a multilayered and partly decentralized economy where prices were allowed to float and private ownership and markets were permitted, but the state still owned most of the major enterprises, and workers were controlled in many other ways.

These changes were partial, conditional, and hesitant, and North Korea has been ambivalent at best about the introduction of markets. After initial surges of prices, particularly of grains, in 2005 the government partially reintroduced the PDS in grains. Although this ostensibly allowed the government more ability to distribute food to the most needy, it also exacerbated the difficulties of creating true price incentives in the markets. Grain prices appear to be somewhat more stable in the most recent years, but North Korea annually remains precariously close to another famine.[47] Without the full introduction of markets and the creation of alternative commercial sectors that can export goods to earn foreign exchange with which to import food from abroad, the domestic agricultural sector is unlikely to ever have the capacity to feed North Korean citizens by itself.

For its part, overall U.S. strategy toward the North Korean economy has generally emphasized isolation, although the United States has occasionally made attempts to open markets in North Korea. Pursuing economic reform in North Korea is complicated by the fact that North Korea is one of the most heavily sanctioned states under U.S. law, and removal of North Korea from the sanctions list is much more difficult than it appears. There are myriad laws and regulations that affect U.S.-DPRK economic, cultural, and political relations, and each of them needs to be dealt with individually. In fact, there are at least forty-two different laws restricting economic activity between the United States and the DPRK.[48]

Some believe that North Korea is most hesitant about opening its market because of the political challenges that would pose to the ruling regime. Others argue that opening economic relations will actually strengthen the regime and argue that the United States should continue to isolate North Korea. In either case, U.S. policy across administrations has been that removal of sanctions and opening of normal trade relations will come only *after* North Korea denuclearizes, and establishing normal trade relations is not a means to influence the nuclear talks. The United States has not therefore consistently pursued economic relations as an active policy tool with which to influence North Korea.

CONCLUSION

There is no need to exaggerate the range of illegal and abusive practices in which North Korea engages. From horrific human rights abuses to regular flouting of international law, North Korea remains beyond and outside international conventions in many respects.

However, measuring illicit activities is inherently difficult. The challenges the United States faces in dealing with North Korea are many and complex, and it appears unlikely that any breakthrough is imminent. Yet these problems are likely to be intensified now that Kim Jong Il has passed from the scene and Kim's third son, Kim Jong Eun, referred to as the Great Successor, has been chosen as the next leader of North Korea. We know very little about Kim Jong Eun: he studied in Switzerland for a few years, can speak English and German, and was evidently his father's favorite. Speculation has naturally followed about whether Kim Jong Eun can maintain power on his own and what this might mean for the future of North Korea.

On the one hand, the regime might survive well into the future. A third generation of Kim leadership could mean a more belligerent North Korea that is less willing to negotiate with the outside, as the young dictator proves to his own military and regime that he is strong enough and capable enough to lead the country. This could mean a depressing return to politics as seen before, with a recalcitrant North Korea yearning for respect and recognition from the outside world.

Yet the odds of continued rule by Kim Jong Eun may not be high, even though the initial change occurred smoothly. Kim Jong Il himself was announced as his father's successor fifteen years before he actually took office in 1994, and this allowed him time and legitimacy to build support among important internal constituencies and also created an aura of inevitability that led North Koreans to accept him as the next ruler. Kim Jong Il also benefited from the era in which he followed his father; this was before the famine of the late 1990s, only a few years after the end of Soviet support for North Korea, and at the beginning of the long nuclear crisis that continues to plague North Korea's relations with the world.

Kim Jong Eun faces a much more difficult situation than did his father. He had almost no time to build an expectation of inevitability within North Korea, and he will have to continually manage and placate numerous competing factions, egos, and interests. Furthermore, his young age would make leadership difficult in any country: he has virtually no experience in political posts and has no proven leadership abilities, and respect for age and elders has particular importance in Korea. Furthermore, the North Korean economy and foreign relations are worse than ever, and Kim will have few financial or material reserves with which to buy support or to respond to a sudden crisis. Although these facts in and of themselves do not mean he will fail, he certainly faces tremendous obstacles to a smooth succession.

What does all this mean for the future of North Korea? For years there was little reason to think that the North might actually collapse. And though Kim Jong Eun may rule for the next twenty years, there is also the increasing possibility that he will be unable to manage the competing international pressures and internal factional demands.

That is, we may be seeing the beginning of the internal collapse of the Kim dynasty, and governments, humanitarian organizations, and individuals around the region might begin reviewing their contingency plans for how to deal with the chaos that such a collapse would surely bring. To add the challenge of collapse or transition to the long list of issues the United States faces with North Korea makes the difficulties even greater for a peaceful resolution of the North Korean problem.

NOTES

1. David L. Asher, "The North Korean Criminal State, Its Ties to Organized Crime, and the Possibility of WMD Proliferation," Nautilus Institute Policy Forum Online 05-92A, November 15, 2005, http://nautilus.org/napsnet/napsnet-policy-forum/the-north-korean-criminal-state-its-ties-to-organized-crime-and-the-possibility-of-wmd-proliferation/ (accessed June 22, 2012).
2. Balbina Hwang, "Curtailing North Korea's Illicit Activities," *Heritage Foundation Backgrounder*, no. 1679 (August 25, 2003), 2, http://www.heritage.org/Research/Reports/2003/08/Curtailing-North-Koreas-Illicit-Activities (accessed June 22, 2012).
3. Staff of U.S. Representative Ed Royce, "Gangster Regime: How North Korea Counterfeits U.S. Currency," March 12, 2007, www.royce.house.gov/uploadedfiles/report.3.12.07.FINAL.GansterRegime.pdf (accessed June 23, 2012); U.S. Library of Congress, Congressional Research Service, *North Korean Counterfeiting of U.S. Currency*, by Dick K. Nanto and Raphael Perl, RL33324, January 17, 2007; U.S. Library of Congress, Congressional Research Service, *North Korean Crime-for-Profit Activities*, by Dick K. Nanto and Raphael Perl, RL33885, February 16, 2007.

4. Stephan Haggard and Marcus Noland, "North Korea's External Economic Relations," Peterson Institute for International Economics Working Paper WP 07-7 (August 2007), 9–10.
5. Michael Merritt, deputy assistant director, Office of Investigations, U.S. Secret Service, testimony before the U.S Senate Committee on Homeland Security and Governmental Affairs on "North Korea: Illicit Activity Funding the Regime," April 25, 2006, 109th Cong., 2nd sess., 48.
6. "Crime in Peru: Printing Money," *Economist*, May 7, 2009, http://www.economist.com/node/13611552 (accessed June 23, 2012); "$43 Million in U.S. Counterfeit Currency Seized in Peru Since January 2009," *Peruvian Times*, May 15, 2009, http://www.peruviantimes.com/43-million-in-us-counterfeit-currency-seized-in-peru-since-january-2009/152893 (accessed June 23, 2012).
7. Bill Powell and Adam Zagorin, "The Tony Soprano of North Korea," *Time*, July 12, 2007, http://www.time.com/time/magazine/article/0,9171,1642898,00.html (accessed June 23, 2012).
8. Lee Chi-dong, "Russia Urges U.S. to Present Evidence on North Korean Counterfeiting," *Yonhap*, March 7, 2006; Leonid A. Petrov, "Australia and the DPRK: The Sixty Years of Relationship," Nautilus Institute Policy Forum Online 08-069A, September 9, 2008, http://nautilus.org/napsnet/napsnet-policy-forum/australia-and-the-dprk-the-sixty-years-of-relationship/ (accessed June 22, 2012).
9. U.S. Department of the Treasury, "Treasury, Federal Reserve and Secret Service Issue Report on High Use, Low Counterfeiting of U.S. Currency Abroad," HP-154, October 25, 2006, 47, http://www.federalreserve.gov/newsevents/press/other/20061025a.htm (accessed June 23, 2012).
10. John McGlynn, "North Korean Criminality Examined: In Search of the Evidence of Currency Counterfeiting and Money Laundering, Part II," *Japan Focus*, http://www.japanfocus.org/-John-McGlynn/2463 (accessed June 23, 2012); "North Korean Supernote R.I.P.," China Matters, January 14, 2008, http://chinamatters.blogspot.com/2008/01/north-korean-supernote-counterfeiting.html (accessed June 23, 2012).
11. U.S. Department of the Treasury, "Treasury Designates Banco Delta Asia as Primary Money Laundering Concern under USA PATRIOT Act," JS 2720, September 15, 2005, http://www.treasury.gov/press-center/press-releases/Pages/js2720.aspx (accessed June 21, 2012).
12. Quoted in McGlynn, "North Korean Criminality Examined."
13. Quoted in ibid.
14. U.S. Department of the Treasury, "Financial Crimes Enforcement Network; Amendment to the Bank Secrecy Act Regulations—Imposition of

Special Measure Against Banco Delta Asia, Including Its Subsidiaries Delta Asia Credit Limited and Delta Asia Insurance Limited, as a Financial Institution of Primary Money Laundering Concern," *Federal Register* 72, no. 52 (March 19, 2007): 12734, http://www.fincen.gov/bda_final_rule.pdf (accessed June 23, 2012).

15. Quoted in McGlynn, "North Korean Criminality Examined."
16. Doug Struck, "Heroin Trail Leads to North Korea," *Washington Post*, May 12, 2003, A1.
17. Petrov, "Australia and the DPRK."
18. Benjamin K. Sovacool, "North Korea and Illegal Narcotics: Smoke but No Fire?" *Asia Policy* 7 (January 2009): 89–111.
19. U.S. Department of State, Bureau of International Narcotics and Law Enforcement Affairs, *International Narcotics Control Strategy Report*, March 1, 2009, 316.
20. Ibid., 8.
21. Sovacool, "North Korea and Illegal Narcotics," 96–97.
22. Haggard and Noland, "North Korea's External Economic Relations," 7.
23. Ron Corben, "UN Reports Rise in Opium Cultivation in Burma," *Voice of America*, December 14, 2009, http://www1.voanews.com/english/news/asia/UN-Reports-Rise-in-Opium-Cultivation-in-Burma-79218497.html (accessed June 23, 2012); United Nations Office on Drugs and Crime, "Opium Amounts to Half of Afghanistan's GDP in 2007, Reports UNODC," November 16, 2007, http://www.unodc.org/india/afghanistan_gdp_report.html (accessed June 23, 2012).
24. Sovacool, "North Korea and Illegal Narcotics," 99.
25. United Nations Office on Drugs and Crime, *2008 World Drug Report* (New York: United Nations Office on Drugs and Crime, 2008), http://www.unodc.org/unodc/en/data-and-analysis/WDR-2008.html (accessed June 23, 2012).
26. Christopher R. Hill, assistant secretary for East Asian and Pacific Affairs, U.S. Department of State, "Recent Developments in U.S.–Democratic People's Republic of Korea (D.P.R.K.) Relations," statement before the Subcommittee on East Asian and Pacific Affairs, U.S. Senate Foreign Relations Committee, July 20, 2006, http://2001-2009.state.gov/p/eap/rls/rm/69259.htm (accessed 23 June 2012).
27. Asher, "North Korean Criminal State."
28. Victor Cha and David Kang, *Nuclear North Korea: A Debate on Engagement Strategies* (New York: Columbia University Press, 2003).
29. For example, Moon Young Park, "Lure North Korea," *Foreign Policy* 97 (Winter 1994–1995): 97–105.

30. Robert Litwak, "Living with Ambiguity: Nuclear Deals with Iran and North Korea," *Survival* 50, no. 1 (2008): 91–118.
31. Suk Hi Kim and Semoon Chang, eds., *Economic Sanctions Against a Nuclear North Korea: An Analysis of United States and United Nations Actions Since 1950* (London: McFarland, 2007).
32. Stephan Haggard and Marcus Noland, "What to Do about North Korea: Will Sanctions Work?" *Oriental Economist,* July 3, 2009, http://piie.com/publications/opeds/oped.cfm?ResearchID=1254 (accessed June 23, 2012).
33. Rüdiger Frank, "The Political Economy of Sanctions Against North Korea," *Asian Perspective* 30, no. 3 (2006): 33.
34. David E. Sanger, William J. Broad, and Thom Shanker, "North Korea Says It Tested a Nuclear Device Underground," *New York Times,* October 9, 2006, http://query.nytimes.com/gst/fullpage.html?res=9E0CE0DC1330F93AA35753C1A9609C8B63&sec=&spon=&&scp=1&sq=%22North%20Korea%20Says%20It%20Tested%20a%20Nuclear%20Device%20Underground%22&st=cse (accessed June 23, 2012).
35. Adam Segal, quoted in Jayshree Bajoria, "The China–North Korea Relationship," Council on Foreign Relations, *Backgrounder,* July 21, 2009, http://www.cfr.org/publication/11097/ (accessed June 23, 2012).
36. Russia has defined "luxury goods" loosely—as watches costing over $2,000 and coats over $9,000. Marcus Noland, "The (Non)-Impact of UN Sanctions on North Korea," *Asia Policy* 7 (January 2009): 61–88.
37. The figures are from U.S. Library of Congress, Congressional Research Service, *North Korea's Second Nuclear Test: Implications of UN Resolution 1874,* by Mary Beth Nikitin et al., R-40684, July 1, 2009, 10–11.
38. Bajoria, "China–North Korea Relationship."
39. Leon Sigal, "Punishing North Korea Won't Work," *Bulletin of the Atomic Scientists,* May 28, 2008, http://www.thebulletin.org/web-edition/op-eds/punishing-north-korea-wont-work; David C. Kang, "The Avoidable Crisis in North Korea," *Orbis* (Summer 2003): 495–510.
40. Quoted on *The NewsHour with Jim Lehrer,* July 28, 2008, http://www.pbs.org/newshour/bb/white_house/july-dec05/rice_7–28.html.
41. Stephen W. Bosworth, "Remarks at the Korea Society Annual Dinner," New York, June 9, 2009, http://www.state.gov/p/eap/rls/rm/2009/06/124567.htm (accessed June 23, 2012).
42. Tessa Morris-Suzuki, "Japan–North Korea Relations: The Forgotten Agenda," *Asia Pacific Bulletin,* no. 28 (February 10, 2009), http://www.eastwestcenter.org/publications/japan-north-korea-relations-forgotten-agenda (accessed June 23, 2012).

43. L. Gordon Flake and Scott Snyder, eds., *Paved with Good Intentions: The NGO Experience in North Korea* (Westport, CT: Praeger, 2003).
44. Stephan Haggard and Marcus Noland, *Hunger and Human Rights: The Politics of Famine in North Korea* (Washington, DC: U.S. Committee for Human Rights in North Korea, 2005).
45. Katharine H. S. Moon, "Beyond Demonization: A New Strategy for Human Rights in North Korea," *Current History* 107 (September 2008), 267.
46. Yukie Yoshikawa, *The Prospect of Economic Reform in North Korea*, DPRK Briefing Book (Berkeley: Nautilus Institute, March 2004), http://nautilus.org/publications/books/dprkbb/transition/dprk-briefing-book-the-prospect-of-economic-reform-in-north-korea/ (accessed June 23, 2012).
47. Stephan Haggard, Marcus Noland, and Erik Weeks, "North Korea on the Precipice of Famine," Peterson Institute for International Economics Policy Brief PB08-6 (May 2008).
48. David C. Kang, "The Next Nuclear Agreement with North Korea: Prospects and Pitfalls" (Report of a meeting held in Washington, DC, October 29, 2007, National Committee on North Korea, January 8, 2008), 6.

CHAPTER 5

Building Food Security in North Korea

W. RANDALL IRESON

For at least the past fifteen years the Democratic People's Republic of Korea (DPRK) has not produced enough food to feed its population, and continuing production shortfalls since 1995 have not been covered by foreign aid or imports. The Food and Agriculture Organization of the United Nations (FAO) estimated a shortfall of about 20 percent for 2010 and 14 percent for 2011.[1] Drought in May and June 2012 will likely affect production negatively for that year. The famine of the mid-1990s has been succeeded by chronic malnutrition. In accord with its *juche* (self-reliance) philosophy, DPRK policy has emphasized self-sufficient food production as its primary approach to achieving food security for the population, and the country did achieve this goal for a period in the 1980s. However, that achievement relied on a substantial energy subsidy obtained through concessional trade with the USSR and China, and when those imports suddenly contracted after 1989, agriculture production collapsed. The DPRK government, assisted by numerous international aid organizations, has been working to revitalize the agriculture sector, with limited success. There are no technical or economic reasons why the DPRK could not attain food security, or even self-sufficient food production, but actions to achieve food security must involve more than the agriculture sector. Needed technical changes to agriculture require the application of best farming practices, but widespread adoption of these practices is impeded by lack of support infrastructure, and by economic policies and planning institutions that discourage more grain production and inhibit investment in and maintenance of productive capital.

This chapter discusses food security in the DPRK, reviews the history of agricultural production and food security, and proposes a means for attaining food security for the DPRK. The discussion covers the key technical and institutional elements of the agriculture sector, its relationship with industry, and the role of government policy in shaping the behavior of cooperative farms and farmworkers. A scenario for self-sufficient food production is proposed, as well as the technical and institutional changes necessary to implement it. Comments with regard to the future trajectory of DPRK agriculture are necessarily somewhat speculative, since the DPRK economy is already undergoing changes, and there are indications the government may modify some policies or regulations. Particularly after the death of Kim Jong Il, it is difficult to predict what policy decisions will be made in the future, and one can only propose actions that could ameliorate the current situation.

FOOD SECURITY AND *JUCHE*

Food security refers to the ability of a population group to have reliable access to nutritious food. The definition adopted by the 1996 World Food Summit is a useful standard for the discussion that follows: "Food security exists when all people, at all times, have physical and economic access to sufficient, safe and nutritious food that meets their dietary needs and food preferences for an active and healthy life."[2] This definition recognizes the importance of distribution and seasonality. National or regional averages for adequate food availability do not substitute for food availability at the individual or household level. Second, both physical and economic access are critical: food must be locally available, and people must have the means of purchasing and physically obtaining it. Distribution systems and the workings of the market are thus integral elements of a food-security system.

The political economy of the DPRK has been based on *juche*, a Korean word usually translated as "self-reliance" but also incorporating the belief that all problems can be resolved by human intervention. In its approach to economic development, the DPRK has emphasized self-sufficient domestic production of all important items, ranging from steel and industrial machinery to consumer goods to food. Following the Korean War, the leaders first emphasized industrial development, but agricultural production also grew rapidly. Relatively isolated economically by international sanctions and its own choices, the DPRK received substantial economic assistance from the socialist bloc countries, which greatly facilitated postwar reconstruction as well as modernization of industry and farming. DPRK policy approached the goal of food security largely in terms of self-sufficient domestic food production and has maintained that approach since the food crisis of the mid-1990s, aided by a concerted effort to make up production shortfalls by means of foreign aid.[3] The emphasis on self-sufficient production of food may have been adaptive given the DPRK's isolationism, but that production relied on imports of critical farm inputs such as fertilizer and fuel, often obtained at highly concessional prices.

In addition to production, distribution must also be considered. DPRK citizens not working on cooperative farms are entitled to receive their food through the Public Distribution System (PDS). Prior to the food crisis, rations were distributed through neighborhood centers, at a rate based on occupation, gender, and age. Until around 1994, the PDS appears to have been relatively effective in collecting grain and other food from the country's farms and distributing it equitably across the entire DPRK population. Shortages were also shared. Income was not an issue, since the economy was essentially nonmonetized. Citizens received housing, clothing, medical care, education, and food directly from the state based on their citizenship and occupational participation. Cash wages were minimal[4] and used for incidental purchases rather than for basic-subsistence needs. Available data suggest that farm production was adequate to meet domestic demand at least in the 1980s.[5] With adequate resources and an operating transportation network of rail and trucks, the PDS was able to collect food from the farms and distribute it throughout the country, including movements from food-surplus to food-deficit areas. One could therefore consider the DPRK to have been food secure during this period.

Since at least the mid-1990s, after the contraction of fertilizer and energy imports, domestic food production has been inadequate for population needs, and food imports (whether purchased or as aid) have not bridged the gap. Deprived of supplies, the PDS has been unable to distribute adequate food rations. Stephan Haggard and Marcus Noland have described in some detail the contraction in daily rations as well as growing regional disparities.[6] The industrial northeast has been especially disadvantaged, having little farmland and being located far from the most agriculturally productive provinces. With fuel also in short supply, it has not been possible to move food to the regions most dependent on the PDS. Although the government has probably made efforts to even out distribution of what food has been available, there have been clear inequalities, and at times the PDS has been completely without food.

Food security is an important factor in regime stability. The DPRK was established with a promise that the state would provide for its citizens. Han Park has noted the central importance of ideology in North Korean society, but as the state has been unable to fulfill its promises, the legitimacy of the ideology and the leadership may be questioned.[7] Sung Chull Kim has proposed the emergence of "systemic dissonance" as the disjunct between ideology and reality grows.[8] Marcus Noland and Benjamin Habib have speculated as to the likelihood of regime change brought about by social unrest caused by economic contraction.[9] The imminent collapse of the DPRK government has long been inaccurately predicted by many analysts. Following the death of Kim Jong Il, the government has strongly emphasized continuity of leadership and of domestic policies, but other paths of change could emerge if economic conditions remain bleak. The government has a vested interest in establishing food security for the population. The possible paths as well as the obstacles to this goal are discussed below.

HISTORY OF AGRICULTURAL DEVELOPMENT IN THE DPRK

Following the end of the Korean War, the DPRK embarked on an agricultural modernization effort that was political as well as technical in scope. Rural land reform, closely followed by the inclusion of virtually all farmland in cooperative or state farms, was accompanied by technical and institutional changes supporting an industrialized agricultural sector. Farm production grew, and during the first two postwar decades the DPRK economy was arguably more dynamic than that of the Republic of Korea (ROK). The population became more urban, so that today 40 percent of the population is rural and 36 percent of the workforce is engaged in agriculture or fisheries.[10]

Under Japanese colonial rule, the Korean economy was organized to produce food and industrial goods for the Japanese economy. John Feffer has dated the systematic development of industrial agriculture from this period.[11] The northern part of the peninsula was more industrialized, and the south produced more food. Thus, after partition the DPRK had fewer inherent farming resources than the ROK but also a smaller population. The FAO has estimated total arable land in the DPRK at about 2 million hectares (ha), of which about 1.4 million ha are suited for grain production or other field crops.[12] The 2008 DPRK census gives a reliable count of 24.05 million persons.[13] The land area suited for staple crop production is thus a very low 0.058 ha/person,[14] which is still about 50 percent greater than the figure for the ROK. The government holds food security as an important national goal. The Korean Workers' Party New Year Editorials have in recent years called agriculture "the main front of socialist economic construction," with similar phrasing in 2006. In the 2010 editorial, the exhortation to "improve the people's standard of living" occurs frequently, and the editorial further states, "Light industry and agriculture are the major fronts in the efforts for improving the people's standard of living." The 2011 editorial says, "The food problem is a burning issue in building a thriving country" but allots only one paragraph to agriculture in a twelve-page document focusing on leadership succession.[15]

Technical Changes

The *juche* ideal of self-reliance through human effort has led the DPRK to emphasize grain production for domestic consumption. In the pursuit of that goal, the agriculture sector was developed in accord with the Rural Technical Revolution: "chemicalization," mechanization, irrigation, and electrification. This is also the basis of modern North

American, European, and South Korean farm technology, but in the DPRK the technology was implemented in a planned economy that was insensitive to economic efficiency and environmental sustainability. Thus, in the mid-1970s chemicalization, referring to the use of mineral fertilizers and synthetic pesticides, included a target application of 2,000 kg/ha of fertilizer on grain crops—a rate higher than anything conceived of by U.S. farmers, even today.[16] Planning documents of this period delineate other elements of this energy-intensive farming strategy: 100 percent irrigation of nonrice upland crops, distribution of one tractor per ten hectares, and an annual production target of ten million metric tons (MT) of grain.[17]

Farm mechanization was based on the simple and robust twenty-eight horsepower Chollima tractor and other farm machines such as rice threshers, rice transplanters, and cargo trucks. This equipment has not been modernized and is now wholly out of date and inefficient. Irrigation of rice was accomplished through extensive canal systems, using a combination of gravity distribution and extensive but inefficient pump networks to bring water from rivers and reservoirs.

DPRK agriculture needed a healthy industrial sector, not just for machinery and distribution but for imports of fertilizer, petroleum feedstock for domestic fertilizer production, and fuel, which were obtained from China and the USSR at concessional prices.[18] Because ideology required that local food production feed the DPRK population, the cost of imported supplies and inefficient use of fuel and fertilizer were not particularly relevant in the effort to squeeze every possible ton of grain out of the fields.

Agriculture scientists developed rice and maize varieties that were high yielding and responsive to fertilizer inputs. These were classic Green Revolution goals, widely implemented in other countries as well. But a side effect of selection for high yield is the need for a long growing period, and most high-yielding DPRK rice and maize varieties now require 150 days or more between planting and harvest. Long maturity creates difficulties given the short growing season and requires additional efforts by farmers. In an earlier paper I provide a more detailed discussion of the technical development of the agriculture sector.[19]

CRISIS AND FAMINE

The outcome was that food production in the DPRK did grow substantially, and at one point met the basic needs of the population. But those achievements collapsed beginning around 1990, and the country suffered famine conditions by the middle of the decade. Although DPRK authorities initially claimed that natural disasters (extensive floods in 1995 and 1996, followed by a widespread drought in 1997) caused the food crisis, the reality is otherwise. The food crisis reflects an energy crisis. The farming system—indeed the entire industrial economy—depended on cheap imports of energy and raw materials from the USSR and China to power tractors, produce fertilizer, run pumps, and manufacture farm equipment.[20] When the USSR dissolved and China moved to a more market-based trade relationship with the DPRK, the DPRK could no longer import the fuel and fertilizer necessary to sustain farm production. The problem was not that DPRK farming was energy intensive—all modern farming is—but that it was energy inefficient and not productive enough to pay full price for the energy needed. The graph in figure 5.1 shows the close link between DPRK fertilizer use and food production, at least through 2002.

Besides the relationship between fertilizer use and production, the graph also shows the consistent shortfall in production below the minimum requirement since 1995. The minimum food requirement curve accepts the WFP/FAO estimate of 167 kilograms of cereal grain or grain equivalent per person per year (460 gm/day), to which is added a 10 to 15 percent estimate of postharvest loss to the crop. An alternative approach, but yielding the same pattern, would be to exclude the losses from the food requirement but similarly reduce the production figures to account for the loss. Haggard and Noland have argued that FAO production estimates between 1988 and 1993 overstate reality, and also that population requirements are lower.[21] Though the peak production figures may be exaggerated, the general pattern of collapse still holds. The WFP/FAO estimates of average consumption requirement are based on the food grain needed to provide 1,600 kcal, or 75 percent of the average minimal dietary need[22] and assume part of the diet is obtained from other sources. In my view this may overestimate the availability of other food resources in the DPRK setting. Production estimates in this

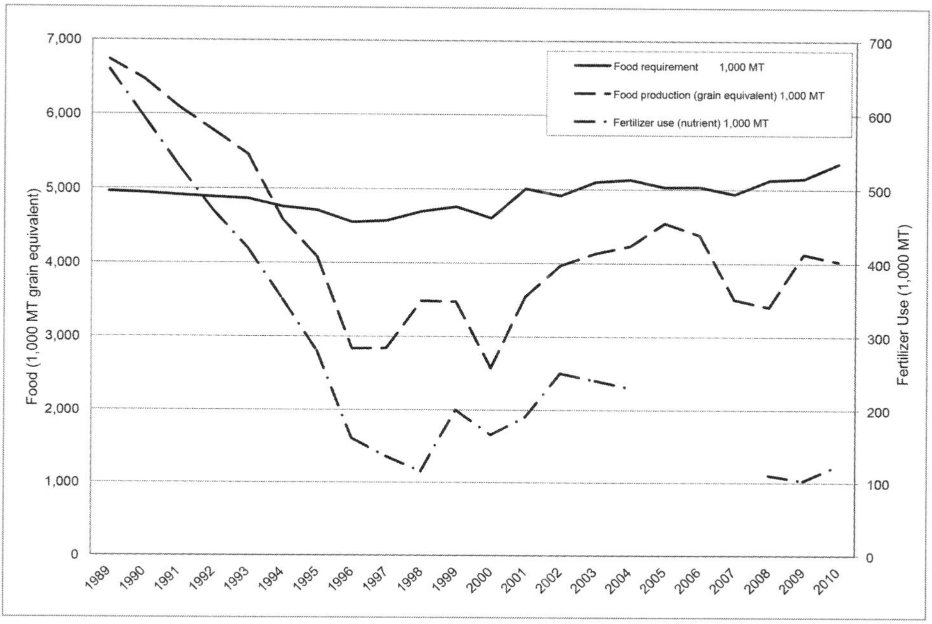

FIGURE 5.1. DPRK food production and fertilizer use, 1989–2010. (Source: The data for this graph are from the multiple FAO/WFP [World Food Programme] crop assessment reports, with the addition of FAO data for the years 2005–2007, when crop assessments were not performed.)

data series do include potato and other tuber crops and in recent years also include estimates of aggregate production from household gardens.

Whatever the actual figures, there is no question that food production shrank dramatically, and that the DPRK experienced famine conditions for at least several years, as well as continuing food shortages both before and after the crisis years. Nutrition surveys of children under age seven were performed in 1998, 2000, 2002, and 2004. In the 1998 survey, fully 74 percent of children aged twenty-five to eighty-four months were stunted[23]—that is, their height to age was in the lowest 2.2 percent of the normal distribution curve. Stunting is a sign of chronic malnutrition, and this statistic reflects the severe long-term food shortages for the general population of the DPRK. Wasting—low weight for height and an indicator of acute malnutrition—was measured in 17 percent of children in the same age range.

The PDS, Coping Strategies, and Markets

Lacking adequate food resources, the PDS was unable to make distributions. Promised rations were reduced, in some months to below 250 grams per day, and in others there was simply no distribution. As food production dropped and as the government reduced the allowance that farm households could retain, hoarding at the farms further cut the grain available for PDS distribution.[24] WFP bulletins during the period track the rise and fall of the announced PDS ration, which never approached precrisis levels and was regularly below the minimal amount of food needed for survival. As the crisis continued, Andrew Natsios has claimed, what food was available was distributed to groups according to their political standing or importance.[25]

Faced with the collapse of their accustomed food source, families were forced to improvise, foraging for wild foods, eating alternative foods such as ground corn cobs, grass, and the inner layer of tree bark, seeking food from relatives living on farms or in China, and trading household goods or dismantled factory equipment across the border with China. In rural areas, farm households had access to household garden plots of about one hundred square meters and cultivated them intensively. Both urban and farm households also cultivated unregulated plots on steep hillsides. All efforts were not enough, and death rates rose, particularly in urban areas and in the provinces without much farmland. Estimates vary between around a half million to as many as three million excess deaths nationally. Probably the true number is around six hundred thousand, but no one will ever know with certainty.[26]

As the PDS collapsed, farmers' markets became more important. Traditionally active three days a month, these markets became daily events, and other informal trade took place on roadsides, under bridges, and in the alleys of towns. But the price of grain in these markets was many times greater than the highly subsidized government prices and completely beyond the means of anyone who had to rely on state wages. Whereas the official price of rice was 0.08 won/kg in 1998, the price in the free market was 77 won/kg.[27]

In 1998, food production began to increase, probably assisted by substantial fertilizer inputs from China.[28] But it was not until 2000 that the effects began to be visible in people's energy and behavior. International assistance to the agriculture sector initially focused on providing the critical inputs (principally fertilizer but also pesticides and good seed) that had been lacking in recent years. With the addition of food aid (3.8 million grain equivalent tons between 1997 and 2000),[29] the crisis began to abate, and PDS distributions began to pick up. But the annual "lean season" in late spring, before the harvest of winter wheat or early potatoes, remained extremely problematic, and PDS distributions contracted or were abandoned during these months. The 2002 and 2004 nutrition surveys of children under seven recorded modest improvements in the incidence of chronic and acute malnutrition compared with the 1998 survey.[30]

Markets remained an important and growing force in the DPRK economy, and in an effort both to restrict their impact and encourage farm production, the government instituted wage and price adjustments in July 2002. The won was effectively devalued by a factor of seventy, wages of all industrial, government, and service workers were raised a commensurate amount, and all official prices were adjusted upward. With regard to food, the price of milled rice was changed from 0.08 to 44 won/kg, close to the contemporary free-market price of 50 won/kg. For maize, a similar adjustment, from 0.06 to 24 won/kg, was made.[31] The intent was to encourage farms (and members of the cooperative farms) to deliver their surplus grain to the government, in order to stock the PDS. It was also hoped that higher prices would encourage more production, but absent the ability to acquire additional farm inputs, the actual increase was marginal. The continuing shortage of food caused free-market prices to rise again, maintaining their substantial premium over the official rates. Rice prices varied between 400 and 1,000 won/kg, and maize between 270 and 350 won/kg in the 2004–2005 period, and the free-market exchange rate went from 220 won/US$ prior to the price reforms to around 1,800 won/US$ in the same period.[32]

Recovering Production

Farm production continued to grow through 2005, except for a sharply reduced harvest in 2000 caused by drought and damage from two typhoons. The government accepted the temporary necessity of markets and allowed many of them to function on a daily basis in settings with permanent tables and roofs, with the sellers regulated and charged a daily permit fee.[33] Around 2004, the government also implemented new policies regarding farm production.[34] Production quotas were set for each sub–work team (SWT) rather than for the whole farm, and any production beyond the quota to be delivered to the government could be used or disposed of by the SWT, including sale at farmers' markets. Farm managers told me that this disaggregation of responsibility increased the accountability and effort of farmworkers, "because they now have to be responsible to their uncles" who lead the SWTs. The ability to profit from grain sales in the market would also be a strong incentive to increase production. However, these changes were announced midseason, when it was too late to make significant changes in the cropping pattern or even in fertilizer application rates. There may have been an effect on 2005 farm plans, but in September 2005 the government decreed that all grain must be sold to the government, at official prices, and no private trade in grain would be permitted.[35] This reversal effectively removed any economic incentive to raise cereals production, though many observers report that an active private trade in rice and maize continues.[36]

The 2005 harvest was the best since before the famine and came within 10 percent, or 50,000 tons, of the FAO calculated minimum population need. It seemed as if the DPRK was on the way to restoring production, and in the fall of that year the government announced that food aid would no longer be accepted, that international aid programs should now emphasize development, rather than humanitarian assistance, and that many nongovernmental organizations could close their operations. Nonetheless, in the following years farm production again dropped, and the PDS continued to struggle to obtain the resources needed for widespread distribution. A typhoon in 2007 severely damaged that year's crop, and the government resumed international food aid in the following year. The WFP/FAO rapid food assessment in June 2008 noted that over three-quarters of households had cut back on food consumption, and over half (70 percent among PDS-dependent households) were eating only two meals a day.[37]

Private trade continued to grow despite regulations attempting to restrict it. Market prices for food remain many times higher than state prices. A dual economy has emerged, with the state-controlled sector characterized by central planning, fixed prices, and resource allocation based on the planning process. The market sector is characterized by small-scale production and trading activities, prices largely determined by supply and demand (typically ten to forty times higher than state prices), and resource allocation based on market forces modified by the absolute scarcity of many key items. The 2010 FAO crop assessment reported that the PDS provided only 52 percent of the calorie requirement to the population that year,[38] but other observers have claimed the PDS has effectively been abandoned, despite all government efforts to maintain it.[39]

Distribution Issues

Overall, the DPRK has not achieved food security at any point in the past two decades, but some population groups have been more affected than others. The DPRK food crisis has often been characterized as an urban famine, since rural families have had somewhat better access to food by being members of a cooperative farm or living where some food can be grown on unregulated (steeply sloping) land. Pyongyang received some special food allocations, but during the worst years of the famine, even ordinary officials in Pyongyang went hungry.

Not all rural areas are equally advantaged, however. The rice-bowl counties on the west coast and in Kangwon Province have the best soils and relatively high productivity. Inland and toward the north, terrain and soils become less productive, elevation rises, and average temperature and growing season correspondingly decrease. In such areas, farm production, especially without accustomed inputs, may not exceed the immediate needs of the farm population. The child-nutrition surveys somewhat validate this analysis: the three northeastern provinces—North and South Hamgyong and Ryanggang—consistently show the highest rates of malnutrition,[40] whether due to triage or simple lack of ability to distribute food from relatively better-off provinces.[41]

However, one must be cautious about an overly simple interpretation of the data. Although county-level statistics are not available, the raw data from individual sampling clusters reveal substantial differences in malnutrition rates between villages or urban wards within a single province. Variance within provinces is greater than variance between provinces, and one must not assume that all locations in the rice-bowl provinces are equally prosperous. For example, prevalence of severe stunting in all children under seven ranged from 23 to 50 percent in sampled *ri* (rural village complexes) or *dong* (urban wards) in North Hamgyong, and from 33 to 55 percent in sampled *ri* or *dong* in South Hamgyong. Sampled units in South Hwanghae, an agriculturally prosperous province, ranged from 10 to 47 percent stunting.[42]

With access to food more and more dependent on access to markets, income-earning opportunities became crucial to household food security. It is difficult to understand where individuals can earn cash, since state administration and production jobs pay only in ration coupons and a minimal wage, enough to buy only a few kilograms of grain per month. Anecdotal reports describe diversion of state goods to the market for private sale.[43] Rural households can sell garden produce and small livestock fed on scraps in their home compounds. Coastal villages have some access to an overexploited fishery, but with very rudimentary equipment. Petty trade in both foodstuffs and imported consumer items can provide a small income, which can augment household food access. But there seems to be little identifiable *productivity* in the market sector that would support its growth or continuation.

PATHS TO FOOD SECURITY

Despite the economic collapse of the 1990s and continual shortfalls in agricultural production, it is possible for the DPRK to achieve food security. Given historic emphasis on self-sufficient food production and lacking dynamic industry, the first step is to raise farm productivity to normal levels. Several possible trajectories depart from that point. A feasible path to improved food security is outlined below. It is not meant as a detailed prescription for development, for that would be little different from the central planning approach that has already proven ineffective. Rather, general technical and economic strategies are recommended that must be adapted and modified for local conditions and as the situation evolves. The DPRK could produce enough food domestically to feed its population, but that production cannot be accomplished in isolation. Regardless of whether food security is accomplished emphasizing local production or with some level of trade for food imports, productive and sustainable farming in the DPRK requires inputs that for the immediate future must be acquired by trade. Autarky is not an option. Some combination of material, industrial, and service exports, probably along with international aid, will be needed to achieve this target. In the longer term, agriculture and industry must become reconnected. Even an environmentally sustainable farming system requires both energy and some level of mechanization. The Korean proverb "Industry must live for agriculture to live" remains accurate.[44]

One must not ignore either the investment or economic policies required for the recommended changes. Recapitalization of the farming sector and purchase of an initial round of consumable supplies would require on the order of a billion dollars over a five-year period.[45] However, rebuilding the industrial sector to generate the exports needed for substantial commercial food purchases would require many times that investment and a longer time frame. Rational price structures, ability to reinvest profits, and permission to import supplies are also central to a revitalized agriculture or industrial sector.

Even with adequate aggregate food production, however, the question of effective food distribution must be addressed. Natsios has correctly noted that food produced does not equal food distributed, and Rüdiger Frank has pointed out that a full marketization of food would leave the newly created poor unable to purchase an adequate diet.[46] Nor does it help to depress farm incomes in order to ensure the diet of the urban population. Balanced economic development, whereby productive industrial and service sectors help produce or fund the inputs needed for agriculture as well as generate income for the urban population to purchase food, would go a long way toward ensuring food security for all. The state may participate in or regulate food trade, but it must buy from the farms at market rates for the farms to remain economically sustainable.

A Scenario for Food Self-sufficiency

Whatever the ultimate configuration of the DPRK economy, the immediate need for improved food production must be addressed. National-level data suggest that if appropriate technical and infrastructure changes can be implemented, food security is possible. Table 5.1 summarizes the food situation in 2010 based on the FAO/WFP report and the 2011 rapid assessment.[47] The data are arranged to more clearly show the impact of postharvest losses and to show the contribution of each crop to dietary protein.

Several changes from prior years bear noting: First, soybean production has expanded substantially, from 48,000 MT in 2005 to over 150,000 MT in 2010. The reported area of 90,000 ha is reported to be in addition to any other crops, which is difficult to accept given the limited arable land in the DPRK. Most soy is planted in fields suited for maize and in rotation with maize. One very common pattern in the DPRK is to plant alternating strips of maize and soybeans—for example eight rows of each, or eight rows of maize alternated with six rows of soybeans. Some farms report increasing the plant density of the maize strips to maintain the same number of maize plants per hectare despite the strips planted to soybeans.[48] Thus, it appears that farms are *reporting* a steady area planted to maize, in accord with planning quotas (583,000 ha between 2004 and 2007, 570,000 ha since 2008), rather than the actual field surface allocated to maize plants.

Second, the FAO/WFP have now adopted a slightly higher food standard, adding 7 kg/year of soybeans to the 167 kg of grains. This is the equivalent of about 7 gm of complete protein per person per day from soybeans—an improvement but still well below the dietary requirement. Grains and potatoes also provide crude protein but must be eaten together with other foods (legumes, meat, or dairy products) that contain the essential amino acids lacking in the grain if the body is to be able to utilize the full protein content.[49]

Third, postharvest losses are estimated differently from previous reports: 15 percent for rice, maize, and potatoes, 10 percent for double crops and soybeans. The 2010 report acknowledges, however, that there have been no studies to quantify these losses. Seed requirements are in line with previous estimates, and the estimated production

TABLE 5.1 DPRK food production, 2010–2011

Crop	*Area (1,000 ha)*	*Average yield (MT/ha)*	*Gross production (1,000 MT)*	*Postharvest loss (1,000 MT)*	*Seed need (1,000 MT)*	*Net production (1,000 MT)*	*Net protein (1,000 MT)*
Rice	570	4.26[a]	1,577	237	56	1,284	83
Maize	503	3.35	1,683	252	23	1,408	113
Other cereal	13	1.46	19	2	3	14	1
Main potato	48	13.0[b]	156	23	30	103	7
Spring potato	133	7.7[b]	256	38	83	134	9
Double crop	104	1.73	180	18	21	141	10
Soybean	90	1.71	154	15	5	133	47
Total	**1,461**		**4,025**	**587**	**221**	**3218**	**270**
Adjustments		Less animal feed				–150	–12
		Plus home gardens and production on slopes				+255	+16
Net food available						**3,293**	**273**
Total per person per day (gm)						**372**	**31**
Percentage of nutritional requirement						**81**	**62**

Sources: FAO, *CFSAR 2010*; WFP, *Rapid Food Security Assessment 2011.*

Note: Gross production, loss, seed, and net production data are in grain equivalent MT.

[a]As paddy; grain equivalent = 65%.

[b]As fresh potato; grain equivalent = 25%.

from household gardens and unscheduled plots on steep hillsides are added to the overall food balance sheet (75,000 MT and 150,000 MT, respectively).

When all is combined, the net locally produced food grain available to the population is 3,293,000 MT, or 372 gm per person per day, well short of the 480 gm minimum. Crude protein availability is about 31 gm/day, or 62 percent of the dietary requirement.

This situation could be substantially improved if crop yields were raised to normal levels and if the crop mix were changed somewhat. Table 5.2 shows one possible future production pattern based on modifications to the 2010 cropping pattern. First, the most important change is to raise production to reasonably attainable levels, which are in line with farm production in neighboring Asian countries.[50] The targets are modest and can be maintained by sustainable farming practices that do not require high applications of mineral fertilizer. Practical methods for achieving these yields are discussed below. Second, postharvest losses are cut to 5 percent across the board by improving crop handling and storage. Third, seed requirements for rice and other small grains can be reduced by better planting technology. Fourth, the area planted to soybeans is further increased, to about half the area now planted to maize. The maize area is correspondingly reduced, reflecting actual cropped area rather than planting quotas. Fifth, the area planted to double crops (winter wheat or barley or spring potato) is substantially reduced. Double cropping is an emergency measure that is not agronomically sustainable without continued fertilizer inputs. Finally, it is assumed that emergency cropping on hillsides ends, and there is no food budgeted from that activity, though the use of household gardens continues.[51] In this scenario, food-grain availability is 482 grams per person per day, with 50 grams of protein. Both figures are above the minimum requirement.

These estimates show that with existing land resources and for the current population, the DPRK could achieve food self-sufficiency and certainly food security. Past obstacles to increased production can be overcome by modifications of agriculture technology, infrastructure, and institutions. Most efforts to date have focused on modifying DPRK agricultural practices to improve efficiency and productivity. These technological changes have been effective, but their scope

TABLE 5.2 Possible DPRK food-production scenario

Crop	*Area (1,000 ha)*	*Average yield (MT/ha)*	*Gross production (1,000 MT)*	*Postharvest loss (1,000 MT)*	*Seed need (1,000 MT)*	*Net production (1,000 MT)*	*Net protein (1,000 MT)*
Rice	570	6.0[a]	2,223	111	26	2,086	136
Maize	300	5.0	1,500	75	14	1,412	113
Other cereal	13	3.0	39	2	2	35	2
Main potato	48	15.0[b]	180	9	30	141	10
Double crop	60	3.0	180	9	9	162	11
Soybean	250	2.2	550	28	15	508	178
Total	**1,241**		**4,672**	**234**	**96**	**4,343**	**449**
Adjustments		Less animal feed				–150	–12
		Plus home gardens only				+75	+5
Net food available						**4,268**	**443**
Total per person per day (gm)						**482**	**50**
Percentage of nutritional requirement						**105**	**100**

Note: Gross production, loss, seed, and net production data are in grain equivalent MT.

[a]As paddy; grain equivalent = 65%.

[b]As fresh potato; grain equivalent = 25%.

and sustainability have been greatly limited by the serious lack of infrastructural support and by an economic environment that inhibits maintenance of and reinvestment in modern technology. The government has supported many of the technical changes discussed and has attempted a variety of other policy changes that have been less successful.[52]

Improving Farming Practices

Many technical changes that would lead to substantially improved farm productivity are already being promoted by international aid organizations, tested at DPRK research centers, and being implemented on some farms. The fact that national grain production has risen since 2002 despite reduced fertilizer application (see figure 5.1) suggests that beneficial changes are already being adopted. A detailed discussion is beyond the scope of this chapter, but some important elements can be listed. DPRK soils have been degraded by overproduction and the previous excessive application of chemical fertilizer, which both acidified the soil and burned out most organic matter.[53] Increased applications of lime to counteract soil acidity can improve production of all crops by 20 to 40 percent;[54] farms need only sufficient fuel and trucks to transport the ground lime. Also, widespread planting of leguminous green manure crops would add nitrogen and organic matter to the soil. Green manures together with increased composting of crop wastes and animal manure are elements of DPRK organic farming policy (*yugi nongpop*), meaning in this case a reduced reliance on chemicals rather than certified organic production.[55] A third general practice, reduced-tillage farming of crops other than rice (sometimes termed conservation agriculture), is a means of reducing fuel and labor requirements and controlling weeds and soil erosion.

For rice, widespread adoption of the agronomic practices commonly labeled SRI (System of Rice Intensification) can increase yields dramatically, all other inputs held constant.[56] SRI also reduces seed requirement by at least half and shortens both the period of seedbed growth and time the crop is in the field, thus reducing some management pressure from long-maturity rice. DPRK farms supported by several international organizations have introduced and are expanding this technology. Shorter-maturity rice and maize crops are under development by the DPRK Academy of Agricultural Sciences, and when suitable varieties are released, they will remove the workload of maize transplanting and reduce the time conflict with overwintering crops such as wheat or green manures.

Good-quality hybrid seed is essential for modern maize production, and domestic seed production must be rehabilitated to meet the farms' need for annual seed replacement. One aid organization has recently established a maize-seed production facility that is managed in an economically sustainable manner and could serve as a model for similar infrastructure support in the future.[57] Local production of *Rhyzobium* bacterial inoculants for soybeans and other legumes would raise yields of these crops. Small production facilities exist but need management assistance.

The past pressure for maximum farm production led to an emphasis on rice and maize and especially did not include soil-enhancing legume crops. Diversification and rotation of crops grown in upland fields would contribute to better diets as well as more sustainable farming practices. Rotation between grain and legume crops such as soybeans is particularly beneficial, and potatoes should be planted in a field no more than once every three years in order to control disease and insect infestations. Again, several projects have been promoting these practices, most notably an International Fund for Agricultural Development (IFAD) project that stimulated improved crop rotation on all upland fields of thirty-seven cooperative farms in four counties.[58]

Reducing postharvest crop losses is one of the simplest tasks and would contribute a 5 to 10 percent food increase across the board. This can be accomplished by improved equipment such as mobile rice threshers and corn hullers, trucks to haul harvested grain to storage before it deteriorates in the field, grain-drying equipment, and improved storage facilities, especially for potatoes and other tubers. These technologies are well understood and well developed in neighboring countries and are already being adopted in the DPRK on a small scale. A reliable energy supply is essential, whether diesel fuel or electricity.

The normal rainfall pattern throughout the DPRK is highly concentrated, with 60 percent of the precipitation falling between mid-June and mid-September and normal spring precipitation inadequate for optimal crop growth. Small-pump systems to provide supplemental irrigation to selected upland fields in early spring would contribute to the maximum growth potential of crops such as maize, winter wheat, soybeans, and summer vegetables.[59] It is difficult to quantify the yield benefit, but at least 10 percent is a reasonable estimate. Again, reliable electrical supply to the pumps would be required.

The list goes on and includes integrated pest management, balanced application of potash and phosphate fertilizers, integration of livestock in farm activities, use of effective seeding equipment to improve germination and plant vigor, and so on. None of these are cutting-edge technologies; they represent the application of best management practices of sustainable and energy-efficient farming to the DPRK situation. These and other changes will increase and stabilize overall farm production and reduce the need for extreme measures such as farming on hillsides and extensive double cropping. Such environmentally damaging practices can be then halted and hillsides replanted in permanent cover (fruit trees, fuelwood species, or other agroforestry schemes).

Infrastructure Needs

All the above technical practices have already been introduced in the DPRK but are not widespread and thus have not brought about the aggregate production increases that are necessary. Farms have difficulty adopting these changes because they lack support infrastructure. Without continual donations from aid agencies, farms cannot obtain repair parts, and imported modern equipment thus has a working life of only a few years. A working transport infrastructure is needed to distribute inputs such as lime, fertilizer, and seed, as well as to move and safely store farm produce.

Other infrastructure needs include reliable electric power and seed-production enterprises (especially expanding the improvements in maize- and potato-seed production already begun). Continued development of irrigation canals fed by diversion of surface water would improve water reliability for rice production.[60] Research in groundwater resources for farm use and drilling relatively shallow wells for early-season irrigation of dryland crops[61] would reduce yield losses resulting from water stress. Modern, appropriate-size, energy-efficient farm equipment is urgently needed: midsize tractors, seed drills, and harvest equipment including bulk handling of grain and effective grain-drying equipment. At first such equipment may need to be imported but should be considered a high priority for domestic production in a revitalized DPRK industrial sector.

As noted above, the investment needed to make these infrastructure improvements will be significant—on the order of a billion U.S. dollars.[62] Many of the changes also require reliable fuel and electricity supplies, but for use in equipment that is much more energy efficient. Most changes can be made incrementally, as has happened with the irrigation-supply canals, the improvements in potato-seed production, the Welthungerhilfe-supported maize-seed factory, and a small ROK-supported rice transplanter assembly plant. Each improvement of the support infrastructure makes improving farm production a bit easier.

Economic Policies

Equally significant, however, are the changes needed in the economic environment. Whether the DPRK will implement widespread economic reform is debated, but there is likely an ongoing policy dialogue at several levels, and the proponents of reform have been able to initiate a number of changes.[63] Detailed discussion of economic policy is beyond the scope of this chapter, however.

Infrastructure cannot be maintained without continual reinvestment. Price controls on grains remove incentives to increase production and inhibit farm or farm-household reinvestment in productivity improvements. Currency controls and import restrictions obstruct farms from purchasing needed inputs, whether fertilizer, fuel, or equipment, and also depress both immediate production and investment in production growth. The 2002 price and wage reforms were an unsuccessful attempt to bring official prices in line with the market and thereby stimulate and capture food production. But continued absolute food shortages caused free-market prices to rise well above the official rates. The 2005 regulation that all grains be sold only to the state at the official price has also been ineffective in acquiring sufficient resources for the PDS. The November 2009 currency revaluation disrupted trade and exchange networks and created further disincentives for investment in improved productivity.[64]

Price controls and prohibition of grain sales in the market encourage farmworkers to put more effort into their private vegetable plots or small-animal raising than into the cooperative maize and rice fields. Yet a completely unregulated market would create new loci of food deprivation. Frank's suggestion of a hybrid or mixed system may well be necessary in the near term.[65] But if the state determines that it must manage and control distribution of food grains, it must also pay market prices to the farms in order to encourage greater production as well as to provide enough incentive not to divert their produce into other channels.

The dual economy and limitations of fertilizer, fuel, and other critical imports probably make farms willing to deliver only enough grain to the state to cover the supplies they actually receive at official prices. Since anything else must be acquired on the market, producers are unwilling to dispose of output at 5 percent (or less) of its market value. It is essential that the DPRK allow farms and other economic actors to trade for production inputs at free-market prices and allow imports adequate to meet the *economic* demand. Such a policy would help establish a reasonable value for the won and provide both incentive and ability for farms to turn immediate production increases into sustainable productivity improvements. Two IFAD-supported projects provide an example of how this can work. Microcredit loans to individual households were used to purchase mostly small animals and feed. With this support, livestock populations grew rapidly, the income of participating households doubled, and all loans were repaid.[66] The eggs, milk, and meat produced in these enterprises were sold through farmers' markets. The same model, absent the microloans, is now seen in other farms as well. For example, a cooperative-farm livestock work team may manage a piggery and distribute the piglets to farm households to raise.[67] Such enterprises are successful partly because they are based on traditional methods of animal raising but especially because all needed inputs are locally available in the market and can be paid for by the sale of animal products, also in the market. Restrictions on currency exchange and import of supplies do not impede production, and since prices are unregulated, profits can be reinvested to buy more baby animals and feed.

In comparison, a farm that at some point produces a grain surplus is now either forced to sell that surplus to the state at a small fraction of its market value, or, if it evades the regulation, it is still unable to use a market-based profit to purchase seed, spare parts, or fertilizer that could be used to further increase production the following year. The same situation holds for industrial enterprises producing farm supplies if they cannot sell them at a cost commensurate with the production costs and secure raw materials in the same manner. *Until these obstacles are removed, any aid, development loans, or investment in either the DPRK agriculture or industrial sectors will be unsustainable.*

It bears noting that collectivization per se is neither a cause of the DPRK food crisis nor an obstacle to increased farm production. Given the likelihood of continuing shortages of machinery, fuel, and other farm inputs, and of investment capital for modernization, organizing farm production at a work-team or SWT level may well be an efficient way to share limited resources. Devolution of economic accountability to the SWT has been a reasonable approach to increase worker incentive while maintaining a level of community responsibility, mutual support, and group-centered management of limited resources. Unbridled individuality is hardly necessary to improve DPRK farm production. But removing restrictions on trade in grain and relaxing land planting quotas to allow the SWTs to make their own management decisions based on local resources and abilities would add an important element of flexibility and responsiveness to the production system and facilitate a more diverse, sustainable, and adaptable cropping system.

Institutional Evolution

The agricultural transformation discussed above will not be static or even develop in a single, predictable trajectory. Management decisions must be decentralized. Farms have reported they cannot grow more soybeans, for example, because they must meet high maize-production quotas. Flexibility to innovate must be allowed. Also, food security cannot be achieved in a closed economic system, and the past reliance on imports from the USSR and China demonstrates that DPRK food production has never been accomplished in a closed system. To achieve sustainable food security on a national scale, foreign exchange must be generated to purchase the needed farm inputs that cannot presently be sourced in the DPRK. This could be accomplished by exporting modern industrial products and services as well as high-value farm or fishery products. The gradual regrowth of industrial and services sectors will also help generate income the nonfarm population will need to purchase food in a marketized economy.[68]

As farm production rises and diversifies and as the necessary domestic industrial-support infrastructure also develops, opportunities for increased international trade will likely affect production choices, investment opportunities, and consumer behavior. Two-way trade in food as well as in industrial products may well develop over time and is not antithetical to food security, so long as North Koreans have adequate purchasing power to meet basic nutrition needs.

The changes discussed above cannot be accomplished without a substantial influx of capital for development. At present, it is difficult to identify sources for the initial investments needed to rehabilitate the farm and industrial sectors. As noted, both sectors must develop in parallel for changes in farm techniques and technology to be sustainable. Economic policies must be implemented that allow production surpluses to be reinvested. A functioning, transparent national financial system is needed, especially for the DPRK to work with the international financial institutions.[69] Difficult international political conflicts must be resolved before adequate aid or investment is likely to be forthcoming, but governments and other potential donors or investors should realize that rebuilding the agriculture sector, including its industrial infrastructure, could encourage engagement and conflict resolution in other spheres. Hopefully the DPRK leadership under Kim Jong Eun will also understand that assistance and market development are not antithetical to *juche* ideology or domestic political stability, and that accepting international contact and cooperation and maintaining a stable domestic polity are not a zero-sum trade-off. Rather, development and sustainable economic growth in an open, flexible, and dynamic economic system benefit all actors compared with the continuing austerity of the past two decades.

CONCLUSION

The ongoing food crisis in the DPRK originated in the loss of foreign energy subsidies to a highly energy-dependent agriculture system. But with the use of appropriate and commonplace modern farm methods, the DPRK could become food secure and indeed food self-sufficient. Sustainable agricultural development requires concomitant improvements in farm and industrial infrastructure, relaxation of central-planning controls, and adoption of economic policies that encourage reinvestment of profits into greater productive capacity and facilitate a rational exchange and pricing mechanism for farm inputs and food. Even with increased farm production, national food security also requires growth of industrial and service-sector wages, both to enable the nonfarm population to purchase food and to provide commensurate income to the farms that produce it. The technical and infrastructure changes can be accomplished incrementally but require an appropriate economic policy environment and domestic financial institutions that can be provided only by the government. The investment needed will be substantial but of the same order of magnitude as past humanitarian donations of food and medical aid. And once begun, agriculture and industrial modernization should generate profits for further investment. With appropriate policy choices, a long-term solution is possible.

NOTES

1. Food and Agriculture Organization, World Food Programme, *Special Report: FAO/WFP Crop and Food Security Assessment Mission to the Democratic People's Republic of Korea, 16 November 2010* (Rome: Food and Agriculture Organization of the United Nations, 2010); Food and Agriculture Organization/World Food Programme, *Special Report: FAO/WFP Crop and Food Security Assessment Mission to the Democratic People's Republic of Korea, 25 November 2011* (Rome: Food and Agriculture Organization of the United Nations, 2011). Subsequent citations to this and other FAO crop and food security assessments will be identified as *CFSAR* and the relevant year. Food and Agriculture Organization of the United Nations, World Food Programme, United Nations Children's Fund, *Special Report: FAO/WFP/UNICEF Rapid Food Security Assessment Mission*

to the Democratic People's Republic of Korea, 24 March 2011 (Rome: Food and Agriculture Organization of the United Nations, 2011).

2. Food and Agriculture Organization of the United Nations, *Food Security*, Policy Briefs, issue 2 (Rome: FAO, June 2006), 1 ftp://ftp.fao.org/es/ESA/policybriefs/pb_02.pdf (accessed December 15, 2010).
3. See chapter 6, this volume.
4. Wages were on the order of 100 to 200 won per month, with an official exchange rate of U.S.$1 = 2.12 KPW and a black-market rate of 150 won per dollar.
5. Stephan Haggard and Marcus Noland, in *Famine in North Korea: Markets, Aid, and Reform* (New York: Columbia University Press, 2007), chap. 2, suggest that production in the 1980s and early 1990s was actually much less than what was reported by the DPRK or estimated by the WFP/FAO; Hazel Smith, in *Hungry for Peace: International Security, Humanitarian Assistance, and Social Change in North Korea*. (Washington, DC: United States Institute of Peace Press, 2006), 66, notes the beginning of "Let's eat two meals a day" campaigns as early as 1990. John Feffer, *Korean Food, Korean Identity: The Impact of Globalization on Korean Agriculture* (Stanford: Shorenstein Asia-Pacific Research Center, 2005), 26, http://iis-db.stanford.edu/pubs/20815/Globalization_and_Korean_Agriculture_John_Feffer.pdf (accessed November 18, 2010), cites other sources describing scarcity in the late 1980s. Nonetheless, it appears that minimal needs were mostly being met through at least 1990. See also Andrei Lankov and Kim Seok-hyang, "North Korean Market Vendors: The Rise of Grassroots Capitalists in a Post-Stalinist Society," *Pacific Affairs* 81, no. 1 (2008): 53–72.
6. Haggard and Noland, *Famine in North Korea*, chap. 3.
7. Han Park, *North Korea: The Politics of Unconventional Wisdom* (Boulder: Rienner, 2002).
8. Sung Chull Kim, *North Korea under Kim Jong Il: From Consolidation to Systemic Dissonance* (Albany: SUNY Press, 2006).
9. Marcus Noland, "North Korea in Transition," *Korean Journal of Defense Analysis* 17, no. 1 (2005): 7–32, http://www.kida.re.kr/eng/publication/pdf/01_Marcus%20Noland.pdf (accessed December 17, 2010); Benjamin Habib, "Climate Change and Regime Perpetuation in North Korea," *Asian Survey* 50, no. 2 (2010): 378–401.
10. Central Bureau of Statistics, *D P R Korea 2008 Population Census National Report* (Pyongyang: Central Bureau of Statistics, 2008).
11. Feffer, *Korean Food, Korean Identity*, 6.

12. FAO, *CFSAR 2010*, 10.
13. Central Bureau of Statistics, *D P R Korea 2008 Population Census.*
14. If all arable land is included, the figure is 0.083 ha/person.
15. Korean Central News Agency, "Joint New Year Editorial," Pyongyang, 2005, http://www.kcna.co.jp/index-e.htm, January 2, 2005 (accessed March 8, 2005); Korean Central News Agency, "Joint New Year Editorial," Pyongyang, 2006, http://www.kcna.co.jp/index-e.htm, January 2, 2006 (accessed February 5, 2006); Korean Central News Agency, "Joint New Year Editorial," Pyongyang, 2010, http://www.kcna.co.jp/index-e.htm, January 1, 2010 (accessed January 6, 2010); Korean Central News Agency, "Joint New Year Editorial," Pyongyang, 2011, http://www.kcna.co.jp/index-e.htm, January1, 2011 (accessed January 1, 2011).
16. In the DPRK, fertilizer rates are almost always discussed in terms of "ammonium sulfate equivalent," which was the most commonly available fertilizer prior to the mid-1990s. Ammonium sulfate contains 20 to 21 percent nitrogen, so this target translates to around 400 kg of nitrogen per hectare. Few U.S. farmers apply more than 250 kg/ha, even on the highest-yielding farms of the corn belt.
17. Woon-Keun Kim, "The Agricultural Situation of North Korea," Food and Fertilizer Technology Center, Taipei, 1999, http://www.fftc.agnet.org/library.php?func=view&id=20110726131553 (accessed March 8, 2005).
18. Jaewoo Choo, "Mirroring North Korea's Growing Economic Dependence on China," *Asian Survey* 48, no. 2 (2008): 343–372.
19. Randall Ireson, *Food Security in North Korea: Designing Realistic Possibilities* (Stanford: Shorenstein Asia-Pacific Research Center, 2006), http://iis-db.stanford.edu/evnts/4140/Ireson_FoodSecurity_2006.pdf.
20. See chapter 2, this volume.
21. Haggard and Noland, *Famine in North Korea*, chap. 2.
22. FAO, *CFSAR 1999.*
23. World Food Programme, *Nutrition Survey of the Democratic People's Republic of Korea* (Rome: World Food Programme, 1998), http://oldsite.nautilus.org/DPRKBriefingBook/humanitarian/nutrition_survery98.pdf (accessed December 19, 2010). Children under two years of age typically are at least partly breast-fed and thus somewhat insulated from food shortages. Therefore, I consider the nutrition status of the twenty-five months to eighty-four months age group as most indicative of food availability.
24. Andrew S. Natsios, *The Great North Korean Famine: Famine, Politics, and Foreign Policy* (Washington, DC: United States Institute of Peace Press, 2001), 111ff.

25. Ibid.
26. See, for example, W. Courtland Robinson, Myung Ken Lee, Kenneth Hill, and Gilbert M. Burnham, "Mortality in North Korean Households: A Retrospective Study," *Lancet* 354 (1999): 291–295, http://reliefweb.int/rw/RWFiles2000.nsf/FilesByRWDocUNIDFileName/ACOS-64BLZ7-NKorea_Health.pdf.pdf/$File/NKorea_Health.pdf.pdf (accessed December 19, 2010); Noland, "North Korea in Transition"; Hazel Smith, "Intelligence Failure and Famine in North Korea," *Asia-Pacific Journal: Japan Focus* (2004), http://www.japanfocus.org/-Hazel-Smith/1634 (accessed December 19, 2010); Daniel Goodkind and Loraine West, "The North Korean Famine and Its Demographic Impact," *Population and Development Review* 27, no. 2 (2001): 219–238.
27. Sung Hun Han, "Poverty Line in North Korea," *Peace Economics, Peace Science, and Public Policy* 11, no. 1, art. 3 (2005): 15, 17, http://www.bepress.com/peps/vol11/iss1/3/ (accessed March 13, 2009).
28. See chapter 6, this volume.
29. World Food Programme, Food Aid Information System Database, http://www.wfp.org/fais/quantity-reporting/overview (accessed December 27, 2010).
30. Institute of Child Nutrition, *DPRK 2004 Nutrition Assessment Report of Survey Results* (Pyongyang: Central Bureau of Statistics, 2005).
31. Prior to the reform, farms received 0.62 won/kg for paddy (unmilled) rice, which given normal 65 percent milling recovery would be valued at 0.95 won/kg for milled rice. The milled rice was distributed through the PDS for 0.08 won/kg. See Han, "Poverty Line in North Korea."
32. Ibid.
33. Institute for Far Eastern Studies, "Pyongyang's 'Unification' Market of Today," Nautilus Institute Policy Forum Online 06-27A, http://www.nautilus.org/fora/security/0627.html (accessed January 26, 2009).
34. Tae-Jin Kwon reports this policy in some provinces beginning in 2003. See Tae-Jin Kwon, "Agricultural Policies Under Reform in the DPRK," Institute for Far Eastern Studies, Seoul, ICNK Forum no. 05–07–13–1, http://ifes.kyungnam.ac.kr/admin/upload_file/icnk_brief/ICNK_FORUM_20050713.pdf (accessed December 30, 2010).
35. John Feffer, "The Right to Food: North Korea and the Politics of Famine and Human Rights," in *Human Rights in North Korea: Toward a Comprehensive Understanding*, ed. Kie-Duck Park and Sang-Jin Han, 67–115 (Seoul: Sejong Institute, 2007).

36. Institute for Far Eastern Studies, "DPRK Abandons Food Rations, Orders Self-Sufficiency," IFES NK Brief no. 10–06–17–1, http://ifes.kyungnam.ac.kr/eng/m05/s10/content.asp?nkbriefNO=369&GoP= 4 (accessed January 2, 2011).
37. World Food Programme, Food and Agriculture Organization of the United Nations, *Democratic People's Republic of Korea Joint WFP/FAO Rapid Food Security Assessment* (Rome: World Food Programme, 2008), 5.
38. FAO, *CFSAR 2010*, 23.
39. Andrei Lankov, "Staying Alive," *Foreign Affairs* 87, no. 2 (2008): 9–16.
40. Central Bureau of Statistics, *Report on the DPRK Nutrition Assessment 2002* (Pyongyang: Central Bureau of Statistics, 2002); Institute of Child Nutrition, *DPRK 2004 Nutrition Assessment Report*.
41. Food distribution to the northeastern provinces was stopped or sharply reduced beginning in 1991. Whether this was a conscious policy of triage or reflected the government's inability to move food to areas of extreme scarcity is debated. See Natsios, *Great North Korean Famine*; Smith, "Intelligence Failure and Famine in North Korea"; Feffer, "Right to Food."
42. International Fund for Agricultural Development, *Coastal Communities Livelihood Support Project: Working Paper 1* (Rome: International Fund for Agricultural Development, 2006), table 2.
43. Lankov and Kim, "North Korean Market Vendors."
44. In Korean, *Sanopi salaya nongopi sanda*. Quoted in L. Gordon Flake and Scott Snyder, eds., *Paved with Good Intentions: The NGO Experience in North Korea* (Westport, CT: Praeger, 2003), 19.
45. In Ireson, *Food Security in North Korea*, 20, I estimated around $840 million to recapitalize all DPRK farms, including the cost of international technical assistance. This estimate did not consider improvements in support infrastructure.
46. Natsios, *Great North Korean Famine*, 89ff. He notes that a dual price structure encourages producers to withhold production from the PDS and encourages those controlling food distribution to benefit their families first. See also Rüdiger Frank, "Economic Reforms in North Korea (1998–2004): Systemic Restrictions, Quantitative Analysis, Ideological Background," *Journal of the Asia Pacific Economy* 10, no. 3 (2005): 278–311.
47. Compared with the 2010 *CFSAR* estimate, the WFP *Rapid Food Security Assessment 2011* projects a spring 2011 harvest that is 232,000 MT less owing to adverse winter and early spring weather.
48. C. J. Nelson, pers. comm., 2009.

49. Crude-protein contributions in the tables are estimated based on accepted average nutritional values of each crop: 6.5 percent for polished milled rice, 8 percent for maize, 7 percent for other cereals, 1.7 percent for potatoes, fresh weight, and 35 percent for soybeans.
50. The national average rice yield in the ROK has been above 6 MT/ha for all but two years since the mid-1980s. Yields in China have climbed from 5.5 MT/ha to 6.5 MT/ha; see International Rice Research Institute, "Rice in China," http://irri.org/our-partners/country-relations/asia-oceania/china/rice-in-china (accessed December 27, 2010), and International Rice Research Institute "Rice in South Korea," http://irri.org/our-partners/country-relations/asia-oceania/south-korea/rice-in-south-korea (accessed December 27, 2010). Japanese yields are slightly higher. ROK maize yields have ranged from 4.1 MT/ha to 5.1 MT/ha, and soybean yields from 1.5 MT/ha to 1.8 MT/ha; see KREI, *Agriculture in Korea 1999* (Seoul: Korea Rural Economic Institute, 1999), 43. Northern Iowa and southern Ontario *organic* farmers regularly attain maize yields of over 8 MT/ha and soy yields of over 2.5 MT/ha in rotation systems.
51. Restoring hillsides to timber, fuelwood, fruit, and pasture production would further benefit the economy and environment and improve diet quality.
52. Feffer, "Right to Food," and Frank, "Economic Reforms in North Korea," among others, discuss the difficult choices the government faces in attempting to balance egalitarian policies, economic control, and effective incentives and support for economic growth.
53. Soil pH has been measured as low as 4, and few farms have soil above pH 6.0. Soil organic matter is typically around 1 percent or less.
54. Swiss Agency for Development and Cooperation, "Maize Yield Estimation in Lime Application Trial Plots in Miru (2008)" (SDC internal project document, Berne, 2008).
55. Management issues related to the use of green manures and compost include coordinating crop-planting dates, local seed production, and availability of animal manure, but they can be resolved.
56. See, for example, http://sri.ciifad.cornell.edu/index.html and its links, such as http://sri.ciifad.cornell.edu/aboutsri/methods/index.html.
57. Karin Janz, "Are We Doing What We Want to Do in the DPRK?" (paper presented at the Conference on Humanitarian and Development Assistance to the DPRK, Seoul, November 15–17, 2010).
58. International Fund for Agricultural Development, *Democratic Peoples' Republic of Korea Uplands Food Security Project: Interim Evaluation,*

report no. 2026-KP (Rome: IFAD, 2008), http://www.ifad.org/evaluation/public_html/eksyst/doc/prj/region/pi/korea/korea.pdf (accessed December 23, 2010).

59. Such systems would not be designed to supply full crop water requirements but only the need during April through early June and then be shut down except in a drought emergency.
60. Three such canals have already been completed: the Kaechon–Taesong Lake canal supplies water from the Taedong River to farms in South Pyongan Province, the Paekma Lake–Cholsan canal feeds North Pyongan farms, and a third canal in the Miru hills serves farms in North Hwanghae Province.
61. An active program of well drilling for domestic water supply is under way. The experience gained should be used in a separate program to develop farm water resources, which require much higher pumping rates than for town supplies.
62. Ireson, *Food Security in North Korea*.
63. See, for example, Robert L. Carlin and Joel S. Wit, "North Korean Reform: Politics, Economics and Security," *Adelphi Papers* 46, no. 382 (2006): 1–65; Patrick McEachern, "North Korea's Policy Process: Assessing Institutional Policy Preferences," *Asian Survey* 49, no. 3 (2009): 528–552; Bradley O. Babson, "Facing Reality: Will North Korea Adopt a More Rational Economic Policy?" 38 North, July 9, 2010 (U.S.-Korea Institute at SAIS, Johns Hopkins University), http://38north.org/2010/07/facing-reality-will-north-korea-adopt-a-more-rational-economic-policy/ (accessed August 10, 2010).
64. The won was devalued by a factor of one hundred, but wages were kept the same and prices adjusted. The price of milled rice sold through the PDS went from 44 won/kg to 24 won/kg (equivalent to 2,400 won in old currency and near the previous market rate), and farms were to be paid 29 won/kg for unmilled rice (equal to 44 won if milled). But a year later the market price of milled rice was around 1,000 (new) won/kg; FAO, *CFSAR 2010*, 6–7.
65. Frank, "Economic Reforms in North Korea."
66. International Fund for Agricultural Development, *Democratic Peoples' Republic of Korea Uplands Food Security Project*.
67. C. J. Nelson, pers. comm., 2009.
68. The DPRK now trades coal for maize, and some fishing vessels sell part of their catch to Chinese processors. Other enterprises export software, animation graphics, and minerals. The Kaesong Industrial Complex is

another model of processing for export, as are weapons sales. Because of the recent lack of farm chemicals, DPRK farm products could be grown to certified organic standards and marketed at a substantial price premium. Efficient production of modern farm equipment might compete with ROK or Japanese machinery.

69. Bradley Babson, "The Rocky Road for Modernizing the North Korean Economy," *Korea's Economy* 26 (2010): 45–51.

CHAPTER 6

The External Dimension of North Korea's Food Security

Securing Outside Supplies of Food, Fertilizer, and Fuel

MARK E. MANYIN

Despite the Kim regime's ideological emphasis on *juche*, or "self-reliance," the outside world has always been essential to food security in North Korea. During the decades of relative plenty, the 1950s through the mid-1980s, North Korea imported, at special "friendship prices," important agricultural inputs such as fertilizer and fuel from patrons such as the Soviet Union. In the famine and postfamine years of the 1990s and the following decade, when domestic food production was woefully short of North Korea's needs, the importance of inflows from the outside world increased. Indeed, a major priority of North Korean diplomacy in these years was identifying donors or sellers of cereals, fuel, and fertilizer. Three countries—China, South Korea, and the United States—were particularly critical in these efforts, which are likely to feature prominently in the foreign policy of the new, Kim Jong Eun regime. This chapter looks at the external component of North Korea's food-security situation, particularly during the famine and postfamine period.

THE PREFAMINE FOOD SYSTEM

Until the late 1980s and early 1990s, the North Korean state was fairly successful in distributing staples, including most food staples, to the North Korean population. In the prefamine period, the Public Distribution System (PDS) supplied food with amounts that were calibrated according to each family's size, rank, type of work, and age.[1] High-ranking government officials, soldiers, and special security forces received the largest daily rations, though families in each of these privileged classes were also supplied by separate distribution systems such as that run by the North Korean Workers' Party.[2] An individual's occupation, as well as region of residence, was often indirectly determined also by an individual's *song-bun*, or "loyalty rating," the result of extensive background checks including the backgrounds of relatives. Those from the "core" class were more likely to be eligible for privileged positions and spots in elite universities, as well as more likely to be allowed to reside in Pyongyang. The "wavering" and "hostile" classes—which today account for around 75 percent of the population combined—found it more difficult, and at times impossible, to attain such privileges.

Under the prefamine PDS, cooperative-farm workers were required to meet production targets and were allocated household rations, which were taken from the harvest before being sold to the government. The sale prices to the government were far below what could be obtained in markets, but in exchange farmers received farming supplies, consumer goods, as well as food through the PDS during the preharvest months. As Stephan Haggard and Marcus Noland have put it, so long as the government maintained its implicit part of the bargain, farmers' incentive to hoard or divert food into the markets remained limited.[3]

Three fundamental characteristics of the food system made it particularly fragile. First, as Randall Ireson describes in the preceding chapter, the system was highly centralized, particularly after food shortages in the early 1970s, making each cooperative less able and likely to adapt crops and techniques to local conditions. Second, it was highly reliant upon industrial inputs, particularly industrially produced fertilizer and pesticides. Overfertilization and high use of pesticides created a vicious cycle as gradually lower soil fertility created an ever-growing need for more chemicals. The system also relied heavily upon electrically powered artificial-irrigation methods. Thus, the system was highly vulnerable to any energy shock. Once domestic sources of energy dried up, outside sources were needed to fill the gap.

Third, and most important, at its core the system was highly dependent upon Soviet and Chinese aid. For much of the Cold War, the Soviet Union not only financed North Korea's chronic current-account deficits but also offered "friendship" prices for essential energy exports like coal and oil. Soviet military technology transfers were also important because North Korea arms exports were, as they continue to be today, significant generators of foreign exchange.[4] Additionally, the Soviets and Chinese shipped fuel at "friendship" prices. The fuel was especially critical for producing fertilizer.

THE FAMINE AND EXTERNAL SOURCES OF FOOD SECURITY

In 1987, Moscow began to cut its aid and reduce its price supports. In 1990, at the same time Moscow was pursuing better relations with South Korea, the Soviet Union insisted that North Korea pay for Soviet goods at world market prices and in foreign currency. Imports from the Soviet Union fell precipitously; by 1993, Nicholas Eberstadt has estimated, they were 10 percent of their 1987–1990 average.[5] China briefly stepped in to fill part of the gap, but by the mid-1990s, it too began to demand cash payment. The Democratic People's Republic of Korea (DPRK) could no longer acquire the energy and other inputs needed to maintain productivity in agriculture or industry. As Haggard and Noland have described it, "in the face of this massive trade shock, the North Korean industrial economy began to implode," taking with it the agricultural system.[6] By one estimate, grain production in 1996 and 1997 fell to about 42 percent of its 1989 peak.[7]

As Haggard and Noland have argued, rather than radically adopting new agricultural policies or shifting strategies to obtain food from the outside world—either through increased exports or appealing for aid—the North Korean government responded first by years of strategies to suppress demand for food. From the time the shortages began in the late 1980s, North Korean propaganda invoked the spirit of Kim Il Sung's deprivations during his "arduous march" against the Japanese colonizers. "Let's Eat Two Meals a Day," North Koreans were urged during one patriotic campaign. The state propaganda machine blamed the shortages on a blockade supposedly imposed by the United States.[8] As the famine worsened, Pyongyang finally issued an appeal, in 1995, to the outside world for assistance and redoubled its efforts to obtain imports of food and key agricultural inputs such as fertilizer and fuel.

Within two years after North Korea publicly turned to the outside world for help, Pyongyang had become adept at ensuring a relatively stable supply of food, fuel, and fertilizer through a combination of assistance and commercial imports. Moreover, as I have discussed elsewhere, the North Korean government continually, and often successfully, sought food-aid donors who would insist on least-onerous monitoring and access conditions.[9]

THE DATA CHALLENGE

The rest of this chapter examines inflows of cereals, fertilizer, and fuel since the worst of the famine years in the mid to late 1990s. One theme that runs throughout is the difficulty in distinguishing between aid to and trade with North Korea (see table 6.1 for an illustration of the challenge). North Korean data are sporadic and questionable, and gaining access to reliable North Korean officials is problematic. Moreover, North Korea's biggest source of the inflows necessary to ensure food security, China, does not publish or release its data on aid to North Korea, except to report to the World Food Programme's International Food Aid Information System (INTERFAIS) database. However, the manner of such reporting makes it impossible to distinguish between China's aid and commercial exports, to say nothing of the extent to which commercial exports are sent at "friendship" prices to North Korea.

An indication of China's attempt to obscure its data is that in 2009, in the months after the UN Security Council passed resolution 1874 imposing tougher sanctions on trade with North Korea, China Customs began reporting a precipitous decline in exports to "North Korea" while simultaneously recording an unprecedented surge in exports to "Northeast Asia."[10] This appeared to be an attempt to make Chinese

TABLE 6.1 The data problem: Aid or trade for leading suppliers of cereals to North Korea, 1995–2009

Country	*Volume (millions MT)*	*Comments*
China	3.6 cereal exported; 3.4 cereal aid	Relationship between trade and aid unclear; China suppressed 2009 data on exports to North Korea.
South Korea	3.3 cereal aid	Provided mostly as low-interest, long-term loans
United States	2.2 cereal aid	
Japan	1.3 cereal aid	Last provided in 2005
Thailand	1.1 cereal exported	Some aid, some trade, some purchased by South Korea and shipped as aid directly to North Korea
Brazil	0.9 cereal exported	Presumably trade

Sources: Global Trade Atlas; USAID; ROK Export-Import Bank, "DPRK Support Fund," via ROK Ministry of Unification.

exports to North Korea look lower. Between 25 and 40 percent of China's exports of cereals, coal, and oil to North Korea in 2009 were recorded in this fashion. After a number of observers complained, China abandoned this practice in 2010. The numbers for "Northeast Asia" and "North Korea" suddenly returned to their customary levels.

EXTERNAL SOURCES OF CEREALS

Aid

Between 1997 and 2008, North Korean diplomacy brought in a rather stable inflow of food aid, cumulatively totaling over twelve million metric tons (MT) (see figure 6.1). Although it is true that annual food-aid inflows varied significantly, this should not obscure the larger point that during this period, except for 2006, over 750,000 MT of food, or around three-quarters of the estimated harvest gap, were brought into the country either gratis or on concessional terms.[11] As shown in table 6.1, according to the INTERFAIS database, four countries—China, South Korea, the United States, and Japan—have dominated the

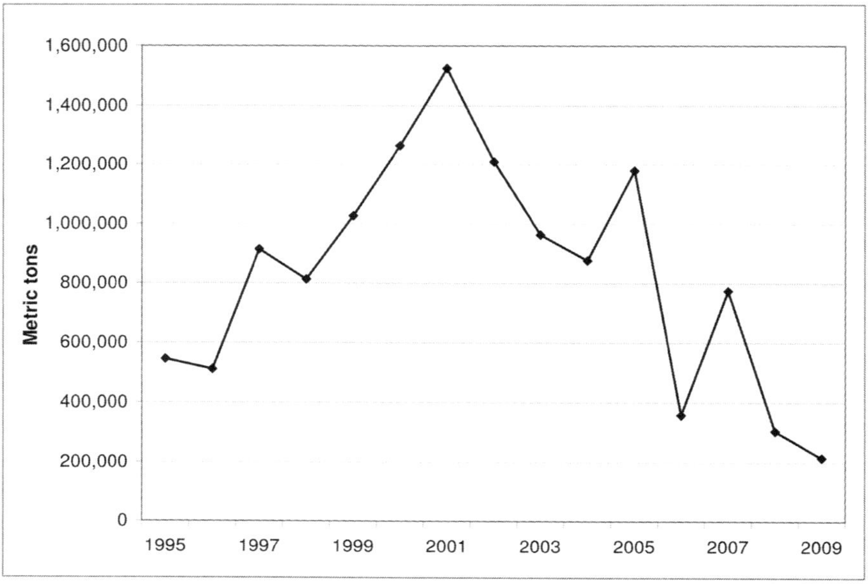

FIGURE 6.1. Food aid to North Korea, 1995–2009. (Source: INTERFAIS database)

provision of food aid to North Korea, accounting for over 80 percent of total donations.

Figure 6.1 and table 6.1 tell much of the story of North Korea's aid diplomacy during the first decade of the twenty-first century. By the middle of that decade, the North Korean government was sufficiently emboldened by its successful food-aid diplomacy and several better harvests to impose new restrictions on the operations of the World Food Programme (WFP) in the country. The WFP had been the main vehicle through which food aid from the United States and a number other countries had been channeled. Food donations from Western countries and Japan stopped as a result of these restrictions, as well as the eruption of the second North Korean nuclear crisis in 2002, the collapse in Japan-DPRK normalization talks, and the realization by donors that the North Korean regime effectively had chosen to remain dependent on food aid instead of expending foreign exchange on imports of food. The virtually unconditional food aid that China and the South Korean government of Roh Moo-hyun provided during the middle of the decade made up for this change and indeed may have enabled

North Korea to insist that the WFP curtail the presence and intrusiveness of its North Korea program. However, this left North Korea vulnerable to a change in government in Seoul.

Food aid fell precipitously after 2007 for a number of reasons. When the conservative Lee Myung-bak was inaugurated as South Korean president in 2008 and demanded better monitoring of food shipments and more reciprocity in North-South relations, Pyongyang reacted negatively and declined to ask for food from Seoul. The same was true for fertilizer aid from South Korea. At the same time, for unknown reasons, food aid from China decreased dramatically. North Korea also experienced some of its worst harvests in a decade. In the spring of 2008, Pyongyang turned back to the United States, negotiating an agreement that allowed for substantial improvement in monitoring and access in return for a pledge of half a million MT of food. Most of this food was to be channeled through a reinvigorated WFP country program. However, the United States had shipped only about a third of the aid before

TABLE 6.2 Major food donors to North Korea, 1995–2009

Year	*China*	*South Korea*	*United States*	*Japan*	*Total for all countries*
1995	—	150,000	—	378,000	544,492
1996	100,000	3,401	23,379	136,702	510,119
1997	150,000	62,393	139,942	791	914,567
1998	153,351	54,056	241,521	67,000	812,383
1999	207,103	12,204	549,611	—	1,026,838
2000	291,349	351,703	317,060	99,999	1,263,564
2001	435,148	198,000	320,795	500,000	1,525,618
2002	350,696	457,800	222,938	—	1,208,953
2003	230,422	542,191	48,162	—	963,794
2004	158,722	406,510	106,437	80,803	877,164
2005	531,416	492,743	27,699	48,084	1,179,812
2006	257,991	79,500	—	—	358,679
2007	312,231	431,280	—	—	773,767
2008	126,784	8,605	147,226	—	305,054
2009	124,067	—	31,016	—	215,780
Total	**3,429,279**	**3,250,386**	**2,175,786**	**1,311,379**	**12,480,583**
Share (%)	27.5	26.0	17.4	10.5	100

Source: INTERFAIS database.

disagreements with the North Korean government led to the program's cessation. This coincided with the collapse of the Six-Party Talks over North Korea's nuclear program.[12] The lack of food-aid donations from the United States and South Korea has led the WFP to drastically curtail its operation in North Korea, despite ongoing food shortages. Even after the WFP negotiated a new protocol with North Korean authorities in the spring of 2011, the size of the agency's program remained a fraction of its former scope. No doubt the WFP and North Korea hoped that negotiations with the Obama administration in late 2011, would lead the United States to resume large-scale food assistance and rejuvenate donations from abroad. These talks, which, according to many reports, were nearing conclusion and were unofficially linked to a North Korean concession on its nuclear program, were halted after Kim Jong Il's death.

Commercial Imports

As for commercial exports of cereals to North Korea, since Pyongyang's statistics are either not available or unreliable, some insights can be gleaned from other countries' export data. An analysis of such "mirror" statistics from the customs services of nearly seventy countries reveals that the leading exporters of cereals to North Korea were China, Thailand, and Brazil.[13]

China has been by far the largest supplier. China Customs reports that between 1995 and the end of 2010, Chinese enterprises exported over 3.7 million MT of cereals to North Korea. By volume, nearly 95 percent of Chinese commercial exports have consisted of corn (about 67 percent) and rice (about 27 percent). As with aggregate food-aid inflows, although annual North Korean imports of cereals from China have varied, they have consistently been significant (see figure 6.2). Aside from 2004 and 2006, inflows of grains from China have always exceeded 100,000 MT. Chinese exports of cereals since 2005 appear to have undergone a significant shift downward. Between 2005 and 2006, shipments of corn and rice fell by a factor of four, from around 330,000 MT in 2005 to under 80,000 MT the following year. Although exports to North Korea nearly doubled in 2007, following flooding and a poor harvest there, they have yet to reach the same level as in the past.

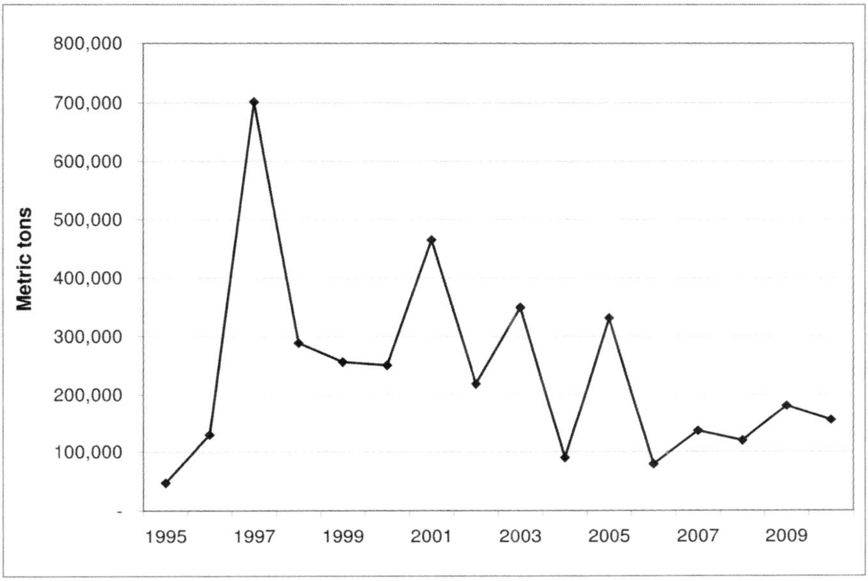

FIGURE 6.2. Chinese cereal exports to North Korea, 1995–2010. (Source: China Customs statistics as reported to Global Trade Atlas)

As mentioned, calculating Chinese food aid is problematic; the way the Chinese government reports its food aid to the WFP makes it impossible for the WFP to distinguish between aid and commercial exports.[14] Because of the opacity of Chinese data and the Chinese government's unwillingness to differentiate between food aid and commercial sales to North Korea, it is unclear to what extent aid and exports overlap (see figure 6.3). Overall, there appears to be a relationship between aid and trade; after 2000, the trend lines for both categories of shipments tend to follow each other closely. However, it is not clear to what extent aid and trade overlap or are sent separately; the 126,000 MT of aid in 2008, for instance, may include or be in addition to the 119,000 MT in reported exports.

China has been known to offer some products to North Korea at "friendship prices" significantly lower than prevailing world prices. Thus, a look at the prices China charges to North Korea for its exports can perhaps shed some light on the question of trade versus aid. As figure 6.4 shows, according to Chinese customs data, it appears that the corn from China is not provided at concessional prices.

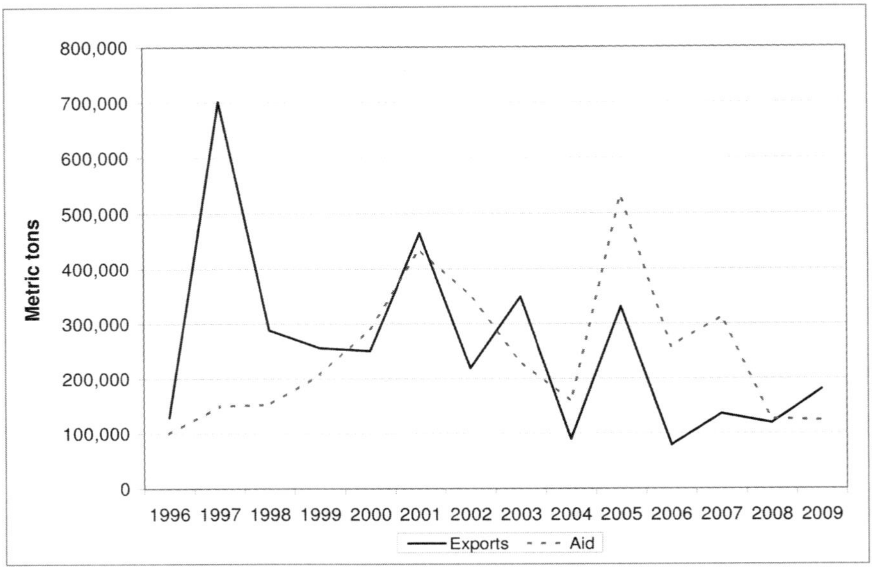

FIGURE 6.3. Chinese cereal aid and exports to North Korea, 1996–2010. (Source: China Customs statistics as reported to Global Trade Atlas)

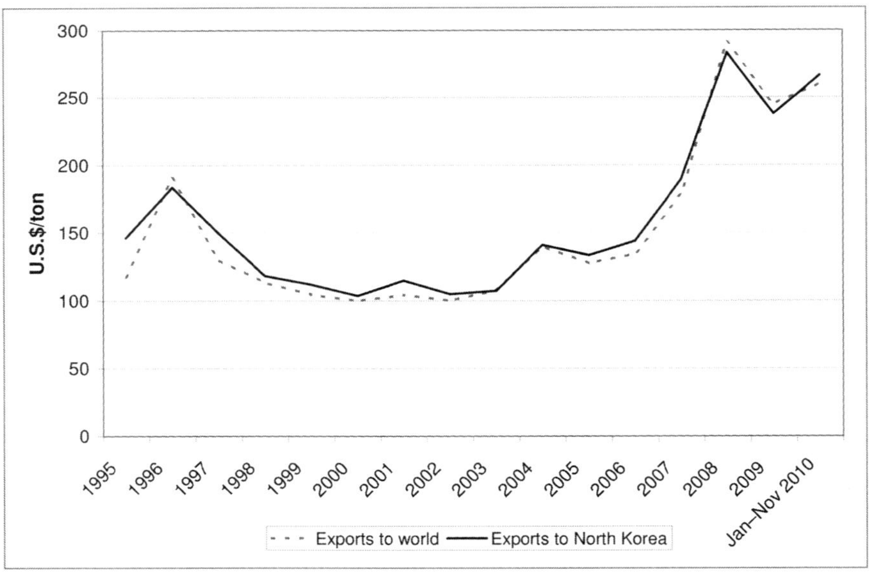

FIGURE 6.4. Chinese corn exports to world and North Korea, in unit prices, 1995–2010. (Source: China Customs statistics as reported to Global Trade Atlas)

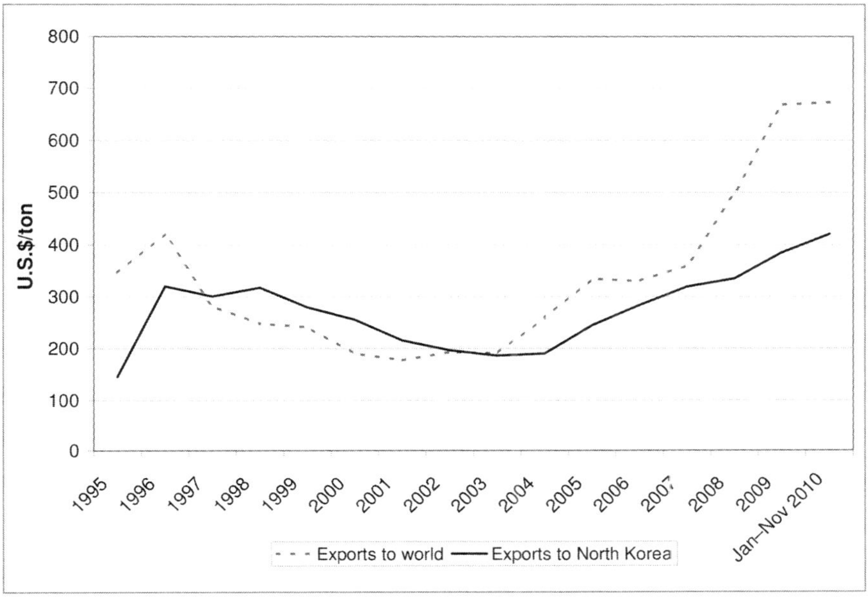

FIGURE 6.5. Chinese rice exports to world and North Korea, in unit prices, 1995–2010. (Source: China Customs statistics as reported to Global Trade Atlas)

In contrast, for much of the past fifteen years, Chinese rice appears to have been shipped to North Korea at prices much below the average prices Chinese rice obtained in the global marketplace (see figure 6.5). This may mean that whereas corn was sold on commercial terms, rice was provided at concessional prices. If accurate, this may indicate that the Kim regime has been able to convince China to help it satisfy the North Korean elite classes' reported preference for rice over other grains.

OUTSIDE SOURCES OF FERTILIZER

Another major source of inputs to North Korea's agricultural system has been fertilizer shipments. Since the peak of the famine, North Korea has imported over 3.5 million MT of fertilizer, virtually all (over 97 percent) of which has come from South Korea and China (see figure

6.6). Every year from 2002 to 2008, North Korea received over 350,000 MT of fertilizer from these two sources.

However, these shipments were far too low for the country's basic needs. According to Haggard and Noland, the North Korean Ministry of Agriculture has estimated that about 700,000 MT of fertilizer is needed for the North Korean farming sector to maintain adequate production levels.[15] Even in the peak years of South Korean and Chinese fertilizer shipments, these two suppliers provided less than three-quarters of this level. Most years, foreign sources were far below this threshold.

South Korean Fertilizer

During the "Sunshine Policy" years, South Korea was the largest shipper of fertilizer, which was sent as assistance (i.e., free of charge). South Korean shipments of fertilizer began in 1999, as relations between the two Koreas thawed a bit. The two sides reached an agreement to permit family reunions in return for South Korea's providing 200,000 MT of fertilizer. The first 100,000 MT were to be given before the reunions took place, with the second shipment happening later. However, in June of that year, just days before the first fertilizer shipment was to depart, North Korean naval vessels crossed the Northern Limit Line, triggering a response from the South Korean navy that sank or crippled at least two North Korean boats. In the aftermath, although the first 100,000 MT were shipped (on June 22), North Korea did not go forward with the reunions, and the second shipment was not sent in 1999.[16]

The following year, the first-ever inter-Korean summit was held, between South Korean president Kim Dae Jung and North Korean leader Kim Jong Il, inaugurating a new era in North-South relations. For the next eight years, under Kim Dae Jung and his successor, Roh Moo-hyun, South Korea pursued its Sunshine Policy of providing largely unconditional aid to North Korea, in the expectation that this would give Pyongyang incentives to change its behavior, reduce the threat level on the Korean Peninsula, and gradually raise North Korea's income level so as to reduce the eventual costs that South Korea would have to pay for reunification. A key component of the Sunshine Policy was providing the North with large-scale amounts of fertilizer through the

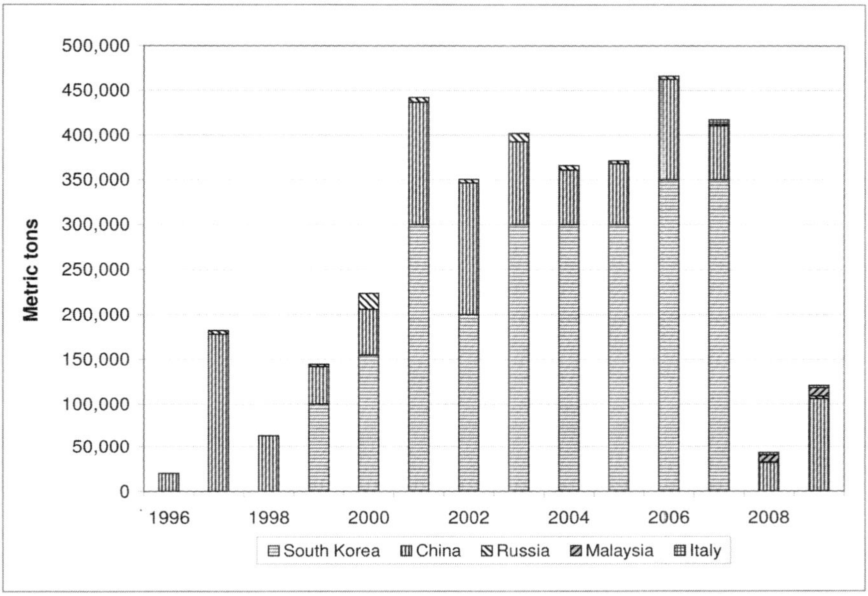

FIGURE 6.6. Major fertilizer exporters to North Korea, 1996–2009. (Sources: ROK Ministry of Unification; Global Trade Atlas)

Korean Red Cross. From 2000 to 2007, South Korea provided North Korea with an average of around 300,000 MT of fertilizer, worth over U.S.$700 million.

However, in 2008 the inauguration of a conservative government led by Lee Myung-bak brought about a change in South Korea's aid policy toward North Korea. The Lee government has established the principle of reciprocity in its assistance policy: large-scale aid, including humanitarian aid, is linked to North Korea's cooperation on other issues, foremost among them progress on denuclearization. The greater the cooperation from Pyongyang, the greater the assistance from Seoul. The Lee government has also reduced aid to South Korean nongovernmental organizations (NGOs) operating in North Korea and has made it more difficult for them to travel to the North.[17]

North Korea did not request humanitarian assistance from the South until the second half of 2009. In response, South Korea pledged in October 2009 a small amount—10,000 MT of corn—but North

Korea did not accept the offer until January 2010. The delay may have been due to South Korea's reported insistence that the aid be subject to greater monitoring. Seoul also came forward with some food aid in the fall of 2010, following localized flooding in North Korea and during the brief thaw in North-South relations that preceded North Korea's late-November shelling of Yeonpyeong Island. Despite these modest exceptions, it appears that the Lee government is linking the provision of large-scale assistance to progress in the nuclear talks.

Chinese Fertilizer

China, along with Russia, is one of the world's top fertilizer exporters, particularly of the nitrogenous fertilizer that, as Ireson discusses in the preceding chapter, North Korea prefers. Virtually all—nearly 90 percent—of China's 1.2 million MT of fertilizer exports to North Korea since 1995 have been nitrogenous matter.[18]

Analyzing China's fertilizer shipments to North Korea since the mid-1990s reveals some interesting patterns. First, there are peaks and valleys to a greater extent than with cereal trade. Fertilizer exports were high, and rose dramatically, in 1997, in the 2001 to 2002 period, in 2006, and in the 2009 to 2010 period. The nearly threefold jump from 2009 to 2010 is particularly noteworthy. The low periods of China's fertilizer shipments, when they were below 50,000 MT, were 1998 to 2000 and in 2008 (see figure 6.7).

The second observation centers on the question of whether these fertilizer shipments were assistance or commercial exports. Comparing China's fertilizer shipments to North Korea with exports to other countries may reveal some clues. Figure 6.8 shows the yearly percentage change in China's shipments of nitrogen fertilizer to North Korea, South Korea, and the rest of the world. It starts in 2001, the year after China began exporting significant amounts of fertilizer to South Korea. The figure shows that China's exports to South Korea have had a strong—and in some years, nearly identical—correlation to its exports to the rest of the world, both in direction and in magnitude. In contrast, changes in China's shipments to North Korea appear to have had almost no relationship to trends in China's nitrogen fertilizer exports to the rest of the world, either in magnitude or direction. For example,

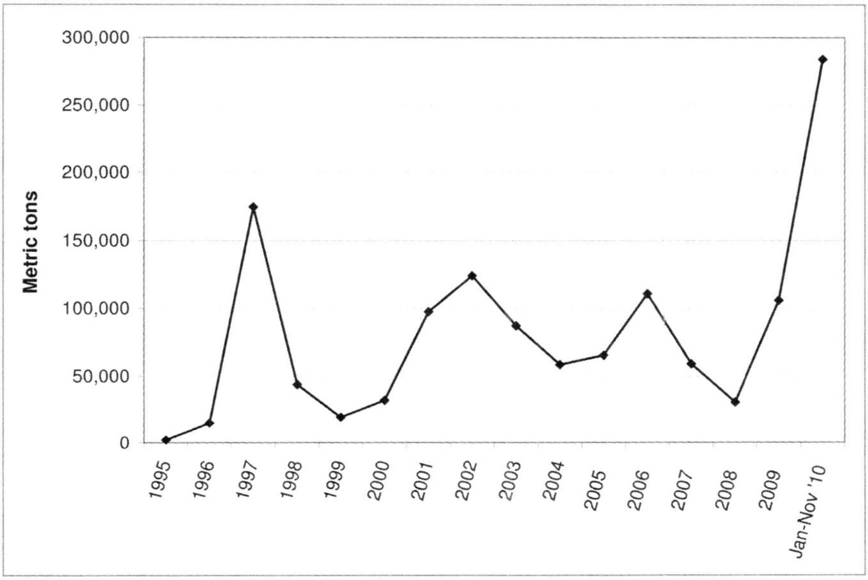

FIGURE 6.7. Chinese shipments of nitrogen fertilizer to North Korea, 1995–2010. (Source: China Customs statistics as reported to Global Trade Atlas)

in 2003 and 2004, China's shipments to North Korea decreased even as its exports to the rest of the world rose. Another striking disconnect occurs in 2009 and 2010, when shipments to North Korea rose dramatically while Chinese global shipments declined (in 2009) and then registered a slight increase (in 2010). This would seem to indicate that something unique has been going on between China and North Korea, though the data alone do not reveal whether the shipments have been assistance or commercial exports. On the other hand, the observation could be simply a reflection of the vagaries of North Korea's need for fertilizer.

Third, looking at the Chinese price data shown in figure 6.9, it appears that in most years Chinese fertilizer exports to North Korea roughly tracked with prices offered to the rest of the world, including South Korea. Three years stand out, however, as exceptions. In 2007, 2009, and especially 2010 Chinese nitrogenous fertilizer seems to have been sold at "friendship prices" to North Korea and thus may have

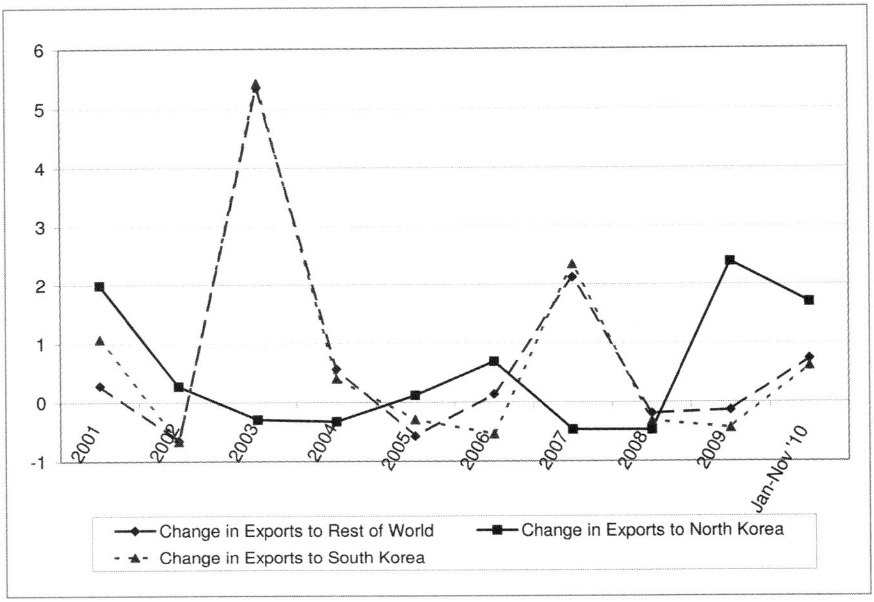

FIGURE 6.8. Yearly percentage change in quantity of Chinese fertilizer exports, 2001–2010. (Source: China Customs statistics as reported to Global Trade Atlas)

constituted Chinese assistance to help compensate for declining food and fertilizer assistance following the cessation of not only South Korean aid but also the end of the WFP and U.S. NGO food aid programs in late 2008 and early 2009, respectively.

EXTERNAL SOURCES OF FUEL

The final external source of food security in North Korea is fuel. A look at mirror statistics reveals that China was by far the largest provider of outside fuel for North Korea between 1995 and 2009, selling over 15.5 million MT of oil and coal and over 56 million kWh of electricity. Revealing Moscow's potential importance to North Korea's meeting its energy needs, Russia was North Korea's number-two supplier of energy, shipping over 7 million MT of fuel, nearly 70 percent of which was in

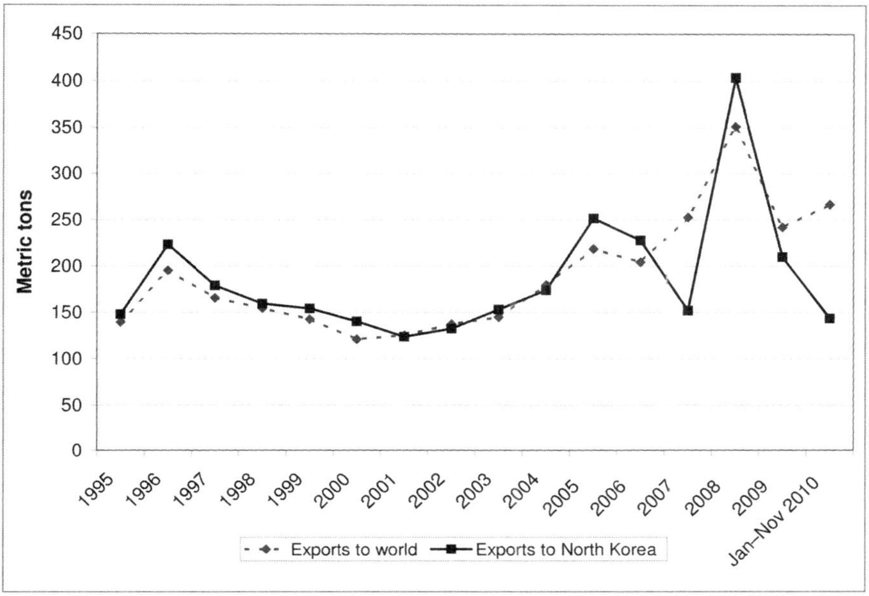

FIGURE 6.9. Chinese fertilizer exports to world and North Korea, in unit prices, 1995–2010. (Source: China Customs statistics as reported to Global Trade Atlas)

the form of coal, and about one-third was oil. Almost half of Russia's total energy exports from 1995 to 2009 came in two years, 2005 and 2006, when around 3.4 million MT of coal were shipped to North Korea. Indonesia, South Africa, and more recently India have also played important, albeit sporadic, roles, with each selling between 240,000 MT and 400,000 MT over the past fifteen years.

Figure 6.10 shows Chinese shipments to North Korea of crude oil, coal, and other petroleum products from 1995 to 2010. After dropping sharply during the famine years, energy inflows stabilized somewhat around the years 2000 to 2002. Strikingly, since 2005 North Korean fuel imports have been virtually unchanged. This would seem to indicate the hand of the government, rather than the market, directing fuel to North Korea, one of many indicators that Beijing continues to ensure that at least a subsistence level of inputs is being shipped to North Korea to maintain the Kim regime in power.

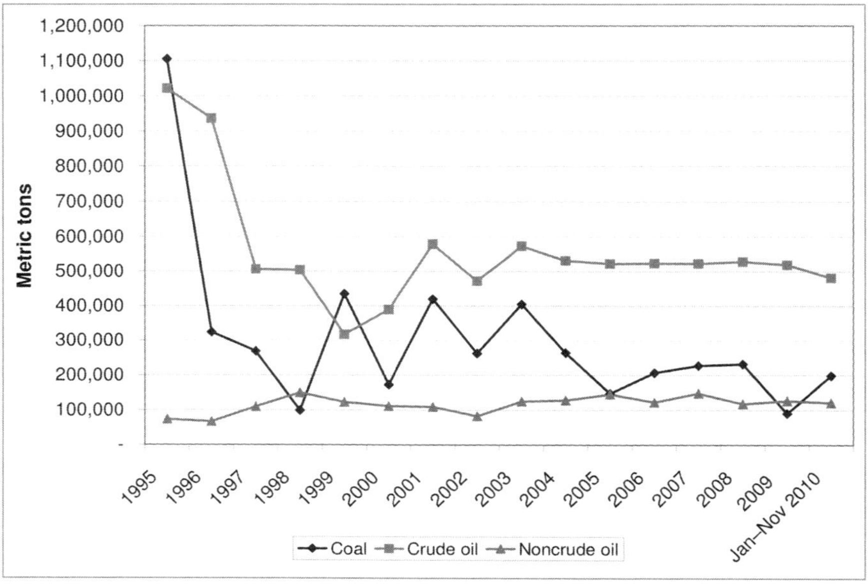

FIGURE 6.10. Chinese energy exports to North Korea, 1995–2010. (Source: China Customs statistics as reported to Global Trade Atlas)

CONCLUSION

The review here of the major external sources of North Korea's food security reveals three implications. The first is the growing importance of China to ensuring a subsistence level of food security for the North Korean economy. In two of the three product categories examined—food, fertilizer, and fuel—China's share of North Korea's imports has ballooned in importance in recent years (see figure 6.11). When it comes to fuel, the story is similar, if a bit more nuanced. China still has a plurality of North Korea's coal and oil imports, but North Korea's success in obtaining coal from India from 2007 to 2009 somewhat lessened Pyongyang's dependence on Beijing.[19]

Second, unless foreign providers dramatically increase their provision or sales of food, fertilizer, and fuel to North Korea, the answer to North Korea's food security will not come from the outside world.

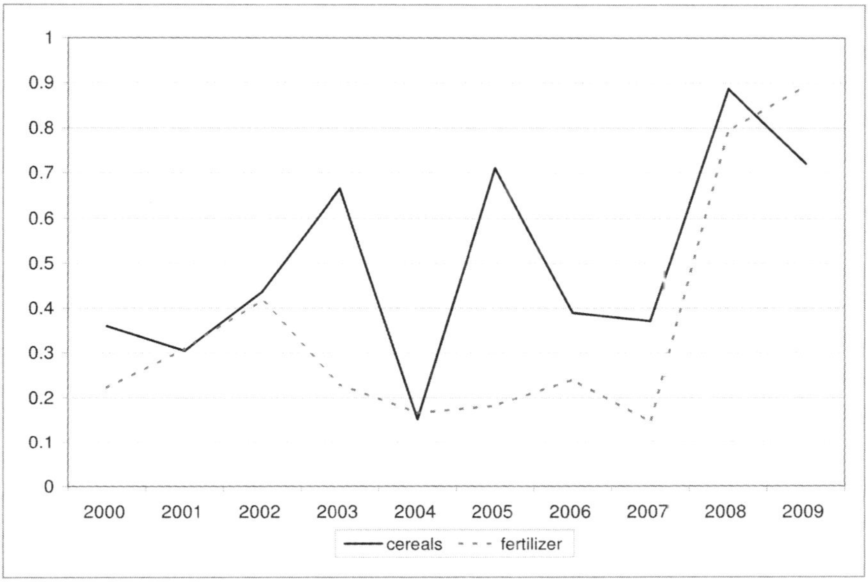

FIGURE 6.11. China's share of North Korean imports of cereals and fertilizer, 2000–2010. (Source: China Customs statistics as reported to Global Trade Atlas)

According to anecdotal reports of the time, the peak of South Korean and Chinese assistance and exports around 2005 coincided with marginal improvements in North Korea's food security, but not wholesale improvements.

Third, looking forward, the prospects for an improved food-security situation in North Korea do not look bright. Despite a greater rhetorical emphasis on economic reforms to make the country into a "great, prosperous, and powerful country," North Korea's domestic moves from 2010 to mid-2012 appear to indicate the government's determination to exert *more*, not less, control over the economy, including agriculture. Few experts, if any, expect the new Kim Jong Eun regime to adopt a reformist stance. This means that unless North Korean authorities make dramatic changes in their agricultural system, for the foreseeable future North Korean food security is likely to continue to depend heavily on inflows of food, fertilizer, and fuel from the outside world.

NOTES

1. As described in Barbara Demick's book *Nothing to Envy: Ordinary Lives in North Korea* (New York: Spiegel & Grau, 2009), North Koreans typically would go to their local food distribution center warehouse on their assigned day every fortnight. After handing in food coupons, a small amount of money, and documents attesting that the requisite number of hours had been fulfilled at work, each recipient would pick up her allotment of food, which would be selected by the PDS officer. Each distribution center generally fed a population of fifteen hundred to three thousand families; see Stephan Haggard and Marcus Noland, *Famine in North Korea: Markets, Aid, and Reform* (New York: Columbia University Press, 2007), 52. Note that even in its current depleted form, the PDS continues to provide North Koreans with an important source of food, and it is the vehicle through which Western food aid is delivered.
2. Haggard and Noland, *Famine in North Korea*, 53–54.
3. Ibid., 56–57.
4. Ibid., 27.
5. As reported in ibid., 28.
6. Ibid., 27, 31–32.
7. Randall Ireson, "Why North Korea Could Feed Itself," 38 North, May 1, 2010 (U.S.-Korea Institute at SAIS, Johns Hopkins University), http://38north.org/2010/05/why-north-korea-could-feed-itself/ (accessed December 25, 2010).
8. Demick, *Nothing to Envy*, chap. 4.
9. Mark Manyin, "Food Crisis and North Korea's Aid Diplomacy: Seeking the Path of Least Resistance," in *New Challenges of North Korean Foreign Policy*, ed. Kyung-Ae Park (New York: Palgrave Macmillan, 2010), 70.
10. For more, see the economic analysis in U.S. Library of Congress, Congressional Research Service, *China–North Korea Relations*, by Dick Nanto, Kerry Dumbaugh, and Mark Manyin, R41043, December 28, 2010.
11. The drop in 2006 was due primarily to South Korea's suspension of humanitarian assistance following North Korea's missile and nuclear tests in July and October 2006, respectively.
12. The participants in the Six-Party Talks are China, Japan, North Korea, Russia, the United States, and South Korea.
13. Global Trade Atlas, using China Customs data (accessed January 10, 2011).
14. Interviews with WFP and INTERFAIS officials, 2005, 2009.
15. Haggard and Noland, *Famine in North Korea*, 32–33.

16. "President Reaffirms Resolve to Achieve Family Reunions between South, North," *Korea Herald*, October 11, 1999.
17. Jong-moo Lee, "The History of South Korean Aid to the DPRK" (paper presented at the Conference on Humanitarian and Development Assistance to the DPRK, Seoul, November 24–26, 2009).
18. Global Trade Atlas, using China Customs data (accessed December 25, 2010).
19. Global Trade Atlas (accessed December 25, 2010).

PART

II

Global Cooperation for Promoting North Korea's Non-Traditional Security

CHAPTER 7

The Responsibility to Protect and Its Limits in North Korea

TSUNEO AKAHA

"Rwanda's genocide, massacres in Srebrenica, Cambodia's killing fields, ethnic cleansing in Kosovo, the Holocaust: these experiences—both their human toll and the political and institutional failures they represent—have seared humanity."[1] The responsibility to protect (RtoP) represents the international community's most recent attempt to prevent the reoccurrence of these man-made crises. It establishes a norm that reaffirms the sovereign state's primary responsibility to protect its own citizens, commits the international community to assist those states that are either unwilling or unable to do so, and authorizes the international community to intervene when the state has clearly failed to protect its citizens and others within its borders.

There are mounting international calls for the international community to apply RtoP to North Korea, including international intervention, because the North Korean government is either unwilling or unable to protect its citizens from the threat to their most fundamental of rights, the right to life. Václav Havel, former president of the Czech Republic, and Kjell Magne Bondevik, former prime minister of Norway and president of the Oslo Center for Peace and Human Rights, in their op-ed to the *New York Times* in June 2010, declared, "North Korea is actively committing crimes against humanity—against its own people" and called for international intervention.[2] In the same month, defectors who had survived torture and near starvation in North Korean prison camps requested a meeting with UN secretary-general Ban Ki-moon to seek advice about the potential remedies for rights abuses in North Korea. Former South Korean president Kim Young Sam and Kjell Magne Bondevik publicly supported their request.[3] Kim Young Sam was quoted as saying North Korea not only threatens the South but "is also a serious threat to its own people and to humankind in terms of humanitarianism, human security and human rights." In their call for deeper UN involvement with the alleviation of human suffering in North Korea, both Kim and Bondevik referred to RtoP.[4]

In this brief analysis, I consider whether the international community is ready to heed the call. I first examine the concept of RtoP, its evolution in the global debate, and various criticisms about its scope and limitations. I then discuss whether it is desirable and possible to apply RtoP to North Korea. I conclude by pointing out the difficulties of implementing the norm in North Korea.

RtoP: The Principle

In December 2001, the International Commission on Intervention and State Sovereignty, cochaired by Gareth Evans, former Australian foreign minister, and Mohamed Sahnoun, a special adviser to the UN secretary-general, issued a report, *The Responsibility to Protect*, articulating RtoP as a norm for the international community to adopt in order to prevent and to react to large-scale human atrocities resulting from the unwillingness or inability of states to prevent them. The 2005 World Summit placed the need to protect populations from genocide, war crimes, ethnic cleansing, and crimes against humanity on the global policy agenda. The UN General Assembly member states embraced RtoP in paragraphs 138 and 139 in the outcome document of the High-Level Plenary Meeting of the General Assembly in September 2005. The two paragraphs read as follows:

> Paragraph 138: Each individual State has the responsibility to protect its populations from genocide, war crimes, ethnic cleansing and crimes against humanity. This responsibility entails the prevention of such crimes, including their incitement, through appropriate and necessary means. We accept that responsibility and will act in accordance with it. The international community should, as appropriate,

> encourage and help States to exercise this responsibility and support the United Nations in establishing an early warning capability.
>
> Paragraph 139: The international community, through the United Nations, also has the responsibility to use appropriate diplomatic, humanitarian and other peaceful means, in accordance with Chapters VI and VIII of the Charter, to help to protect populations from genocide, war crimes, ethnic cleansing and crimes against humanity. In this context, we are prepared to take collective action, in a timely and decisive manner, through the Security Council, in accordance with the Charter, including Chapter VII, on a case-by-case basis and in cooperation with relevant regional organizations as appropriate, should peaceful means be inadequate and national authorities are manifestly failing to protect their populations from genocide, war crimes, ethnic cleansing and crimes against humanity. We stress the need for the General Assembly to continue consideration of the responsibility to protect populations from genocide, war crimes, ethnic cleansing and crimes against humanity and its implications, bearing in mind the principles of the Charter and international law. We also intend to commit ourselves, as necessary and appropriate, to helping States build capacity to protect their populations from genocide, war crimes, ethnic cleansing and crimes against humanity and to assisting those which are under stress before crises and conflicts break out.[5]

On April 28, 2006, the Security Council unanimously adopted resolution 1674 on the protection of civilians in armed conflict, reaffirming the provisions of paragraphs 138 and 139. In February 2008, Secretary-General Ban Ki-moon appointed Edward Luck as a special adviser and tasked him with leading the preparation of a report on implementing the commitment of RtoP.[6] Then, in May 2008, the Security Council reaffirmed "the responsibility of States to comply with their relevant obligations to end impunity and to prosecute those responsible for war crimes, genocide, crimes against humanity and serious violations of international humanitarian law."[7]

In January 2009, the secretary-general released the report, *Implementing the Responsibility to Protect*, in which he put forth a three-pillar approach, one he had articulated in a speech in Berlin in July 2008.[8] The three pillars are as follows:

1. the primary and continuing legal obligations of States to protect their populations—whether citizens or not—from genocide, war crimes, ethnic cleansing, and crimes against humanity, and from their incitement;
2. the commitment of the international community to assist States in meeting the above obligations; and,
3. Member States' responsibility to respond in a timely and decisive manner, in accordance with the United Nations Charter, to help protect populations from the four listed crimes and violations.

The secretary-general recommended that the General Assembly meet to consider how member states would take the 2005 World Summit commitment forward.

In July 2009, the General Assembly debated RtoP based on the secretary-general's report. The ninety-two member states and two observers who spoke demonstrated strong interest in the norm and support for implementing the 2005 commitment. On September 14, 2009, the General Assembly adopted resolution A/RES63/308, taking note of the report of the secretary-general and the debate in the General Assembly and agreeing to continue its consideration of RtoP. This was a remarkable achievement by the international community in view of the fact that only a few years earlier there had been much disagreement about RtoP.[9]

However, RtoP remains an emerging norm, not yet a universally accepted rule or principle under international law. The international community needs to continue to debate the concept, refine it, and establish it either as an international practice or legal principle if it is to be legitimately applied to North Korea or elsewhere in the world. There are criticisms that the advocates of RtoP need to counter and limitations to the concept that the international community must overcome before the idea can be said to be an established universal norm.

Criticisms and Limitations of RtoP

The first of the three pillars outlined by the secretary-general—the principle that the state has the primary responsibility for protecting its citizens from the worst atrocities—has long been established under international human rights and humanitarian law.

"Genocide" is defined in Article 2 of the 1948 UN Convention on the Prevention and Punishment of the Crime of Genocide as "any of the following acts committed with intent to destroy, in whole or in part, a national, ethnical, racial or religious group, as such: killing members of the group; causing serious bodily or mental harm to members of the group; deliberately inflicting on the group conditions of life calculated to bring about its physical destruction in whole or in part; imposing measures intended to prevent births within the group; [and] forcibly transferring children of the group to another group."[10]

"War crimes" defies a simple definition, but according to Courtois, Werth, Panné, Paczkowski, Bartošek, and Margolin, they are "violations of the laws or customs of war," including "murder, the ill-treatment or deportation of civilian residents of an occupied territory to slave labor camps," "the murder or ill-treatment of prisoners of war," the killing of hostages, "the wanton destruction of cities, towns and villages, and any devastation not justified by military, or civilian necessity."[11]

"Ethnic cleansing" has been defined by a UN commission of experts reporting to the Security Council as involving "the planned deliberate removal from a specific territory, persons of a particular ethnic group, by force or intimidation, in order to render that area ethnically homogeneous."[12]

The concept of "crimes against humanity" has evolved since the first significant early reference to it in the context of World War I (by the Allied powers of Britain, France, and Russia against members of the Ottoman government). In the aftermath of World War II, the principle was defined in the London Charter of the International Military Tribunal, which was drafted in preparation for the Nürnberg trials, and applied in the International Military Tribunal for the Far East (Tokyo trials). In 1976, the General Assembly recognized apartheid in South Africa as a crime against humanity.

According to Article 7 of the Rome Statute establishing the International Criminal Court (the court was established in 2002), "crimes against humanity" refers to "any of the following acts when committed as part of a widespread or systematic attack directed against any civilian population, with knowledge of the attack: (a) murder; (b) extermination;

(c) enslavement; (d) deportation or forcible transfer of population; (e) imprisonment or other severe deprivation of physical liberty in violation of fundamental rules of international law; (f) torture; (g) rape, sexual slavery, enforced prostitution, forced pregnancy, enforced sterilization, or any other form of sexual violence of comparable gravity; (h) persecution against any identifiable group or collectivity on political, racial, national, ethnic, cultural, religious, gender, or other grounds that are universally recognized as impermissible under international law, in connection with any act referred to in this paragraph or any crime within the jurisdiction of the Court; (i) enforced disappearance of persons; (j) the crime of apartheid; and (k) other inhumane acts of a similar character intentionally causing great suffering, or serious injury to body or to mental or physical health."

What is new is that the international community has accepted for the first time the collective responsibility to act should states fail to protect civilians from genocide, ethnic cleansing, war crimes, or crimes against humanity.[13] It is this innovation in norm building—and its implementation—to which both concern and criticism have been directed.

Selectivity and Use of Double Standards

At the General Assembly debate on RtoP in 2009, some member states expressed concerns regarding the selectivity and the use of double standards in the implementation of the norm, the use of force and unilateral intervention, the restraint on the use of the veto by the permanent members of the Security Council in RtoP situations, and the respective roles of the General Assembly and the Security Council in implementing RtoP.[14]

The concern regarding selectivity and double standards is not limited to RtoP. In fact, every international norm, principle, rule, or standard is subject to selectivity and double standards in its application.[15] North Korea was one of the countries that raised this issue at the 2009 General Assembly debate. As the ambassador of Chile stated during the debate, however, the international community's failure to apply international norms consistently everywhere should not be reason to apply RtoP nowhere.[16]

Veto by Security Council Members

A related concern is about the veto by the permanent members of the Security Council. This is a realistic problem. Although a large number of countries echoed the recommendation of the secretary-general's report calling on the permanent Security Council members to refrain from using the veto in RtoP situations,[17] the concern is likely to continue as part of the debate on UN reform. Among the permanent members, China is the most likely to veto a resolution calling for international intervention in North Korea for purposes of protecting its people.

International Intervention versus the Principle of Noninterference

Another concern expressed by some member states during the 2009 General Assembly debate related to pillar three, international intervention in the face of a state's failure to protect its own citizens and others within its territory. In their view, the pillar violates the cardinal principle of noninterference on which the international system is built. By contrast, Iceland endorsed the view expressed in the secretary-general's report that the third pillar consisted of more than military intervention and included such measures as mediation, enhancing international-justice mechanisms, the imposition of financial and travel sanctions, restrictions on the flow of arms, and peace-enforcement missions under Chapter VII of the UN Charter. Japan argued that if consent was not forthcoming and the most serious violations continued, collective action, including the use of force, had to be taken by the Security Council according to the UN Charter.[18] North Korea, Venezuela, Iran, and Pakistan charged that RtoP was a license for the powerful to intervene unilaterally in a country. Sudan stated that RtoP amounted to unilateral "humanitarian intervention." In response, South Korea argued that RtoP was distinct from humanitarian intervention because it was based not on unilateral actions but on collective actions, in accordance with the UN Charter.[19] Questions were also raised by a number of countries about the threshold that would trigger international intervention, the meaning of "timely response," who would decide whether a situation constituted one of the four core crimes, and the need to formulate clear exit strategies for interventions.

The Roles of the Security Council and General Assembly

The question of the respective roles of the Security Council and the General Assembly regarding RtoP was also a point of contention in the General Assembly debate, with some countries expressing concern about the principle granting additional authority to the Security Council and others arguing that the Security Council would be the organ to respond to RtoP situations. South Korea endorsed the secretary-general's position that the UN Charter already provided the definitive guide on the respective roles of the General Assembly and the Security Council. South Korea also supported the secretary-general's idea that the General Assembly should conduct a periodic review of what member states had done to implement RtoP.[20]

Sovereignty versus International Intervention

Objection may be and has been raised that RtoP contradicts state sovereignty inasmuch as it authorizes international intervention. Secretary-General Ban Ki-moon has responded by stating, "Properly understood, RtoP is an ally of sovereignty, not an adversary. Strong States protect their people, while weak ones are either unwilling or unable to do so. Protection was one of the core purposes of the formation of States and the Westphalian system. By helping States meet one of their core responsibilities, RtoP seeks to strengthen sovereignty, not weaken it."[21] It is doubtful, however, that the secretary-general's statement would allay fears of some states that are jealously protective of their sovereignty and opposed to any international intervention.

Another criticism is that RtoP infringes on state sovereignty inasmuch as the international intervention it authorizes can be used as a pretext for other, national interest–based purposes. Secretary-General Ban Ki-moon has said in response, "The responsibility to protect does not alter the legal obligation of Member States to refrain from the use of force in conformity with the Charter. Rather it reinforces this obligation. By bolstering United Nations prevention, protection, and response and rebuilding mechanisms, RtoP seeks to enhance the rule of law and expand multilateral options."[22]

Among the Northeast Asian countries, South Korea was the most ardent supporter of the secretary-general's report to the General Assembly. In addition to its positions noted above, South Korea stressed the importance of effective domestic-dispute resolution mechanisms, candid self-reflection, searching dialogue, and periodic risk assessment; it spoke in favor of the strengthening of early warning; and it supported the key role of the special adviser on the prevention of genocide and that of the secretary-general's adviser on RtoP. South Korea also emphasized the importance of mediation and rapid-reaction capacity and supported introducing criteria relating to RtoP into regional peer-review mechanisms.[23]

In contrast, North Korea—along with Malaysia, Iran, Pakistan, and Sri Lanka—showed a most negative attitude toward RtoP. Among other points raised by North Korea was that RtoP would be used to justify military attacks on humanitarian pretexts.[24]

China stated it was open to discussion of the application RtoP but added that the new norm could not be used to place pressure on states because it remained a concept and lacked the force of international law and that ultimately action could be taken only with the consent of the state involved.[25] Japan was largely supportive of RtoP, placing some emphasis on the distinction between RtoP and human security, a point taken up in the next section.

According to Ambassador Gert Rosenthal, permanent representative of Guatemala to the United Nations, 80 percent of the statements made by member states "reflected positive attitudes both towards paragraphs 138 and 139, the Secretary-General's report, and the need for the GA to continue its consideration of R2P."[26] Juan Méndez, former special adviser to the secretary-general on the prevention of genocide, has echoed the optimistic assessment, stating, "The norm of R2P is close to being crystallized."[27]

Clearly, the General Assembly needs to and plans to continue to debate these issues so that international consensus can be reached on RtoP as a norm and then translate it into a universally binding legal principle. However, some states will continue to undermine the universal acceptance of RtoP as a principle and reject its application within their own borders. North Korea will surely be one of them.

RtoP VERSUS HUMAN SECURITY

One of the major limitations of RtoP is that it does not apply to the entire range of human-security issues facing many countries around the world but rather is restricted to four crimes and violations, genocide, war crimes, ethnic cleansing, and crimes against humanity. In defending the narrow focus of RtoP as adopted by the UN General Assembly and the Security Council, Secretary-General Ban Ki-moon stated, "Our conception of RtoP . . . is narrow but deep. Its scope is narrow, focused solely on the four crimes and violations agreed by the world leaders in 2005. Extending the principle to cover other calamities, such as HIV/AIDS, climate change or response to natural disasters, would undermine the 2005 consensus and stretch the concept beyond recognition or operational utility." He further stated, "At the same time, our response should be deep, utilizing the whole prevention and protection tool kit available to the United Nations system, to its regional, subregional and civil society partners and, not least, to the Member States themselves. As the Summit urged, we need to enhance UN early warning mechanisms, integrating the system's multiple channels of information and assessment. We need to strengthen the capacities of States to resist taking the path to genocide, war crimes, ethnic cleansing and crimes against humanity." As far as capacity building is concerned, he stressed, "a range of areas—from development, good governance and human rights to gender equality, the rule of law and security sector reform."[28]

One of the most ardent advocates of human security, the United Nations Development Programme (UNDP) issued a report, *Delivering Human Security through Multi-level Governance,* in which it sounds a critical note on the narrow focus of RtoP. Released in March 2009, the report states, "In recent years, human security has often been more closely associated with the concept of responsibility to protect, thus emphasizing individuals' freedom from fear. Yet if the international community is willing to protect civilians—and indeed has accepted international responsibilities in that regard—then it should also accept that people's needs and vulnerabilities go far beyond their freedom from fear. The international community should be prepared to act in different and additional spheres of human security, adopting a comprehensive approach that takes account of the differing sources of vulnerability and human security risks."[29]

The UNDP report welcomes the acknowledgment, in the 2004 report of the secretary-general's High-Level Panel on Threats, Challenges and Change,[30] of development and human security as "indispensable foundations for a collective security system and fundamental tools to help combat poverty, infectious disease and environmental degradation that threaten human security" and applauds the secretary-general's incorporation of this understanding in his report *In Larger Freedom: Towards Development, Security and Human Rights for All*, submitted to the General Assembly in 2005.[31] The UNDP report then asks, "Why has the responsibility to protect been confined only to cases of violent threats to physical security?" "In this sense," the report continues, "the principles related to the responsibility to protect, being limited to physical security, take into account just some components of freedom from fear, leaving aside, for instance, the whole spectrum of non-physical violent security threat." "What about the other constitutive principles of human security? The concept of responsibility to protect does not include epidemics or mass starvation for example, even though these may cause the death and destitution of millions of individuals."[32]

The UNDP report further discusses people's economic vulnerabilities, such as those being experienced under the ongoing financial crisis and related economic downturn, as well as environmental security, natural disasters, climate change–related disasters, food security, and community security in terms of threats to people's religious and ethnic identities. Having given a broad range of human-security problems, the report suggests, "If a wider understanding of the responsibility to protect envisaged in this paper is considered reasonable, then one can derive from that that the international community should not only have a mandate but also the responsibility to protect all human beings through facilitation or the provision of essential global public goods such as a reliable international economic and financial order, sustainable development frameworks, international peace, climate stability, sufficient food availability to all, human rights enhancement and protection systems and more."[33]

The report concludes, "The limited interpretation and application of the responsibility to protect concept to genocide, war crimes, ethnic cleansing and crimes against humanity, pertaining to the freedom from fear sphere, is well justified by the need to confirm acceptance, secure consolidation and early implementation of this basic principle. However, the present prevailing understanding of the responsibility to protect does not allow the international community to apply the same sense of compelling obligation to prevent and remedy extreme sufferings such as mass starvation, epidemics, or other massive life threats falling under the category of freedom from want. The ongoing debate and the discussion that will follow the recently released report of the Secretary-General of the UN on Implementing the Responsibility to Protect should also link those major insecurities to an explicit responsibility of the States and the International Community."[34]

APPLYING RtoP TO NORTH KOREA

The criticism in the UNDP report has obvious implications for the human-security situation in North Korea. The applicability of RtoP to the North Korean situation will be severely limited if the principle is confined to genocide, war crimes, ethnic cleansing, and crimes against humanity and if, in implementing RtoP, the international community, namely the United Nations (principally the Security Council), cannot agree that the North Korean government's unwillingness or inability to protect its citizens from the human-security problems they are experiencing indeed amounts to one of the four listed crimes or violations.

The question is basically threefold. First, is there evidence that the North Korean government is unwilling or unable to protect its citizens from the four crimes or violations? Second, does the United Nations (i.e., the Security Council) accept the evidence as warranting the invocation of RtoP, requiring international intervention? Third, is the international community willing and able to contribute the necessary resources for intervention? I examine each of these questions in the remainder of this chapter.

What evidence is there that supports the claim that the North Korean government is unwilling or unable to protect its citizens from the four crimes or violations to which RtoP as currently defined applies?

In June 2010, *Foreign Policy* magazine published the "Failed States Index 2010," in which North Korea was ranked seventeen, with its human rights record receiving the fourth worst score after Somalia, Chad, and Sudan.[35] In February 2005, the U.S. Department of State's Bureau of Democracy, Human Rights, and Labor described the North Korean government's human rights record as "extremely poor" and noted, "It continued to commit numerous serious abuses. Citizens did not have the right to change their government. There continued to be reports of extrajudicial killings, disappearances, and arbitrary detention, including of many persons held as political prisoners. Prison conditions were harsh and life-threatening, and torture reportedly was common. Pregnant female prisoners reportedly underwent forced abortions, and in other cases babies reportedly were killed upon birth in prison." The country report continued, "The regime subjected citizens to rigid controls over many aspects of their lives. . . . Citizens were denied freedom of speech, the press, assembly, and association; all forms of cultural and media activities were under the tight control of the KWP. . . . The Government restricted freedom of religion, citizens' movement, and worker rights."[36]

Although independent verifications of these and other numerous descriptions of human rights abuses in North Korea have been and continue to be difficult because of poor access, we can safely state at a minimum that more recent attempts at documenting North Korea's human rights situation and its humanitarian conditions give ample evidence to warrant formal investigation by international human rights organizations, including the Office of the High Commissioner for Human Rights, the UN Human Rights Council, and the UN High Commissioner for Refugees (UNHCR).

Among the growing number of reports on the human rights situation in North Korea is *Failure to Protect: A Call for the UN Security Council to Act in North Korea*, released in 2006.[37] The report was commissioned by Václav Havel, Kjell Magne Bondevik, and Elie Wiesel and prepared by the global law firm DLA Piper and the Committee for Human Rights in North Korea. Havel, Bondevik, and Wiesel concluded, "The evidence and analysis contained in this report is deeply disturbing. Indeed, it is clear that Kim Jong Il and the North Korean government are actively committing crimes against humanity. North Korea allowed as many as one million, and possibly many more, of its own people to die during the famine in the 1990s. Hunger and starvation remain a persistent problem, with over 37 percent of children in North Korea chronically malnourished. Furthermore, North Korea imprisons upwards of 200,000 people in its modern-day gulag, and it is estimated more than 400,000 have died in that system over 30 years." They urged the Security Council to "take up the situation of North Korea" and exclaimed, "Protecting the people of North Korea requires nothing less."[38] Two years later, Havel, Bondevik, and Wiesel commissioned a follow-up report, *Failure to Protect: The Ongoing Challenge of North Korea*, and in it they stated, "The situation remains unchanged" and "the international community has far too long neglected the human rights situation in North Korea because of the nuclear threat. It is the purpose of this report to emphasize that human rights should be part of all international involvement with the country. The people of North Korea deserve nothing less."[39] Unfortunately, the Security Council has so far not taken up the issue of human rights abuse in North Korea.

Systematic human rights abuse and dire humanitarian conditions in North Korea have also been discussed in such reports as *Hunger and Human Rights: The Politics of Famine in North Korea*[40] and *The North Korean Refugee Crisis: Human Rights and International Response*,[41] both published by the U.S. Committee for Human Rights in North Korea. The former report states, "A famine in the 1990s killed as many as one million North Koreans or roughly five percent of the population," "the government was culpably slow to take the necessary steps to guarantee adequate food supply," and "the regime blocked humanitarian aid to the hardest hit parts of the country during the peak of the famine and curtailed commercial imports of food once humanitarian assistance began." It further states, "At virtually every point, the North Korean government has placed roadblocks in the way of the donor community, and more than 10 years into this process, the relief effort remains woefully below international standards in terms of transparency and effectiveness. Up to half of aid deliveries do not reach their intended recipients." The report concludes, "These problems cannot be separated from the underlying political situation in the country; it is misguided to separate the humanitarian and human rights discourses."[42] On the last point the report further states, "The failure of the North Korean government to guarantee adequate supplies of food to its population is inextricably linked to the government's denial of a battery of rights to its citizens: to confront public officials with their shortcomings; to publicize information that allows government officials to know the extent of distress; and to organize collectively in the face of injustice and deprivation."[43] The report asks, "How does the outside world deal with a regime that, in effect, holds its own population hostage to the humanitarian impulses of outsiders?"[44] In short, according to the report, the famine and the continuing hunger among the people of North Korea are a result not simply of the inability of the government in Pyongyang to provide adequate supplies of food for its population but also of its unwillingness to do so, and, moreover, the dire humanitarian condition is also a consequence of the government's abuse of the human rights of its own people. That is, the North Korean government has failed in its responsibility to protect. Furthermore, by severely restricting international aid access to the people in need, Pyongyang is preventing the international community from its responsibility to assist North Korea in capacity building.

The continuing outflow of North Korean citizens into neighboring countries, particularly China, because of the dire economic situation, which is systemic in nature, including chronic food shortages, as well as the absence of political freedom in North Korea, has also been documented by international human rights organizations. This phenomenon may reasonably be seen as a crime against humanity, hence subject to RtoP, inasmuch as it is the result of the North Korean government's inability or refusal to provide for the basic necessities of its citizens.

The editors of the report *The North Korean Refugee Crisis: Human Rights and International Response* conclude that the North Korean citizens who have fled their country for safe haven and better economic conditions in China and elsewhere are refugees. They state, "Despite the importance of economic motivations, and the government of China's desire to portray them as 'economic migrants,' they must be considered refugees on the basis of their well-founded (and well-documented) fear of persecution should they return to North Korea." They assert that the situation "raises important policy issues, most centrally for China and South Korea, but also for the United States, the UN, and other concerned parties. Yet subsequent discussion of the issues confronting these outside actors should not obscure the central point: *it is North Korean government policy—political repression, economic incompetence, and the denial of the most basic human rights, including the criminalization of exit—that creates the refugee problem.*"[45] The editors recognize China's legitimate concern about border control with respect to the illegal inflow of North Korean citizens into its territory but contend, "There is no reason why Chinese policy could not move on two tracks: upholding its international obligations with respect to North Korean refugees; and continuing its preferred strategy of political and economic engagement with North Korea with respect to the border security issues on the peninsula."[46] They are critical of what they consider the South Korean government's "increasingly unwelcoming" attitude toward North Korean defectors in South Korea, pointing out that even though the number of refugees entering the country has increased, it is still "trivial by any reasonable metric." They also note that the cash grants given by Seoul to the North Koreans who make it to South Korea have been reduced, making it harder for the refugees to finance their journey—often through Southeast Asia or Mongolia—and also increasing the prominence of criminal gangs in the migration process.[47] They welcome the North Korean Human Rights Act passed by the U.S. Congress in 2004 as a "laudable first step with respect to the refugee issue" but note that it "faces bureaucratic difficulties in implementation."[48] The editors of the report acknowledge the difficult challenge the UNHCR faces in balancing its need to "continue its constructive activities in Beijing on behalf of the North Korean refugees" and the need to "induce the Chinese government to grant access to the border region." "In the end," the editors conclude, "it is North Korea that is central, and it is unlikely that the root causes of the problem can be rectified without significant political change in North Korea. Indeed, it is important to recall that the refugee problem is only the very small tip of a much larger iceberg of repressive conditions within North Korea itself."[49]

The UN Human Rights Council has also been alarmed by increasing reports of the serious human rights situation in North Korea, but its ability to conduct its own assessment has been compromised by the North Korean government's refusal to recognize the mandate of the special rapporteur on the situation of human rights in North Korea or to extend full cooperation to him and allow him access to the country. On March 22, 2010, the Human Rights Council adopted resolution 13/14 on the "situation of human rights in the Democratic People's Republic of Korea," in which the council expressed deep concern "at the continuing reports of systematic, widespread and grave violations of civil, political, economic, social and cultural rights in the Democratic People's Republic of Korea and at the unresolved questions of international concern relating to the abduction of nationals of other States" and deplored "the grave, widespread and systematic human rights abuses in the Democratic People's Republic of Korea, in particular the use of torture and labor camps against political prisoners and repatriated citizens of the Democratic People's Republic of Korea." The resolution also stated that the council was "alarmed by the precarious humanitarian situation in the country." It further urged the North Korean government "to ensure full, rapid and unimpeded access of humanitarian assistance that is delivered on the basis of need, in accordance with humanitarian principles, coupled with adequate monitoring."[50] It should be highlighted that both China and Russia voted against this resolution.

Earlier, on December 18, 2009, the UN General Assembly had adopted resolution 64/175 on the "situation of human rights in the Democratic People's Republic of Korea." The resolution expressed the General Assembly's "very serious concern" at the "persistence of continuing reports of systematic, widespread and grave violations of civil, political, economic, social and cultural rights in the Democratic People's Republic of Korea."[51] Reported violations include the following:

(i) Torture and other cruel, inhuman or degrading treatment or punishment, including inhuman conditions of detention, public executions, extrajudicial and arbitrary detention; the absence of due process and the rule of law, including fair trial guarantees and an independent judiciary; the imposition of the death penalty for political and religious reasons; collective punishments;

and the existence of a large number of prison camps and the extensive use of forced labor;

(ii) Limitations imposed on every person who wishes to move freely within the country and travel abroad, including the punishment of those who leave or try to leave the country without permission, or their families, as well as punishment of persons who are returned;

(iii) The situation of refugees and asylum-seekers expelled or returned to the Democratic People's Republic of Korea and sanctions imposed on citizens of the Democratic People's Republic of Korea who have been repatriated from abroad, leading to punishments of internment, torture, cruel, inhuman or degrading treatment or the death penalty, and, in this regard, urges all States to respect the fundamental principle of non-refoulement, to treat those who seek refuge humanely and to ensure unhindered access to the United Nations High Commissioner for Refugees and his Office, with a view to improving the situation of those who seek refuge, and once again urges States parties to comply with their obligations under the 1951 Convention relating to the Status of Refugees[13] and the 1967 Protocol thereto[14] in relation to refugees from the Democratic People's Republic of Korea who are covered by those instruments;

(iv) All-pervasive and severe restrictions on the freedoms of thought, conscience, religion, opinion and expression, peaceful assembly and association, the right to privacy and equal access to information, by such means as the persecution of individuals exercising their freedom of opinion and expression, and their families, and on the right of everyone to take part in the conduct of public affairs, directly or through freely chosen representatives, of his or her country;

(v) The violations of economic, social and cultural rights, which have led to severe malnutrition, widespread health problems and other hardship for the population in the Democratic People's Republic of Korea, in particular for persons belonging to particularly exposed groups, inter alia, women, children and the elderly;

(vi) Continuing violations of the human rights and fundamental freedoms of women, in particular the trafficking of women for the purpose of prostitution or forced marriage and the subjection of women to human smuggling, forced abortions, gender-based discrimination, including in the economic sphere, and gender-based violence;

(vii) Continuing reports of violations of the human rights and fundamental freedoms of children, in particular the continued lack of access to basic economic, social and cultural rights for many children, and in this regard notes the particularly vulnerable situation faced by, inter alia, returned or repatriated children, street children, children with disabilities, children whose parents are detained, children living in detention or in institutions and children in conflict with the law;

(viii) Continuing reports of violations of the human rights and fundamental freedoms of persons with disabilities, especially on the use of collective camps and of coercive measures that target the rights of persons with disabilities to decide freely and responsibly on the number and spacing of their children; and,

(ix) Violations of workers' rights, including the right to freedom of association and collective bargaining, the right to strike as defined by the obligations of the Democratic People's Republic of Korea under the International Covenant on Economic, Social and Cultural Rights, and the prohibition of the economic exploitation of children and of any harmful or hazardous work of children as defined by the obligations of the Democratic People's Republic of Korea under the Convention on the Rights of the Child.[52]

The General Assembly has also expressed very serious concern at the North Korean government's refusal to recognize the mandate of the special rapporteur on the situation of human rights in North Korea or to extend cooperation to him.

CONCLUSION

It is tempting to conclude—and it may very well be the case—that the North Korean government, by omission and by commission, has failed to protect its own citizens from the four crimes and violations subject to RtoP, that the government has been the main culprit of the appalling humanitarian conditions and systematic human rights abuses in the country, and that there is both moral and legal justifications for international intervention on humanitarian grounds. All the evidence available to the international community appears to lead to that conclusion. Of the wide-ranging atrocities allegedly committed by the North Korean regime against its own citizens, the large-scale food deprivation and the prison system may rise to the level of "crimes against humanity" subject to the RtoP norm. However, the ultimate answer on this question must be provided by the United Nations as the highest and the most comprehensive representative of the international community. Perhaps more important, the narrow focus of RtoP noted in this chapter prevents us from concluding that international intervention under this principle is justified. To reiterate, RtoP applies only to genocide, war crimes, ethnic cleansing, and crimes against humanity and does not apply to a whole range of other human-security problems; and it is mostly regarding the latter for which we have mounting if imperfect evidence.

So, is there evidence that North Korea has committed genocide? The Convention on the Prevention and Punishment of the Crime of Genocide (Article II) defines "genocide" as "any of the following acts committed with intent to destroy, in whole or in part, a national, ethnic, racial or religious group, as such: (a) killing members of the group; (b) causing serious bodily or mental harm to members of the group; (c) deliberately inflicting on the group conditions of life calculated to bring about its physical destruction in whole or in part; (d) imposing measures intended to prevent births within the group; and (e) forcibly transferring children of the group to another group."[53] As horrific as the tales of survivors of famine in North Korea in the 1990s are, we have no evidence to suggest that the famine was intended to destroy a national, ethnic, racial, or religious group.

Among the four violations subject to the RtoP principle, North Korea may be charged with the murder or ill-treatment of prisoners of war during and following the Korean War, but our judgment must wait for the conclusion of a permanent peace treaty replacing the armistice and subsequent investigation of this possible war crime.

As noted, "ethnic cleansing" has been defined by a UN commission of experts reporting to the Security Council as involving "the planned deliberate removal from a specific territory, persons of a particular ethnic group, by force or intimidation, in order to render that area ethnically homogeneous."[54] Inasmuch as the North Korean regime's atrocities do not appear to be committed against a particular ethnic group, we cannot charge Pyongyang with ethnic cleansing as such.

How about crimes against humanity? Do we have conclusive evidence that the North Korean government has committed or is committing this crime? The body of evidence that has been compiled in the various reports noted above seems to suggest that the North Korean government may be charged with acts under (a), (c), (d), (e), (f), (g), (h), (i), and (k) under Article 7 of the Rome Statute establishing the International Criminal Court, as noted earlier. However, in order to bring the North Korean government to the International Criminal Court, the North Korean government, as well as the country wishing to bring charges against Pyongyang, must accept the jurisdiction of the court. As of July 18, 2008, Japan and South Korea had ratified the Rome Statute, but North Korea, China, and the United States had not.[55]

Moreover, as noted, RtoP is still an emerging norm, not an established legal principle under international law. We must wait for the General Assembly's continued debate and hope that the body will be able to adopt RtoP as a universal principle. We must also wait for the United Nations to develop operational guides for implementing the principle. The General Assembly must resolve the question of authority—under whose authority the international community would be permitted to intervene in the face of the failure of a state to protect its own people from the four crimes and violations. Further, the United Nations must establish the threshold of gravity beyond which international intervention would be justifiable, as well as the criteria to be used for assessing the gravity.

Even if RtoP were to become a universally established principle, there is no guarantee that North Korea would accept it or, even if it did, comply with it. In fact, most of the legal basis for RtoP is found in existing international human rights and humanitarian law, and yet the country has not responded to the international call for investigation into the alleged crimes and violations, and the human rights condition and humanitarian situation in the country remain dire. International human rights and humanitarian laws relevant to RtoP include but are not limited to the Covenant on Economic, Social and Cultural Rights; the Covenant on Civil and Political Rights; the Convention on the Elimination of All Forms of Discrimination against Women; and the Convention on the Rights of the Child. North Korea is a party to all of these conventions.[56] However, this has apparently not prevented the nation from violating the fundamental human rights enshrined by the conventions. Nor is North Korea a party to many other international laws pertinent to RtoP, including the International Convention on the Protection of the Rights of All Migrant Workers and Members of Their Families; the 1951 Refugee Convention; the Protocol Relating to the Status of Refugees; the Convention against Transnational Organized Crime; the Protocol to Prevent, Suppress and Punish Trafficking in Persons, Especially Women and Children, supplementing the Convention against Transnational Organized Crime; and the Protocol against the Smuggling of Migrants by Land, Sea and Air, also supplementing the Convention against Transnational Organized Crime.

If the General Assembly were to develop a consensus on RtoP with clear guidelines for its implementation, would the international community be willing and able to apply the principle in North Korea? The first of the three pillars of RtoP outlined by Secretary-General Ban Ki-moon—the primary responsibility of each state to protect its own citizens—would depend on the willingness and capacity of the North Korean government to carry out that responsibility, but all available evidence suggests the government in Pyongyang has neither the willingness nor the capacity to do so. Moreover, if past experience is any guide, the second pillar—international assistance in capacity building—would likely be blocked by the North Korean government. The third pillar—international intervention in the face of the state's failure to protect its own citizens against the four crimes and violations—would, at a minimum, require consensus among the permanent Security Council members, but China (and probably Russia as well) would be likely to oppose intervention, be it of a military or some other coercive nature.

Consequently, the international community would have no recourse other than to continue to press China to do all it can to alleviate the human suffering visiting the tens of thousands of North Korean citizens who have fled their country and who now live within their territory, to call on Pyongyang to accept the humanitarian assistance the international community is ready to offer to its citizens, and to remind the North Korean leadership that it is its responsibility to respect and protect the fundamental human rights accorded to its citizens by international human rights and humanitarian law. Once RtoP is established as a global norm and an international legal principle, the international community must also remind North Korea that it has the responsibility to protect its own citizens from the four crimes and violations to which the new principle applies.

NOTES

1. " 'Implementing the Responsibility to Protect,' Responding to the UN Secretary-General's Report on the Responsibility to Protect Populations from Genocide, War Crimes, Ethnic Cleansing and Crimes against Humanity," Global Centre for the Responsibility to Protect, Ralph Bunche Institute for International Studies, CUNY Graduate Center, New York, June 2009, 1.
2. Václav Havel and Kjell Magne Bondevik, "Forget Not Their Abominations," Opinion, *New York Times*, http://www.nytimes.com/2008/09/19/opinion/19iht-edhavel.1.16308272.htm (accessed June 25, 2010).
3. Agence France-Presse, "Defectors Seek to Meet UN on North Korea," June 14, 2010, http://news.smh.com.au/breaking-news-world/defectors-seek-to-meet-un-on-north-korea-20100614-ya50.html (accessed June 20, 2010).
4. Agence France-Presse, "Defectors Seek to Meet UN."
5. UN General Assembly, Sixtieth Session, *2005 World Summit Outcome*, September 15, 2005, A/60/L.1, 31.
6. " 'Implementing the Responsibility to Protect,' Responding to the UN Secretary-General's Report," 1.
7. UN Security Council, "Statement by the President of the Security Council," May 27, 2008, S/PRST/2008/18, 1, http://www.securitycouncilreport.org/atf/cf/%7B65BFCF9B-6D27-4E9C-8CD3-CF6E4FF96FF9%7D/Civilians%20S%20PRST%202008%2018.pdf (accessed June 20, 2012).
8. The text of his speech is reproduced in United Nations, Secretary-General, *Secretary-General Defends, Clarifies "Responsibility to Protect'" at Berlin Event. On "Responsible Sovereignty: International Cooperation for a Changed World,"* SG/SM/11701, July 15, 2008, http:/www.un.org/News/Press/docs/2008/sgsm11701.doc.htm (accessed June 25, 2010).

9. Gareth Evans and Mohamed Sahnoun, cochairs of the International Commission on Intervention and State Sovereignty, noted in 2002 "continued disagreement about whether there is a right of intervention, how and when it should be exercised, and under whose authority." See Evans and Sahnoun, "The Responsibility to Protect," *Foreign Affairs*, November/December 2002, http:/www.foreignaffairs.com/articles/58437/gareth-evans-and-mohamed-sahnoun/the-responsibility-to-protect (accessed June 25, 2010).
10. See http://www.hrweb.org/legal/genocide.html (accessed June 12, 2011).
11. Stéphane Courtois, Nicolas Werth, Jean-Louis Panné, Andrzej Paczkowski, Karel Bartošek, and Jean-Louis Margolin, *The Black Book of Communism: Crimes, Terror, Repression* (Cambridge, MA: Harvard University Press, 1999), 5.
12. Quoted in Cathie Carmichael, *Ethnic Cleansing in the Balkans: Nationalism and the Destruction of Tradition* (London: Routledge, 2002), 2.
13. " 'Implementing the Responsibility to Protect,' Responding to the UN Secretary-General's Report," 3.
14. The concerns are summarized by Mónica Serrano, executive director, Global Centre for the Responsibility to Protect, in "Meeting Summary: Uniting to Support the Responsibility to Protect; Preserving the Spirit of the 2005 Agreement, Thursday, 25 September 2008, Millennium UN Plaza Hotel, New York," 1, http://www.responsibilitytoprotect.org/files/Summary%20Report%20-%20Uniting%20to%20Support%20the%20%20Responsibility%20to%20Protect.pdf (accessed June 20, 2012).
15. "Implementing the Responsibility to Protect: The 2009 General Assembly Debate; An Assessment," Global Center for the Responsibility to Protect, Ralph Bunche Institute for International Studies, CUNY Graduate Center, New York, August 2009, 6.
16. Ibid.
17. Ibid.
18. Ibid., 7.
19. Ibid.
20. Ibid., 8.
21. United Nations, *Secretary-General Defends, Clarifies*, 3.
22. Ibid., 2.
23. "Implementing the Responsibility to Protect: The 2009 General Assembly Debate," 8–9.
24. Ibid., 10.
25. Ibid.

26. Serrano, "Meeting Summary. Uniting to Support the Responsibility to Protect: Preserving the Spirit of the 2005 Agreement, Thursday, 25 September 2008, Millennium UN Plaza Hotel, New York," Global Centre for the Responsibility to Protect, 2.
27. Ibid., 3.
28. United Nations, *Secretary-General Defends, Clarifies*, 2.
29. UNDP and United Nations University CRIS, *Delivering Human Security through Multi-level Governance*, March 2009, vii.
30. United Nations, *A More Secure World: Our Shared Responsibility; Report of the Secretary-General's High-Level Panel on Threats, Challenges and Change*, http://www.un.org/secureworld/report2.pdf (accessed June 12, 2011).
31. UNDP and United Nations University CRIS, *Delivering Human Security*, 12.
32. Ibid., 15.
33. Ibid., 16–17.
34. Ibid., 67.
35. North Korea tied Zimbabwe and Guinea in the magazine's assessment of the human rights record of countries around the world in 2010. "The Failed States Index 2010," *Foreign Policy*, http://www.foreignpolicy.com/articles/2010/06/21/2010_failed_states_index_interactive_map_and_rankings (accessed June 25, 2010).
36. U.S. Department of State, Bureau of Democracy, Human Rights, and Labor, "Korea, Democratic People's Republic of," February 28, 2005, http://www.state.gov/g/drl/rls/hrrpt/2004/41646.htm (accessed June 25, 2010).
37. DLA Piper and U.S. Committee for Human Rights in North Korea, *Failure to Protect: A Call for the UN Security Council to Act in North Korea*, 2006.
38. Václav Havel, Kjell Magne Bondevik, and Elie Wiesel, "Foreword," in *Failure to Protect: A Call for the UN Security Council to Act in North Korea*.
39. Václav Havel, Kjell Magne Bondevik, and Elie Wiesel, "Foreword," in DLA Piper, U.S. Committee for Human Rights in North Korea, and the Oslo Center for Peace and Human Rights, *Failure to Protect: The Ongoing Challenge in North Korea*, 2008.
40. Stephan Haggard and Marcus Noland, *Hunger and Human Rights: The Politics of Famine in North Korea* (Washington, DC: U.S. Committee for Human Rights in North Korea, 2005).
41. Stephan Haggard and Marcus Noland, eds., *The North Korean Refugee Crisis: Human Rights and International Response* (Washington, DC: U.S. Committee for Human Rights in North Korea, 2006).

42. Haggard and Noland, *Hunger and Human Rights*, 8.
43. Ibid., 10.
44. Ibid., 11.
45. Haggard and Noland, *North Korean Refugee Crisis*, 73 (emphasis in original).
46. Ibid., 75.
47. Ibid.
48. Ibid., 76.
49. Ibid.
50. UN General Assembly, Human Rights Council, Thirteenth Session, Agenda Item 4, *Human Rights Situation That Requires the Council's Attention, Resolution Adopted by the Human Rights Council 13/14, Situation of Human Rights in the Democratic People's Republic of Korea*, April 15, 2010, A/HRC/RES/13/14, http://www2.ohchr.org/english/bodies/hrcouncil/docs/13session/A.HRC.RES.13.14_AEV.pdf (accessed June 20, 2012).
51. UN General Assembly, Sixty-fourth Session, Agenda Item 69 (*c*), *Resolution Adopted by the General Assembly. Situation of Human Rights in the Democratic People's Republic of Korea*, March 26, 2010, A/RES/64/175, 2, http://www.mofat.go.kr/mofat/htm/issue/nk_humanrights64_ga.pdf (accessed June 20, 2012).
52. Ibid., 2–4.
53. "Convention on the Prevention and Punishment of the Crime of Genocide," Article 2, http://www.hrweb.org/legal/genocide.html (accessed June 20, 2012).
54. "Implementing the Responsibility to Protect: The 2009 General Assembly Debate," 10.
55. Coalition for the International Criminal Court, "States Parties to the Rome Statute of the ICC," http://www.iccnow.org/documents/RatificationsbyUNGroup_18_July_08.pdf (accessed June 28, 2010).
56. North Korea is not a party to the Convention on the Elimination of All Forms of Racial Discrimination.

CHAPTER 8

International Legal Perspectives on North Korean Refugee Issues

SHIN-WHA LEE

Under conditions of extreme poverty and devastating famine, many North Koreans have defected. If they make it to South Korea, they are almost always granted asylum and citizenship under the South Korean constitution. However, direct defection by means of crossing through the Demilitarized Zone (DMZ), dotted with land mines, razor wire, and a heavy American and South Korean troop presence, is often an unfeasible choice. Most defectors have chosen an alternative route, illegally fleeing into mainland China. The number of defectors is widely estimated, ranging from several thousand, according to the South Korean government's estimation, to hundreds of thousands, as estimated by nongovernmental organizations (NGOs).

Unless North Korea's economy fails entirely, or the regime collapses, those who attempt to escape from the North are likely to be constrained by several factors, such as Pyongyang's tight control of the internal movement of ordinary citizens and stepped-up border security, the financial burden of securing an escape route, and the risk of being captured on the Sino–North Korean border or in China itself. However, given the widespread economic hardships and food crisis in the North and uncertainty about the newly launched Kim Jong Eun regime they will continue to seek this perilous passage to China and beyond.

The North Korean defector problem began to come under the international spotlight as the result of several deliberate defection attempts that were often, since the first years of the twenty-first century, facilitated by international NGOs. Consequently, the number and whereabouts of North Korean escapees, their safety, the causes of their flight, the limitations of international law on refugees in relation to them, and the position taken and policies adopted by concerned governments have become topics of debate among interested international parties. Furthermore, with the passage of the North Korean Human Rights Act, signed by U.S. president George W. Bush in 2004, the adoption of North Korean human rights–related resolutions by the United Nations every year since 2005, and various accusations by NGOs over human rights violations in North Korea, the country's human rights record has drawn significant international attention. In this vein, the North Korean defector problem has been considered both a refugee issue and a human rights concern.

Conversely, there have been certain observations suggesting that North Korean human rights issues, including the defector problem, might instigate a regime change in North Korea. With the development of its nuclear and missile programs, Pyongyang has faced international pressure, including UN Security Council resolutions 1718 and 1874, which imposed sanctions against North Korea in order to get the country to halt its nuclear tests and that required it to suspend all ballistic missile–related activity. In response, North Korea has offensively criticized the UN resolutions as a political conspiracy by the United States, Japan, and the European Union to overthrow its regime and ideology. Thus, arguments have arisen over whether or not human rights issues in the North should be related to political and security agendas.

Still, it should be noted that the flight of these defectors itself is a lagging, not leading, indicator of serious food and economic crises in North Korea.[1] North Korean escapees must experience severe economic suffering and starvation, which is a serious human rights problem, before deciding to defect. Upon entering China, these defectors need to find their way to another country, mostly into South Korea, as they face the danger of being forcibly returned to North Korea by Chinese authorities, who regard them as illegal migrants. Those repatriated back home are subject to severe punishment and, in some cases, even death. Furthermore, of those defectors who are not captured or sent back to North Korea, many are exposed to human trafficking, sexual assault, and labor exploitation in China. Nevertheless, these crimes remain unspoken out of fear of arrest and repatriation.

Although it is important to deal with the North Korean defector problem from the perspective of human rights and humanitarian challenges, we need to consider that the problems and classifications of these people have become multifaceted, since they make up a very complex and diverse population. It is not easy to deal with the issue of defectors living abroad, since it requires a comprehensive assessment of the legal and political challenges involved in order to assess the possibility of protecting them. In addition, the future of the Kim Jong Eun regime, the possible mass exodus of people out of North Korea, the geostrategic interests of the countries involved, and the role of the United Nations and NGOs need to be collectively considered. If managed poorly, the escapee problem may bring about a host of unwelcome political and strategic ramifications.

This chapter therefore seeks legal and political solutions to the plight of North Korean defectors. With special emphasis upon the situations of asylum seekers in China, this chapter discusses the legal measures available to them under international laws related to human rights, humanitarian issues, and refugee protection. China's obligations are called for, as a responsible global stakeholder, to observe international laws to which it is a signatory. This chapter also acknowledges that the international community should help alleviate North Korea's dire food and economic circumstances and hence eliminate the reason for escape. For this, the defector issue is not considered just from a humanitarian standpoint but also from the perspective of the entire host of North Korean problems, including Pyongyang's development of nuclear weapons, its ill-managed economic policies, and the uncertain political situation under the reign of the young new leader. A bilateral and multilateral political and diplomatic approach by regional countries and international organizations is also required to develop strategies for legal reforms and policy changes related to the North Korean defector problem and beyond.

DEVELOPMENTS OF NORTH KOREAN REFUGEE PROBLEMS

The term *talbukja* has been widely used to refer to individuals who have fled North Korea. After the partition of Korea in 1945, North Koreans, mainly male soldiers and political elites, defected to South Korea for political and ideological reasons. South Korea welcomed them as *gwysunja* or *gwysunyongsa*, meaning individuals or brave soldiers who have returned to the right path, that is, the South. In the midst of the Cold War rivalry and military tension between the two Koreas, their lives before and after defection were publicized to boast of the supremacy of the South Korean system and to consolidate anticommunist sentiment.

During the past fifteen years, there has been a noticeable change in the nature and scope of North Korean defections. The great famine in the 1990s reportedly led to the deaths of two to three million people, left more than half of the North Korean population malnourished,[2] and motivated famine-stricken people to leave the country. Though denial of human rights, political oppression, and fear of brutal treatment of those facing imprisonment remain as important reasons for the flight, acute food shortages and economic hardships have caused the rise in North Korean defections since the mid-1990s. Their food and economic problems were caused not only by floods and droughts but also by the country's failed economic policies and the collapse of its special trading relationship with China and the former Soviet Union.

According to the Korean Ministry of Unification, the number of North Korean defectors to the South began to increase dramatically in the late 1990s, and as of December 2011, 23,100 defectors were in South Korea. Many of them were ordinary North Koreans who came with family members, and the substantial increase in the number of female defectors (70 percent of the total) is noteworthy (see table 8.1).

Yet direct flight to South Korea through the tightly guarded DMZ is usually an impractical option, and instead most North Korean defectors have attempted to seek asylum in China across the country's northern border at the Yalu and Tumen rivers. This journey is fraught with peril, since escapees risk being shot and killed by North Korean soldiers.

When famine in North Korea was at its peak and the rush of defectors at its height between 1996 and 1999, the influx of international relief aid into the country meant that border control was relatively unrestricted. This meant that North Koreans, particularly those living in the provinces in the northeastern part of the Korean Peninsula adjacent to China, increasingly sought to cross the border. At the time, *joseonjok* (Chinese people of Korean descent) living near the border were

TABLE 8.1. Number of North Korean defectors entering South Korea, 1989–2011

	1989	*1993*	*1998*	*2001*	*2002*	*2003*	*2004*	*2005*	*2006*	*2007*	*2008*	*2009*	*2010*	*2011*	*Total*
Male	562	32	235	563	506	469	626	423	509	570	612	666	579	819	7,171
Female	45	2	71	480	632	812	1,268	960	1,509	1,974	2,197	2,261	1,800	1,918	15,929
Total	607	34	306	1,043	1,138	1,281	1,894	1,383	2,018	2,544	2,809	2,927	2,379	2,737	23,100

Source: Republic of Korea, Ministry of Unification, "Policy on North Korean Defectors: Recent Status" (in Korean), http://www.unikorea.go.kr/CmsWeb/viewPage.req?idx=PG0000000365.

As of December 2011.

sympathetic to the plight of North Koreans. Many defectors crossed without any outside assistance; bribing North Korean soldiers watching the border was commonplace, and Chinese officials were indifferent to the escapees. Religious organizations actively helped them as well.[3]

Until the late 1990s, many of the defectors aimed to return to their families in the North once they had obtained food, medicine, or money. The area that the defectors sought for short-term residency was primarily the Yanbian Korean Autonomous Prefecture, which is densely populated by *joseonjok*. On the other hand, defectors looking for long-term accommodations traveled farther north, to areas such as Liaoning, Jilin, and Heilongjiang provinces (see table 8.2).

Over the past decade, however, an increasing number of North Korean escapees have opted to remain in China until the food and economic situations at home improve, or migrate to other countries, mostly South Korea, for permanent resettlement. However, the Chinese government has labeled the vast majority of North Korean defectors as illegal aliens or economic migrants at best, although several defectors have qualified for political refugee status. The defectors seized by Chinese authorities, referred to as *jyogyo* (ethnic North Koreans in China), have been forcibly repatriated to North Korea based on the National Border Treaty signed by the two countries in 1962. Beijing wishes to avoid any deterioration in its relations with North Korea and also intends to prevent the possible mass exodus of North Koreans into

TABLE 8.2. Duration of residence of North Korean defectors in China, 1997–1999 (%)

Duration / *Place*	*Less than 3 months (50.3)*[a]	*More than 6 months (28.8)*[b]
Yanbian	74.6	11.4
3 northeastern provinces	19.4	48.8
Other areas	6	39.8
All of China	100	100

Source: Joeun Beotdeul, *Report on Status and Human Rights of North Korean "Food Refugees"* (in Korean) (Seoul: Joeun butdeul, 1999), 3.

[a]Percentage of short-term North Korean defectors.

[b]Percentage of long-term North Korean defectors.

China that might occur if they were to be recognized as official refugees. China deals with North Korean defectors based not on whether the cause of defection is political or economic but on whether or not the applicant is an illegal immigrant.[4]

Several *kihwek mangmyong* (premeditated defection) attempts by North Koreans took place with the help of NGOs after China, under international pressure, released a North Korean family of seven, known as the Gil Su family, that sought refuge at the UN High Commissioner for Refugees (UNHCR) office in Beijing in 2000. In the face of growing worldwide scrutiny of the North Korean refugee issue, China has endeavored to avoid international criticism of its policy regarding these defectors. However, it has reinforced its repatriation policy by developing a net of systematic search protocols and house-to-house arrests and by imposing heavy fines on those who help North Korean escapees and giving rewards for reporting their presence. Consequently, unless an incident seizes international attention, such as the cases of the Gil Su family and the rush of twenty-five North Koreans into the Spanish embassy in Beijing in March 2001, most defectors in China face forcible return. Therefore, many remain in isolation, hiding in huts or caves and emerging only to search for food.[5]

For those defectors who have managed to live among the Chinese population, they often face human rights violations, such as labor exploitation and sexual harassment, and yet for fear of being arrested and sent home they tend to remain silent. Women constitute two-thirds of all North Korean escapees. About 80 percent of these women have been sold through human trafficking into commercial sex exploitation, enslaved marriage, and exploitative labor.[6] They are often forced to marry widowers, older bachelors, disabled and mentally ill men, or obsessive gamblers, who are unable to find wives through traditional means. They are not only often beaten or imprisoned but also suffer from prejudice and the stigma of having sold their bodies. Meanwhile, male escapees have little choice but to undertake hard labor for less than the proper amount of remuneration. They cannot speak out because revealing their identity would lead to repatriation.[7]

The North Korean government, which is primarily responsible for the plight of these people, has linked the defector problem with the sustainment of its communist regime. Although North Korea signed the International Covenant on Civil and Political Rights in 1981, it nonetheless regards defectors as antisocialists and criminals that have illegally fled the country, and it has therefore strengthened control and punishment measures. Repatriates are subject to imprisonment and torture in North Korea's gulags and, at times, execution without trial.[8]

Flaws in international law concerning refugees contribute to the agony of North Korean defectors in China. They are not officially categorized as refugees because a defector must meet the requirement of being forced to leave owing to a well-founded fear of being persecuted for political reasons before a decision can be made on whether an individual asylum seeker is granted refugee status, according to the 1951 UN Convention Relating to the Status of Refugees and the 1967 Protocol Relating to the Status of Refugees. Unfortunately, North Korean "food refugees" have been trapped by this legal restriction.[9]

Since asylum in China and entry into South Korea via China have become too difficult, North Koreans have increasingly been moving to Inner Mongolia and Southeast Asian countries such as Vietnam, Thailand, Laos, and Myanmar, often participating themselves in human trafficking or joining criminal groups to keep their identities hidden.[10] During the past few years, the largest number of North Korean defectors have followed the latter pattern of fleeing to Southeast Asia, and in July 2004, seven hundred defectors amassed in the region traveled to South Korea on a chartered plane.[11] The defectors using this Southeast Asian route are less vulnerable to forced repatriation because of the distance of travel, cost, and lower levels of government control. They nonetheless face apprehension, bribery requests for release, and harassment by the border guards in the countries they attempt to enter.[12]

Some argue that the overall figure of North Korean escapees has decreased because of increased enforcement along the North Korean border and strengthened surveillance in China, as well as restricted migration to third-party countries.[13] Others argue that the number has increased not only because of economic difficulties and the food crisis but also because the process for entry into South Korea through countries other than China is less difficult than in the past. Additionally, more defectors have left with their families, assisted by relatives and friends who have already succeeded in settling in South Korea or elsewhere.[14]

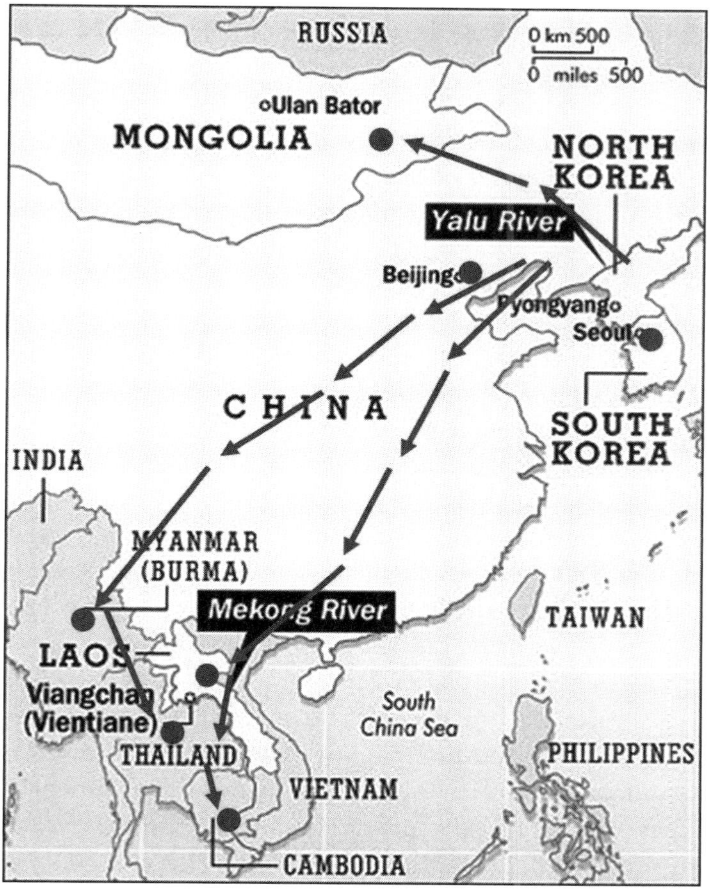

FIGURE 8.1. Routes of North Korean defectors. (Source: Radio Free Asia)

No matter which argument reflects reality, there have been many defectors who have testified that the flight to China is still better than life in North Korea. Networks assisting defectors have thus become more complex and diverse. An increasing number of those who attempt defection are procuring money and establishing contacts before they flee. This means that the most destitute and helpless in North Korea have little means and choice but to suffer from the food shortages and economic hardship at home.

Recently, the food and economic conditions in North Korea have deteriorated not only because of reduced foreign aid but also because of international sanctions as a result of North Korea's missile and nuclear tests. The disastrous revaluation of its currency in 2009 and aggravated inter-Korean relations as a result of the shooting death of a South Korean tourist at North Korea's Mount Kumgang resort in July 2008, the sinking of the South Korean naval ship *Cheonan* in March 2010, and the bombardment of Yeonpyeong Island in November 2010 have not helped, either. There have been reports that the number of North Korean soldiers fleeing into China as a result of food shortages is increasing. The desertion of soldiers, who, in the military-first North Korean system, are better fed than ordinary people, is clear evidence that the country is suffering from a serious food shortage and economic failure.[15]

The flight also relates to the changing mind-set of the younger generation, including young soldiers, in the tightly controlled and closed society of the North. They have gradually realized the "truth" through information that has filtered back from returning refugees, clandestine Internet searches, or by watching black-market South Korean TV programs. Recently, a group of North Korean defectors residing in South Korea developed "stealth USB" memory sticks, which store South Korean soap operas, political information, and other data, and distributed hundreds of them into North Korea. These memory sticks are programmed to appear to contain no contents when going through North Korean customs searches, but with the passage of time, the contents are automatically activated.[16]

Meanwhile, the number of defectors attempting to enter South Korea directly through a sea passage is on the increase. Those who make it into the South are granted South Korean citizenship per its constitution, unless they have committed international crimes. By law, Koreans residing in North Korea are also citizens of South Korea, and North Korean escapees in foreign states are therefore citizens living abroad. Also, according to the Law Regarding the Protection and Settlement Assistance of North Korean Escapees, which has been in force since July 1997, provisionary protection measures must be taken whenever a request is received for protection from North Korean defectors abroad. Negotiations with the receiving state must be carried out according to humanitarian principles to bring them to South Korea.

However, owing to political and diplomatic circumstances, flaws in international law, and overly bureaucratic procedures, many North Koreans still await entrance into South Korea or are admitted only on a selective basis. The adaptation by refugees to the South Korean way of life is also not easy, causing some social problems. In addition, the possibility of North Korean spies operating in the guise of refugees has become a concern to the South Korean government.[17]

In particular, the "progressive" administrations of South Korean presidents Kim Dae Jung and Roh Moo-hyun between 1998 and 2007 practiced "quiet diplomacy" on the issue of North Korean escapees in China by requesting that they be provided with special treatment based on humanitarian principles, while respecting the rights of China under international law. Many North Korean escapees voiced their right to defect to the South, but Seoul was not eager to help them for fear of causing diplomatic tension with China and obstructing inter-Korean relations.

The growing number of North Korean defectors will ultimately become a grave concern. For instance, in October 1999 the director of the UNHCR's Asian bureau acknowledged the existence of some one hundred to one hundred fifty refugees among North Korean defectors in China. This acknowledgment was immediately followed up by an announcement from the South Korean minister of foreign affairs stating that his government was ready to host "all" North Korean refugees.[18] It remains doubtful whether South Korea or other countries can accommodate the North Korean refugees if the number acknowledged by the UNHCR is increased to the levels that NGOs claim, possibly hundreds of thousands of people.

The UNHCR and several countries began to grant refugee status to a small number of North Korean escapees in early 2000, with immense international media attention, but in general they have been reluctant to talk about the status of North Korean defectors in China. This is mainly because they wish to stay away from any conflict between international refugee laws and China as a sovereign state. According to UNHCR statistical information, as of January 2011, 1,195 North Koreans were reported as "populations of concern to UNHCR," among them 917 North Korean refugees and 278 asylum seekers. Many of these "populations of concern" have settled in Western states (see table 8.3).[19]

TABLE 8.3. Worldwide resettlement of North Korean refugees, 2000–2010

	2000	*2001*	*2002*	*2003*	*2004*	*2005*	*2006*	*2007*	*2008*	*2009*	*2010*
Australia	3	4	4	3	3	6	8	15	14	15	25
Belgium				0		0	0	7	9	13	22
Canada	0	0		3	4	4	4	4	4	4	23
Denmark	2	2	7	7	7	7	7	8	8	9	9
Germany	0	0	225	258	276	193	239	204	180	156	146
Ireland		1	5	5	5	5	5	6	6	6	6
Israel								2	2	2	2
Kyrgyzstan							2	5	6	7	3
Luxembourg									0	0	
Mexico						1	1	1	1	1	1
Netherlands	3	7	9	14	15	18	20	27	29	31	32
New Zealand		1	1	1	1	1	0	1	1	1	1
Norway	3	3	3	3	3	4	5	9	13	14	14
Russia							0		6	10	14
Sweden			2	2	2	6	7	7	7	8	8
Switzerland		1	2	1	1	1	6	6	6	4	4
Thailand	0										
United Kingdom				0	17	33	64	281	570	574	581
United States	2			7	9	9	30	22	23	25	25
Uzbekistan			1	0							
Yemen									1	1	1

Source: UNHCR, "2012 Regional Operations Profile: East Asia and the Pacific; Democratic People's Republic of Korea," 2012, http://www.unhcr.org/pages/49e488f56.html.

As of January 2011.

INTERNATIONAL LEGAL APPROACHES TO THE NORTH KOREAN DEFECTOR PROBLEM IN CHINA

The current North Korean defector problem must be considered from the standpoint of international law, for at least three major reasons. Above all, the fundamental cause of defections is the failure of the North Korean regime to provide its people with public goods. As noted, since many North Koreans have decided to flee because of economic afflictions and famine caused by failed policies adopted by the government, the defectors must not be regarded as migrants merely seeking individual economic gain. Also, they are defined by the North Korean government as political criminals and face severe punishment if repatriated. Therefore, North Korean escapees, including those that defect merely for economic reasons, must all be protected from political persecution.[20]

Second, many North Korean defectors fall victim to human rights violations during the course of defection or while living in China. More specifically, defecting North Korean women are being abducted, trafficked, and sexually violated. Even without referring to the international law on refugees, these issues violate international laws prohibiting crimes against humanity, particularly the UN Protocol to Prevent, Suppress and Punish Trafficking in Persons, Especially Women and Children, supplementing the Convention against Transnational Organized Crime.[21]

Third, although the list of destination countries for North Korean escapees goes beyond China and includes other nations such as Russia, Mongolia, Southeast Asian countries, the United States, and Europe, consistent principles and rules concerning the protection and treatment of these escapees applicable to all these countries and regions are still nonexistent. Not only does this expose the defectors to constant danger but also, with no internationally agreed-upon norms and rules, countries often choose to either repatriate or detain the defectors, or to relocate them to a third country. Whichever option countries dealing with the issue choose, it imposes political pressure on them. Furthermore, a mass defection to a certain country may provoke conflicts between the countries involved. Therefore, building consensus between states on how to cope with North Korean defection is crucial in order to deal with several sensitive aspects of the problem regardless of the larger discussion on the relation between state sovereignty and international law. In other words, providing North Korean defectors legal status based on the consent of relevant countries involved is important not only in protecting the defectors but also in providing concerned countries with a guiding principle for handling them while broadening policy options.

When considering the North Korean defector problem with regard to international law, the question of granting them refugee standing should be given first attention. Countries signatory to international laws on refugees are obliged to protect people who are in danger of persecution because of race, religion, nationality, membership of a particular social group, or political views. China, which joined the UN refugee convention in 1982 and whose constitution stipulates the offering of asylum to refugees from political oppression (Article 32), should not turn away from North Korean escapees.[22]

Nonetheless, the nature of defection from North Korea has ambiguous and complex aspects, and thus it requires more specific considerations in order for the countries involved to reach an agreement on granting the defectors refugee status.

First, there are differences relating to how countries distinguish economic migrants from refugees. According to international law, economic migrants are governed by their own nations, whereas refugees are protected by the country they escape to.[23] Those who support the Chinese government's position in defining North Korean defectors as illegal economic immigrants underscore the fact that these people entered China merely in order to gain food and thus are not eligible for refugee status.[24] However, this argument is losing persuasiveness. As former UN special rapporteur on the situation of human rights in the Democratic People's Republic of Korea Vitit Muntarbhorn stated in 2005, the North Korean defector problem has obvious political aspects, since, at the time, several had defected in order to escape complex calamities caused by political and economic factors at home.[25] As for repatriated defectors, even if they crossed the border only in search of food, they are likely to be charged with antinational crimes rather than illegal exit and thus face severe punishment. Therefore, the fear deriving from such punishment can in itself fulfill the requirements listed in Article 1A of the UN refugee convention.[26]

Second, there are controversies over whether the punishment given to returned defectors by the North Korean government is persecution or prosecution. If the defectors are considered simple illegal emigrants, the punishment imposed upon them can be regarded as domestic law enforcement. However, considering the fact that the North Korean economic crisis was intensified for certain social classes in pursuit of ulterior political agendas, the economic hardships suffered by the defectors can be understood as persecution. This argument leads to whether famine should be regarded as a form of persecution. Famine endangers human survival and therefore is a violation of basic human rights. For the argument that North Korean defection to avoid famine can be justified as grounds for the granting of refugee status, one must prove that famine occurred asymmetrically in North Korea. There have been numerous reports that the distribution of food and commodities by the North Korean government has favored those who are obliging and valuable to the maintenance of the regime, such as party executives, core-industry workers, and the military.[27]

Third, there is the issue of South Korean national law. If North Korean defectors are granted the status of refugees, it may conflict with the South Korean law that acknowledges all North Koreans as South Korean citizens and may also cause problems of dual nationality. According to the UN refugee convention, people bearing multiple nationalities are excluded from international protection because they can be given protection by the state of which they have another citizenship. North Koreans cannot exercise their "South Korean rights" when they are situated in the North or when they are not protected by South Korean jurisdiction. In this case, their South Korean citizenship can be considered dormant, thus allowing them to be protected internationally. This principle was confirmed by the passing of the U.S. North Korean Human Rights Act in 2004, which proclaims that the South Korean law will be respected and the U.S. government will accept North Korean defectors. However, it further proclaims that when practical salvation of the defectors is impossible, the international community should lend its assistance.[28]

Fourth, there is the issue of the special relationship between North Korea and China. Chinese repatriation of North Korean defectors is perfectly legitimate within the alliance between the two states and therefore does not violate any international law. However, numerous treaties and conventions related to human rights that both China and North Korea have joined clearly stipulate that refugees caused by human rights violations, as well as any inhumane prosecution resulting from repatriation, are exempt from any particular agreement.[29] In the case of the alliance between South Korea and the United States, social-activist groups in the United States continually followed human rights issues in South Korea, and these issues were a source of rifts between the two allies in the past. For example, in the 1970s U.S. president Jimmy Carter reduced American forces stationed in South Korea on the basis that it was wrong to protect a country that violated human rights, and succeeding administrations have all pressured Seoul by linking human rights issues with the alliance.[30] This argues that sacrificing human rights for the sake of security contradicts domestic and international norms. In other words, the argument that a bilateral alliance comes before international principles regarding human rights cannot be justified.

Acknowledging North Korean defectors as refugees and applying international standards is important. But more pivotal than logical ideals is the problem concerning the implementation process of state policies within international relations. Current international law stipulates not only the obligations but also the rights of individual states. In the principle prohibiting repatriation of the UN convention, there is an exceptive clause that permits countries to reject refugees if they are deemed a threat to national security. This has been highlighted in the "war on terror" carried out by the United States and its allies after 9/11. For example, several major Western states have asserted the principle of "refusing potentially dangerous people for the mere sake of protecting the human rights of refugees" in an effort to stop the flow of terrorists entering their countries under the cover of refugees.[31] In other words, because of the clash between refugee rights to "be protected from their motherland" and national rights to "be protected from refugees," the universal norm for accepting refugees in order to protect human rights has weakened, and this can apply to North Korean defectors as well.

Taking into consideration all the legal and practical problems discussed here, efforts to protect North Korean defectors under international law can be specified according to four aspects. First, persuading the North Korean government to pardon illegal border crossers is a viable option. Repatriating refugees after the danger of persecution has been eliminated and the possibility of pardon has been secured is a solution endorsed by the UNHCR. An official statement declaring amnesty for defectors will likely decrease planned defections in the form of forced entry into official residences of foreign countries. It will also relieve China of its diplomatic burden and reduce tension along the border. For this measure to be implemented, several international organizations, including the UNHCR, must convince both China and North Korea of the international value of adopting such measures while assisting and monitoring the actual procedure.

Second, it is practical to adopt a gradual approach in which direct criticism of North Korea and China is avoided while tackling the most serious human rights violations first. Since many aspects of international law entail broad definitions and concepts, requiring China to abide by general refugee rules and national obligations will not only lack persuasiveness but may also give the false impression that the international community is hostile toward it. Therefore, international organizations need to develop close relations with China in order to argue compellingly that repatriating North Korean defectors violates international law, and they need to cooperate with China so that it will provide temporary refugee status while the UNHCR arranges for the defectors to be relocated to a third country.[32] In particular, it would be wise to start to pursue limited goals such as the prohibition of repatriation by central and local governments and the protection of the defectors from human rights violations within China rather than requiring China to guarantee the complete settlement of North Korean defectors. On this front, the efforts of both the international community and NGOs have been rewarded with some progress, inasmuch as it was reported that Chinese officials had ceased repatriation of North Koreans late last year.[33]

Third, there is a need to procure UNHCR access to North Korean defectors and to educate the defectors about their rights. Though planned defection in the form of forced entry into official residences of foreign countries seems to be the most effective method of defection, domestic surveillance and border control are being strengthened, and the overall situation is deteriorating as a result. Therefore, it is important to persuade Beijing that allowing the defectors to contact the UNHCR is a way to decrease forced-entry attempts and lighten their diplomatic burden.[34] Also, considering the fact that most defectors do not understand their rights and the various methods of settlement, educating them on such matters would help the defectors protect themselves from human rights violations in China.

Finally, there is a need to apply the international laws on refugees and human rights simultaneously. As stated, one of the main reasons that North Korean defectors are not entitled to refugee status is because the Chinese government regards them as illegal economic immigrants. As a result, the status of the defectors is in limbo, and they become vulnerable to various human rights violations. Applying international human rights law can protect defectors from numerous crimes they face in China, even without refugee status. Furthermore, the universal principle of protecting human rights can be used as a legal basis to prevent forced repatriation. Specifically, the various monitoring organizations of international law, such as the Committee Against Torture, can be utilized to protect defectors in the absence of an international institution prohibiting repatriation.[35]

INTERNATIONAL LEGAL APPROACHES IN THE EVENT OF MASS DEFECTION

Discussions regarding how to apply international law in the event of mass defection from North Korea are closely related to the future of North Korea. There are at least three clear and separate contingency situations that could produce a massive refugee exodus from the North: the complete collapse of the North Korean regime, the North Korean regime's "muddling through" a serious crisis, and armed conflict.

In the event of complete regime collapse, providing international protection on the grounds of international law related to refugees may be simple owing to the fact that there would no longer remain a government holding jurisdiction over the North Korean people, and therefore the defectors could be granted refugee status. Yet the situation may become complicated with the intervention of China. In the event of the collapse of the North Korean regime, there is a possibility that the Chinese army and police would enter North Korean territory in order to prevent a mass exodus.

On the other hand, if the North Korean regime is maintained despite significant crises, calls for international protection based on humanitarian law will seem less persuasive to the international community, while the role of neighboring countries will increase in importance. Nonetheless, China may cooperate with Pyongyang in order to suppress the flow of defectors or aggressively repatriate North Korean defectors regardless of how diminished the North Korean regime is, and this, in turn, increases the possibility of unnecessary military intervention or inhumane acts.

Finally, in the case of mass defection as a result of armed conflict, human rights law, international humanitarian law, and international law related to refugees can all be applied to the defectors. International human rights law states that human rights are guaranteed to all people, including those who do not possess legal rights, and that this principle transcends the jurisdictions of sovereign states. International humanitarian law seems more meaningful in this scenario. North Korean defectors in this case could receive practical and effective protection through the principle of civilian protection, as specified in Convention (IV) Relative to the Protection of Civilian Persons in Time of War.[36] International humanitarian law has been developed and refined over centuries, dating back to the medieval laws on war, and it has exhibited a high level of standardization regarding civilian protection.[37] The Geneva Conventions of 1949 consist of four treaties, including Convention (IV), and are considered the cornerstone of current international humanitarian law. In particular, the fourth treaty specifically sets the standards in international law for humanitarian treatment of the victims of war, and this could be applied to North Korean defectors if violent conflict erupts.[38]

Applying international law related to refugees would also be easier in a time of armed conflict. It would be difficult for countries to find grounds to reject North Korean asylum seekers, since the situation would be the result of a definite political event, a war. In the case of a war-caused exodus, having predetermined definitions and understanding of the characteristics of mass defection would be pivotal for the effective management of the situation. Meanwhile, the application of international law related to refugees would depend on whether the North Korean regime was able to sustain itself during or in the wake of a conflict. If the regime persisted, the mass defection problem would be handled bilaterally between North Korea and China, and North Korea would be able to reject all international requests on the grounds that it was a domestic issue.

In the case of a mass defection occurring without any violent conflict, international laws related to human rights and refugees would have to be applied comprehensively based on previous experience. The causes of the flight of large numbers of North Koreans in the 1990s persist, and any future mass defections would most likely have the same causes. Consequently, international laws related to the protection of refugees would need to be applied to the case of mass defection from the North. Also, basic human rights must be protected in accordance with international human rights laws to all people, including those with ambiguous legal status. Actual outcomes may differ depending on the existence or not of the North Korean regime. If it persists, countries supporting North Korea will hesitate to grant defectors refugee status. If it collapses, the grounds for rejecting North Korean defectors will weaken. Moreover, the collapse of a regime is itself a political event, and defections that occur as a result are entitled to protection by the international community under obligations to the UN refugee convention.

In all cases, the most fundamental aspect is how individual countries will fulfill their international obligations, as well as how doing so will affect their national interests. Basically, countries are all reluctant to accept the inflow of refugees and will wish to minimize this burden, so it is necessary to install international legal mechanisms and advance interstate cooperation to protect the rights of refugees. In this regard, international cooperation and burden sharing are required to supplement the process in certain aspects, such as coordinating different states' positions and acquiring sufficient resources.

More specifically, based on past experiences of special administrative institutions and international conferences established to deal with large-scale refugee problems, a multilateral organization or an international conference on mass North Korean defections can be created to discuss, coordinate, and implement specific details regarding information exchange and financial cost sharing. For this, the "First International Conference Regarding the Refugees on the Indochina Peninsula," a multilateral meeting held in 1979 to deal with the refugees from Vietnam, can be taken as a guide. Through this conference, the Orderly Departure Program (ODP) was established, offering an official route for the safe and legitimate migration of Vietnamese refugees while decreasing the incentives for the flow of refugees by strictly abiding by third-country relocation application dates and by closing several refugee camps. As a result, the number of refugees in Southeast Asia decreased by nearly half by the mid-1980s.[39]

Furthermore, at the second conference, held in 1989, the legal justification behind the repatriation of Vietnamese refugees was emphasized, and the UNHCR initiated modification of the ODP to create the Comprehensive Plan of Action for Indochinese Refugees (CPA).[40] Neighboring countries of Vietnam participating in the CPA, namely Thailand, Malaysia, Indonesia, Hong Kong, and the Philippines, were all reluctant at first to accept Vietnamese refugees. However, these countries eventually agreed to the UNHCR request to provide temporary shelter, and with financial aid from the United Nations and Western countries, they provided temporary accommodations for the refugees until they were repatriated or relocated to Western countries.[41] Ways to constructively apply this precedent to mass North Korean defection scenarios should be sought.

CONCLUSION

Humanitarian aid and protection are not adequately granted to North Korean "food refugees" because of the political or diplomatic considerations of host countries and inadequately defined international law. According to the 1951 UN refugee convention and the 1967 protocol, only those who have crossed an international border for political reasons qualify as legitimate refugees. The UNHCR rationale for this legal criterion is that victims of economic difficulty and environmental disaster can be accommodated, at least in part, by their own nations, whereas political refugees fleeing war or persecution have no choice but to rely on the international community for protection.

Nonetheless, people of many underdeveloped countries have experienced problems of "complex displacement," generated by combined effects such as natural disasters, economic hardships, government incapacity or repression, and violent conflicts. Those suffering from complex displacement should be distinguished from people subject to "simple displacement," which is driven by somewhat less-dire circumstances, and who are thus considered as "persons of concern to the UNHCR." At this time, North Korean defectors may not be eligible to receive refugee status by law, but the UNHCR and the international community should apply the standards for complex displacement to North Korean food refugees based on the precedent of protecting groups such as the victims of the 1984–1985 famine in Ethiopia.[42]

In addition, given the fact that repatriated North Korean defectors face persecution, the UNHCR's principle of nonrefoulement, which proscribes the expulsion or return of refugees, must be applied to these defectors. Although they should first obtain legal refugee status in order to rely on this principle, the 1977 UNHCR resolution, which expanded the scope of this principle, enables the international community to apply it to those who are likely to be persecuted upon the forcible return to their country of origin, regardless of whether they possess legal recognition as refugees.[43] Therefore, China's forced deportation of North Koreans back to North Korea violates international law.

As mentioned, however, direct criticism of the Chinese government will likely backfire. Efforts must be made to implement instruments to persuade or press China to handle the North Korean defector problem from a humanitarian perspective. Beijing cannot afford to stand by and watch the number of North Korean escapees increase, whether in consideration of its relations with Pyongyang or of its own domestic order. In any case, transnational efforts must first be made to persuade China to refrain from repatriating defectors and to deal firmly with human rights violations to North Koreans in China, and act in a manner befitting its growing influence on the international stage. If China comes around to accommodating the defectors, both the relevant countries and the UNHCR should work actively on developing legal and institutional apparatuses for political asylum.[44]

Finally, in the event of mass defection from North Korea, the problem becomes more than a humanitarian issue and acquires a more complicated interrelation with politics and diplomacy, since it would affect the entire East Asian region. Therefore, the problem must be regarded as a major regional security issue. A timely and efficient response to the problem is important considering that one of the largest obstacles to humanitarian assistance in crisis situations is the overlap and delay caused by uncoordinated actions or interactions between numerous contributors. To ensure that global and regional responses and cooperation in addressing a mass exodus from North Korea are not confounded, and to ensure that the effectiveness of action is not lost in the process, preparations must be made for a systematic and consistent international response. Coordinating interests, positions, and roles of individual states, as well as dividing the responsibility with other actors, including international organizations and NGOs, must be accomplished beforehand through the establishment of a legal framework to guide careful and vigorous planning and implementation.

NOTES

1. Shin-wha Lee, "International Engagement in North Korea's Humanitarian Crisis: The Role of State and Non-state Actors," *East Asia: An International Quarterly* 20, no. 2 (Summer 2003): 74–93.
2. United States Committee for Refugees and Immigrants, *U.S. Committee for Refugees World Refugee Survey 2002—North Korea*, June 10, 2002, http://www.unhcr.org/refworld/country,,USCRI,,PRK,4562d8cf2,3d04c15318,0.html; World Food Programme, *Korea, Democratic People's Republic (DPRK)*, http://www.wfp.org/countries/korea-democratic-peoples-republic-dprk.
3. International Crisis Group, *Perilous Journeys: The Plight of North Koreans in China and Beyond*, Asia Report no. 122, October 26, 2006.
4. Ibid.
5. Lee, "International Engagement in North Korea's Humanitarian Crisis."

6. Mark P. Lagon, "A Struggle for Survival: Trafficking of North Korean Women" (speech given at the Woodrow Wilson International Center for Scholars, Washington, DC, March 3, 2008).
7. Jane Kim, "Trafficked: Domestic Violence, Exploitation in Marriage, and the Foreign-Bride Industry," *Virginia Journal of International Law* 51, no. 2 (2011): 443.
8. Chol-hwan Kang and Pierre Rigoulot, *The Aquariums of Pyongyang: Ten Years in a North Korean Gulag* (New York: Basic Books, 2001).
9. Lee, "International Engagement in North Korea's Humanitarian Crisis."
10. Stephen Haggard and Marcus Noland, eds. *The North Korean Refugee Crisis: Human Rights and International Response* (Washington, DC: U.S. Committee for Human Rights in North Korea, 2006).
11. Bruce Klingner, "The Tortuous North Korean Refugee Triangle," *Asia Times*, September 22, 2004, http://www.atimes.com/atimes/Korea/FI22Dg01.html.
12. Haggard and Noland, *North Korean Refugee Crisis*.
13. U.S. Committee for Refugees and Immigrants, *World Refugee Survey 2008*, June 19, 2008, http://www.unhcr.org/refworld/country,,,,PRK,,485f50ca7b,0.html.
14. Hyun-kyung Kang, "Rush to Freedom Creates Stereotypes of NK Defectors," Korean Sentry Forum, April 26, 2010, http://forum.koreansentry.com/viewtopic.php?t=2427.
15. "North Korean Soldiers Defect to China Fuelling Fears of Imminent Military Clash," *Telegraph*, July 12, 2010, http://www.telegraph.co.uk/news/worldnews/asia/northkorea/7885642/North-Korean-soldiers-defect-to-China-fuelling-fears-of-imminent-military-clash.html.
16. "After the Jasmine Revolution: Waging Information Battles in and out of North Korea," *WL Central*, March 14, 2011, http://wlcentral.org/node/1467.
17. Ji-Sook Bae, "North Korea's Female Spy Caught," *Korea Times*, August 27, 2008.
18. Sang Chol Kim, "Current Status of North Korean Refugee Protection" (in Korean), Korea Development Research Center, no. 103, 1999, http://www.hanbal.com/review/review103/jumgum1.htm.
19. UNHCR, "2012 Regional Operations Profile: East Asia and the Pacific; Democratic People's Republic of Korea," 2012, http://www.unhcr.org/pages/49e488f56.html.
20. Joshua Kurlantzick and Jana Mason, "North Korean Refugees: The Chinese Dimension," in Haggard and Noland, *North Korean Refugee Crisis*, 34–52.

21. U.S. Department of State, *Trafficking in Persons Report 2009* (Washington, DC: U.S. Department of State, 2009).
22. Constitution of the People's Republic of China, http://english.peopledaily.com.cn/constitution/constitution.html.
23. UN High Commissioner for Refugees, *Refugee Protection: A Guide to International Refugee Law* (Geneva: UNHCR, 2001), 41.
24. James D. Seymour, *China: Background Paper on the Situation of North Koreans in China*, 2005, http://www.nautilus.org/napsnet/sr/2005/0527A_Seymour.pdf.
25. Vitit Muntarbhorn, *Question of the Violation of Human Rights and Fundamental Freedoms in Any Part of the World: Situation of Human Rights in the Democratic People's Republic of Korea*, E/CN.4/2005/34, 12–13.
26. Human Rights Watch, "North Korea: Human Rights Concerns for the 61st Session of the U.N. Commission," http://www.hrw.org/legacy/english/docs/2005/04/04/nkorea10410_txt.htm.
27. Sophie Delaunay, "Aid and Accountability: A Necessary Debate," Médecins Sans Frontières, May 24, 2011, http://www.doctorswithoutborders.org/publications/alert/article.cfm?id=5274&cat=alert-article.
28. The White House, Office of the Press Secretary, "President's Statement on the North Korean Human Rights Act," October 21, 2004, http://merln.ndu.edu/archivepdf/northkorea/WH/20041021-22.pdf (accessed June 26, 2012).
29. Human Security Centre, University of British Columbia, *Human Security Report 2005: War and Peace in the 21st Century* (New York: Oxford University Press, 2005).
30. Kang Choi and Joon-Sung Park, "South Korea: Fears of Abandonment and Entrapment," in *The Long Shadow: Nuclear Weapons and Security in 21st Century Asia*, ed. Muthiah Alagappa, 373–402 (Singapore: NUS Press, 2009).
31. Jane McAdam, ed., *Forced Migration, Human Rights and Security* (Oxford: Hart, 2008).
32. Petrice R. Flowers, "Failure to Protect Refugees? Domestic Institutions, International Organizations, and Civil Society in Japan," *Journal of Japanese Studies* 32, no. 2 (2008): 333–361.
33. "China Halts Repatriation of N. Korean Defectors," *Chosun ilbo*, April 19, 2012, http://english.chosun.com/site/data/html_dir/2012/04/19/2012041900780.html (accessed July 25, 2012).
34. Benjamin Neaderland, "Quandary on the Yalu: International Law, Politics, and China's North Korean Refugee Crisis," *Stanford Journal of International Law* 40 (2004): 159.

35. Junghyun Cho, "The Possibility of Protection of North Korean Defectors through International Human Rights Law" (in Korean), *Kukjebuphakhwoi nonjip* 43, no. 1 (2009): 183–206.
36. "Convention (IV) Relative to the Protection of Civilian Persons in Time of War" is an international humanitarian law adopted at the Diplomatic Conference in Geneva on August 12, 1949, http://www.icrc.org/ihl.nsf/385ec082b509e76c41256739003e636d/6756482d86146898c125641e004aa3c5.
37. Roberta Arnold and Noëlle Quénivet, eds., *International Humanitarian Law and Human Rights Law* (Nijhoff: Brill, 2008).
38. For general information on war and international humanitarian law, see ICRC, "War and International Humanitarian Law," http://www.icrc.org/eng/ihl.
39. Judith Kumin, "Orderly Departure from Vietnam: Cold War Anomaly or Humanitarian Innovation?" *Refugee Survey Quarterly* 27, no. 1 (2008): 104–117.
40. United Nations, "Comprehensive Plan of Action for Indo-Chinese Refugees to End in June," press release, REF/1135, March 6, 1996, http://www.un.org/News/Press/docs/1996/19960306.ref1135.html.
41. Richard Towle, "Processes and Critiques of the Indo-Chinese Comprehensive Plan of Action: An Instrument of International Burden-Sharing?" *International Journal of Refuge Law* 18, no. 3–4 (September/December 2006): 537–570.
42. Shin-wha Lee, "International Organizations and the Inter-Korean Peace Process: Traditional Security Versus Nontraditional Security," in *Inter-Korean Relations: Problems and Prospects,* ed. Samuel S. Kim, 175–196 (New York: Palgrave, 2004).
43. UN High Commissioner for Refugees, *Note on Non-refoulement (Submitted by the High Commissioner),* August 23, 1977, EC/SCP/2, http://www.unhcr.org/refworld/docid/3ae68ccd10.html.
44. International Crisis Group, *Perilous Journeys.*

CHAPTER 9

The Role of Nongovernmental Organizations in Protecting Pyongyang's Non-Traditional Security

SCOTT SNYDER

In a globalized and interconnected world, the role of civil society has expanded to the extent that nongovernmental actors have established agency in one form or another in an effort to address global problems, especially in the area of human security. Non-traditional security challenges are particularly amenable to problem-solving efforts on the part of nonstate actors, individuals, and associations precisely because the essential ingredient in addressing many of these problems is the building of capacity to address specific human needs, a response that does not depend exclusively on the state and may be more effectively provided at the level of the individual. Increasingly, it is possible to mobilize that capacity through grassroots campaigns among interested and motivated people without intermediation at the state level.

However, North Korea's system poses unique challenges to the role of individual and nonstate actors in responding to specific human needs in North Korea, precisely because the state remains the essential intermediary regulating person-to-person or other grassroots interactions, while the individual role is subordinated to that of the state in the North Korean system. Although North Korean officials have shown a guarded and somewhat inconsistent stance toward international humanitarian and development assistance in recent years (accepting international assistance and then deciding to terminate it and going hot and cold on the types of assistance they are willing to accept), they have also continually worked in limited forms with a select group of foreign nongovernmental organizations (NGOs) on a variety of projects. These NGOs have developed a consistent track record and have built up trust and credibility with authorities inside North Korea. Although a distinguishing feature of these NGO efforts in the case of the United States, and to a certain extent South Korea, has been that they have pursued their work without regard to government-to-government relationships, the official state of inter-Korean and U.S.–North Korean relations has been a factor that has both enabled and limited ongoing work of these NGOs with North Korean counterparts at various times.

As a result, the role and influence of foreign NGOs working inside North Korea are double-edged, and the capacity of foreign NGOs to perform their appointed tasks can never be separated entirely from the political context in which they operate as defined by the quality of the government-to-government relationship between North Korea and the home government of the foreign NGO.

At the same time, another portion of the international NGO community has focused its attention on international activism in the area of promoting consciousness regarding North Korean human rights, an adversarial approach to the North Korean state that poses a direct challenge to North Korean authorities. These NGOs have been highly successful in building an international coalition of partners focused on promoting human rights in North Korea—especially by advocating with governments and working to promote activity regarding North Korea in the UN Human Rights Council, but there is little likelihood that these NGOs will be able to work together with North Korean counterparts, and they have no means other than "naming and shaming" by which to contribute to the material improvement of human rights conditions inside North Korea.

A third focus of humanitarian and human rights activity, led primarily by a small coalition of South Korean NGOs with some degree of international support, has developed around the task of bringing refugees out of North Korea and providing support for resettlement mainly in South Korea but also in the United States. These NGOs are service providers whose work focuses chiefly on assistance to North Korean citizens who have left their country and face the task of integrating themselves into a new state and society. Such NGOs play a critical role outside North Korea in facilitating North Koreans' arrival in a new home country and in providing assistance in integrating North Korean citizens into a new society. Since it is considered a crime to leave North Korea without authorization, North Korean authorities view these groups as hostile, even though they operate outside North Korea's control and do not take an overtly adversarial position toward the North. NGO-led human rights and refugee-resettlement activities are not addressed in this chapter both because they are covered elsewhere in this volume and because the impact of these activities on human security may be considered ambiguous and self-contradictory, depending on the perspective of the individuals involved and the impact that their exit may have on others inside North Korea.

This chapter surveys the activities of U.S. NGOs working in North Korea and evaluates their respective contributions and scope as they relate to the promotion of non-traditional security in North Korea. On the basis of this set of case studies, the chapter concludes that NGOs are well positioned to play catalytic roles in meeting North Korean human needs and promoting knowledge sharing for North Koreans who are allowed to travel outside North Korea, but that the state-to-state relationship remains an important contextual factor that often stands in the way of NGOs' abilities to achieve these roles to their full potential. In addition, the ability of NGOs to be perceived as interlocutors that act independently from government authorities on both sides is a factor that influences their ability to work as intermediaries and catalysts for transformational change in North Korea.

NGO ROLES AND CONTRIBUTIONS TO NORTH KOREA'S HUMANITARIAN AND DEVELOPMENT SITUATION

The seeds of NGO involvement in North Korea can be traced to primarily the famine of the mid-1990s. At that time, a distinguishing feature of the international response was the establishment and involvement of a number of NGOs in North Korea alongside the UN system in the effort to respond to the humanitarian crisis caused by the famine. At the time, humanitarian aid agencies were unprepared for the unique circumstances they would face in North Korea, a country that had faced a dramatic economic collapse but where the government maintained strong political control. This situation provided a different working environment for humanitarian agencies used to operating in environments where economic collapse was a by-product of the collapse of mechanisms for maintaining political authority. Unique challenges that humanitarian aid agencies faced in North Korea included the monopolistic role of the government in channeling aid, the omnipresent role of the central government as an intermediary with local authorities and people on the ground, the ongoing political confrontation between the two Koreas and between North Korea and the United States, the inability to independently identify and verify quantitatively the scope of need or to independently determine which populations faced the greatest needs, and the relative lack of media coverage of the North Korean crisis in comparison with other humanitarian crises.[1]

Some of the NGOs became involved in North Korea as a result of the availability of government funding for NGO famine-response efforts, but others were driven by private-sector interest in the North Korean situation, especially among the Korean-American community and selected religious communities. These communities established NGOs focused on responding to the humanitarian situation in North Korea. Because many of them were primarily privately funded, they were less subject to political constraints and able to expand their work beyond the narrow task of monitoring food assistance to other, small-scale development projects that came out of their observations and North Korean expressions of need in nonfood sectors. NGOs dependent on governments, such as the U.S. government, for the bulk of their work found themselves constrained to monitoring humanitarian assistance because of U.S. government restrictions on development projects in North Korea, and they ultimately left North Korea once U.S. government funding ceased.

Privately funded NGOs in the United States found that there was widespread need and opportunity for work in North Korea that extended beyond provision and monitoring of food assistance, especially in the areas of promoting improved agricultural methods and enhancing food production through capacity building and provision of higher-quality inputs and in the upgrading of medical facilities by means of both equipment and medicine. Many of these projects naturally created opportunities to be involved in joint and local community development efforts aligned more closely with North Korean needs than what could be accomplished under a strictly humanitarian aid–based approach.

Moreover, the structure of the humanitarian-aid relationship with North Korea was inherently adversarial because of its focus on monitoring assistance in order to discourage diversion, whereas development projects were inherently focused on working together to accomplish specific project objectives. It was possible for individual NGOs to mobilize private funding to take on specific projects that were beyond the scope of work that the U.S. government was able to fund because of legal restrictions on financial support for development versus provision of humanitarian food assistance in North Korea. As private NGOs became involved in these projects, they established relationships with North Koreans that in turn enabled them to pursue other projects and deepened their working experience in the North.

When the U.S. government became involved once again as a donor of food and energy assistance to North Korea in the context of the implementation of the February 13, 2007, Six-Party agreement with North Korea and of a worsening of North Korea's food situation in May 2008, the U.S. government turned to the handful of privately funded NGOs that had ongoing programs with North Korea for assistance in managing two major projects. The first involved the provision and setup of generators at major hospitals in North Korea, initially conceived of as part of the provision of heavy fuel oil equivalent that the six parties committed to provide in return for the freezing and disabling of North Korean nuclear facilities. The second concerned monitoring 100,000 MT of food assistance to be delivered to North Korea as part of a commitment to deliver up to 500,000 MT of assistance (the remainder was to be delivered and monitored via the UN World Food Programme [WFP]). The Congressional Research Service has valued U.S. energy assistance related to the Six-Party Talks at $140 million. The generator project, categorized as medical assistance provided during 2009, is valued at $4 million, and food assistance provided both to the WFP and NGOs during 2008 and 2009 at slightly over $100 million.[2]

These involvements created an opportunity for selected NGOs to strengthen their relationships and credibility in North Korea as the provider of larger-scale energy assistance, but they also imposed an additional challenge for U.S. private NGOs. Involvement with U.S. government–funded projects by NGOs that had cultivated their own relationships with North Korean government authorities ran the risk of politicizing the NGO relationships with North Korea that had previously existed at arm's length from U.S. government policy. On the one hand, selection by the U.S. government to deliver energy or food assistance served to affirm the roles of these NGOs as trusted intermediaries—or at least as trusted service providers—for both governments. On the other hand, there was a risk that political circumstances might intervene in ways that could subject the relationships that U.S. NGOs had independently cultivated with North Korean authorities to new constraints.

The United States Agency for International Development (USAID) contacted four American NGOs, each with long-standing experience in North Korea, to deliver and install generators at North Korean hospitals around the country. Each NGO was contracted to provide and install twenty generators at designated hospitals in regions close to existing projects where those NGOs were already working. The NGOs were responsible for procuring generator equipment, primarily from China, shipping it into North Korea, and sending technical personnel to North Korea to install it. USAID was the project funder. The project was implemented during 2008 and 2009 and faced no apparent political difficulties in the course of implementation.

USAID was also the primary funder behind the far larger effort to deliver 500,000 MT of food assistance to North Korea in May 2008. Funding was handled through a consortium of five NGOs, led by Mercy Corps International. The other NGOs were World Vision, Samaritan's Purse, Christian Friends of Korea, and Global Resource Services. This project required the five NGOs to work together closely as a team in managing in-country monitoring and to coordinate externally in such a way that it was possible to meet the project requirements of USAID while also interacting effectively with North Korean interlocutors. During ten months of operations, the NGO consortium delivered and monitored 71,000 MT of food assistance, almost meeting the full goal of providing 100,000 MT to be delivered through U.S. NGOs. Sixteen representatives from the five NGOs served as staff on the ground to monitor food deliveries in North Pyongan and Chagang provinces. As a result of a failure to raise funds from the international community for assistance to North Korea and continuing disputes with North Korean counterparts over monitoring issues, the WFP was able to deliver only 98,000 MT of assistance of a projected 400,000 MT by the time the North Koreans announced the end of the project in March 2009.[3]

Thus, the NGO community has faced a dual challenge as it has carried out efforts to meet the humanitarian needs of the North Korean people. The first has been the need to manage its relationship with North Korean authorities in such a way that its work can be carried out to the satisfaction of both private donors and North Korean local communities. The second is managing the relationship with the home government so as to maintain a stable environment for continuation of exchanges without falling victim to political constraints resulting from periods of tension in the government-to-government relationship with North Korea.

MANAGING THE RELATIONSHIP WITH THE NORTH KOREAN GOVERNMENT

NGOs committed to providing humanitarian assistance have faced challenges working in North Korea since their arrival there in the 1990s. The North Korean regime has historically been deeply suspicious of the outside world because of its potential to undermine the regime's tight control over its populace. Initially, lack of experience in dealing with NGOs and North Korean suspicions that some NGOs were closely coordinating with the U.S. government prompted the North Korean government to view NGOs as Trojan horses or spies from the United States. Because of these concerns, North Korean authorities carefully monitored the activities and access of NGOs that it allowed into the country while refusing entry to organizations that publicly criticized the regime or were involved in activities deemed threatening to it. In addition, North Korea lacked familiarity with international standards of provision of humanitarian assistance and had only the experience of receiving assistance from socialist countries, so the categories, descriptions, methods, and purposes under which humanitarian aid was provided created ample room for misunderstanding between North Korea and the international community.[4]

NGOs and UN organization representatives faced many restrictions on their activities in the late 1990s, including a North Korean ban on Korean-speaking monitors and at least one week's advance notice of the schedule for conducting food-monitoring activities. Moreover, the sites for food delivery could not be chosen based on an independent assessment by NGOs of greatest need but instead were set by the government. A longtime UN official has described North Korea's distribution system in the following way: "It's very efficient; I mean it works. But we are not naïve. We have 300 monitoring visits a month. They don't mean anything, because there are no random visits."[5] The North Korean government was involved in all aspects of NGO relief efforts and provided local minders for monitoring, which only increased mutual distrust between North Korea and the United States, since NGOs demanded greater transparency and monitoring to ensure proper delivery of aid at the same time that North Korea attempted to monitor the monitors in order to avoid contamination of North Korean society by outside influences deemed harmful to the regime. Other challenges that NGOs faced in the late 1990s related to the price of entry into North Korea, as a result of which some NGOs felt that they were paying for the access and the right to monitor delivery of assistance, and to North Korean resistance to a long-term presence in North Korea, which has required U.S. NGOs to manage projects remotely through frequent visits to the country rather than through offices in the North.[6] Moreover, humanitarian assistance to North Korea came to be seen as linked to the Clinton administration's political strategy; that is, that humanitarian assistance was necessary to grease the wheels for political engagement. This perception, especially on Capitol Hill, opened up NGO humanitarian assistance to increased scrutiny and political attacks.[7]

Because of North Korean efforts to limit the broader social impact of NGO activities in North Korean society, the maintenance of relationships with NGOs carried with it a management burden for North Korean authorities, who had to maintain communications with NGO counterparts, prepare to host visitor delegations, accompany in-country NGO staff at almost all times, and respond to internal questions and criticisms that might arise regarding foreign assistance to North Korea.

NGOs attempting to work with North Korea faced a highly constricted operating environment that made some projects impossible. Most notably, North Korean authorities were slow to accept projects that might involve large-scale contact between foreigners and average North Koreans and long resisted direct contact between outsiders and end users of foreign assistance on a person-to-person level. Several NGOs, such as Médecins Sans Frontières, left North Korea in the late 1990s because of these restrictions. However, North Korean authorities have allowed contacts with professional counterparts as necessary and desirable in the course of aid delivery or project installation.

Despite the challenges and restrictions imposed by the North Korean government, NGOs that maintained programs in North Korea after the food crisis of the 1990s developed on-the-ground experience and relationships inside North Korea by pursuing local joint-development projects. These projects enabled NGOs that continued their work in the North to maintain long-standing professional or institutional contacts with individual representatives of partner institutions and to expand technical contacts in ways that have also required greater interaction and involvement in local communities. Foreign NGO assistance efforts have thus expanded the capacity of individual organizations in North Korea authorized to work with foreign NGOs and have enabled the establishment of direct, long-term relationships with managerial and technical professionals at the local level. Moreover, the product of this cooperation has resulted in greater capacity by local organizations to produce goods for local consumption or to meet health needs of particular communities at the local level.

In some respects, the decision by participating NGOs to accept U.S. government funding for humanitarian assistance programs in North Korea in 2009 might be regarded as a setback compared with the pursuit of joint-development projects, precisely because delivery of humanitarian assistance emphasized an inherently adversarial approach that requires outside monitoring of aid delivery versus the cooperative approach on which joint-development projects are premised. But renewed humanitarian assistance was also the only viable channel for U.S. government support to North Korea given the existing restrictions on U.S. government funding for development projects in the North. With over a decade of experience in North Korea, the U.S. NGOs that were selected to monitor delivery of U.S. food aid had long-standing relationships that allowed them to take the rough edges off the adversarial nature of monitoring arrangements; at the same time, the fact that the work plan for the provision of U.S. food aid to North Korea had been negotiated between the two governments also meant the NGOs bore limited responsibility for any conflicts arising from implementation of the project.

The U.S. government was able to win concessions regarding the role and responsibilities of monitors participating in the consortium that approximated international standards. Mercy Corps International president Nancy Lindborg described the program as providing "an important model for how we might normalize humanitarian assistance [to North Korea] based on international humanitarian standards" and allowing the U.S. NGOs to "mount a program based on identified humanitarian need and international standards, with significant levels of access to all points of food delivery." The involvement of U.S. NGOs in the monitoring program "demonstrated the spirit and goodwill of the people of the United States toward the people of North Korea."[8] By the end of the project, U.S. NGOs claimed that "we have ensured that food reached almost one million vulnerable children, pregnant and nursing mothers, and the elderly."[9]

A shortcoming of the monitoring regime as implemented during 2008 to 2009 was that monitors did not have firsthand access to local markets, despite the fact that, in contrast to the late 1990s, the markets had become the primary mechanism for distribution of food in North Korea. Without market access, monitors had no capacity to assess the impact of food assistance on prices and no independent capacity to observe potential diversion to the markets after food had been delivered to the mutually agreed upon locations. Although the North Korean government would surely resist efforts by U.S. NGOs to monitor food distribution in the markets, the enhanced role of the markets in North Korean daily life and the impact of food distribution on local market prices are an important collateral impact of external provision of food assistance that should be monitored more carefully in future efforts to provide food assistance to North Korea.

In a 2005 article, Edward Reed identified five prerequisites for effective NGO operations in North Korea: (1) the need for "an effective counter-part development-oriented North Korean governmental unit, (2) simplified regulations that facilitate effective NGO operations in North Korea, (3) the ability to gather survey and observational data in connection with planned projects, (4) greater opportunities for aid worker interaction with local populations, and (5) the ability of NGOs to independently select and supervise national staff."[10] The U.S. NGO experience, through both the U.S. government food-aid project and other, small-scale development efforts, suggests modest progress in the direction of meeting these criteria. The North Koreans have established the Korean-American Private Exchange Society as a primary counterpart organization for U.S. NGOs and allowed U.S. NGO representatives to engage in a monitoring process that involved greater cooperation with local-level authorities and visits to private households. However, it is still hard for NGOs to work in North Korea, and neither NGOs nor UN agencies have full control over local staff hiring.

At the same time, it is clear that maintenance of active relationships with U.S. NGOs does provide North Korea with opportunities to attain tangible benefits from outside sources for the welfare of the North Korean people. If North Korean authorities assess that the return on investment is negative in terms of time or cultural influences deemed detrimental to the North Korean population, they retain the right to curtail or suspend foreign-funded projects, as they did when they suspended U.S. NGO and WFP provision of U.S.-funded food assistance to North Korea in March 2009. However, it is important to note that in this case, because each of the NGOs involved in the consortium were also engaged in other projects in North Korea, it has been possible for the NGOs to continue their work on projects in other areas beyond food monitoring.

MANAGING THE RELATIONSHIP WITH THE U.S. GOVERNMENT

The relationship between American NGOs that have developed longstanding relationships with North Korea and the U.S. government has been double-edged. On the one hand, U.S. private NGOs need to cooperate with the U.S. government in order to secure travel permission for North Koreans they may invite to the United States for technical visits or other consultations regarding program development. In addition, the opportunity to secure U.S. government funding for new projects that might further NGO objectives of enhancing the human-security environment in North Korea by pursuing local-level development projects is a potentially useful one, since it provides contact with new actors with whom the U.S. NGOs may not otherwise have occasion to work with, for example, in the medical field.

However, U.S. government funding for such projects also raises the possibility of politicizing the image of U.S. NGOs in the eyes of their North Korean counterparts, or that U.S. NGO representatives might find themselves enmeshed in intractable conflicts between the two governments not related to the main work of their projects, especially to the extent that these representatives are perceived by North Korea as representing U.S. government interests in ways that conflict with North Korean interests. Representatives of NGOs involved in the consortium needed to ensure that their identity and role were perceived in North Korea as independent of the U.S. government while at the same time meeting U.S. government requirements for delivery of food assistance.

The U.S. government was well served by the decision to approach NGOs that had extensive experience working with North Korea. The use of NGO staff with long experience dealing with North Koreans cut down on North Korean suspicions regarding U.S. government intentions by bringing familiar faces into the food-monitoring and generator-delivery efforts. U.S. NGO experiences with specific obstacles in North Korea and North Korean preferences regarding how to manage such work probably eliminated many potential areas of misunderstanding that could have stalled the project. The prior experience of the U.S. Private Voluntary Organization Consortium (PVOC) of the mid-1990s served as a negative model for how both misunderstanding regarding North Korean preferences and internal conflicts among American NGOs could derail cooperation on successful project implementation. The 2007–2008 experience of American NGO cooperation appeared to go more smoothly and has received credit for successfully monitoring the delivery of over 70,000 MT of food assistance with sufficient levels of professionalism that the operation did not arouse Congressional concerns, in contrast to the experience of the late 1990s.

In this case, it probably helped that the U.S. government conducted its own negotiations with North Korean representatives regarding the parameters and conditions for renewal of food assistance to North Korea prior to involving NGO representatives. However, the prior negotiation did imply that the U.S. NGO role was primarily that of a subcontractor to the U.S. government and thus had a limited policy role or responsibility for determining terms of implementation. The U.S. government had taken a similar approach in the mid-1990s but at that time did not have sufficient understanding of specific issues that might emerge on the ground during the course of implementation. As a result, American participants in the PVOC found that many important implementation issues remained unresolved and that they had no power to revise the terms of an agreement that had come of prior negotiations between governments. Based on their extensive experience working inside North Korea, the U.S. NGOs were better prepared in 2008 to undertake monitoring and had a better understanding of their roles and obligations.

The existence of a U.S. NGO consortium is itself a relatively unique by-product of the complexities and challenges of working with North Korea. Thus, an added burden (and opportunity) for NGOs was the need to work together on project implementation (and budgeting) more closely than would otherwise be necessary. Although the existence of a consortium enhanced communication among NGOs working in North Korea, it also created the need to resolve issues internal to the consortium in a manner that did not leave members of the consortium subject to manipulation by North Korean counterparts. A positive aspect of the U.S. NGO consortium experience during 2008 to 2009 was that the NGOs worked together more effectively than they had in the late 1990s, when they were more competitive with one another and worked less effectively as a team. The difficulties of the experience of the late 1990s provided lessons learned that enabled more successful management of inter-NGO cooperation during 2008 and 2009.

The accumulated experience of U.S. NGOs in North Korea also meant that they were able to listen more effectively to North Korean complaints and frustrations regarding the U.S. program, including U.S. preferences for delivery of corn-soy blend over grains that were better suited to the North Korean diet. U.S. NGOs were able to convey North Korean frustrations but were unable to overcome the rigidity of U.S. laws regarding procurement and procedures for delivery of humanitarian assistance. Their experience on the ground in North Korea also enabled them to find and propose solutions to specific misunderstandings rather than allowing them to spin out of control and be dealt with at higher levels or between governments. This experience kept the program running efficiently in accord with the negotiated terms of reference between the two countries and in part explains why U.S. NGOs were able to avoid some of the problems that the WFP was unable to overcome and that ostensibly led to North Korea's determination to terminate the program in March 2009.

MANAGING DIFFICULTIES IN THE INTERNATIONAL POLITICAL ENVIRONMENT

Given the intractability of the disputes between the United States and North Korea and the wide gap between the positions of the two governments, the need for effective intermediaries is high and the likelihood that such an impetus will be government led is low on either side. With globalization, nongovernmental actors have sought greater participation, but they can act only under enabling conditions that must be provided by governments. At the same time, the roles and contributions of NGOs in resolving fundamental problems such as North Korea's food problem, overcoming North Korea's political isolation, or solving the North Korean nuclear issue are quite limited. Nonetheless, U.S. NGOs should, to the extent possible, be catalysts and enablers for the promotion of positive changes both in North Korea and in its contacts with the outside world. NGO contributions to the promotion of North Korean reform occur primarily in proportion to the capacity of NGOs as bridge builders, both to provide training for North Koreans from the international community and to expose North Koreans more broadly to international standards and best practices. Such contributions can support the efforts of international financial institutions to engage in a more broad-ranging dialogue about reform in North Korea and promote closer university ties through exchanges and training programs with American university programs.[11]

NGO potential to act in the current context is constrained by the difficult political situation and by government policies on both sides that hamper NGOs in achieving a fully active catalytic role. Both the U.S. and North Korean governments constrain NGO activities for their own reasons as a result of the current political environment, rather than providing an environment of predictability and transparency in which NGOs could better accomplish their objectives. To the extent that NGOs can establish a role for themselves that is nonpolitical, they can also serve as both a conduit and a rationale for promoting a more stable relationship, but under current circumstances, NGO contributions and scope of action remain constrained by politics.

On the U.S. side, one of the most difficult issues NGOs face is the fact that the U.S. government confines itself to humanitarian assistance, despite the fact that provision of humanitarian aid at the expense of development assistance teaches North Korean counterparts the wrong lessons about interactions with the international community and essentially keeps North Korea on welfare and away from building local capacity to solve local problems. Thus, the nature of U.S. assistance is increasingly out of sync with the locally focused community development efforts that U.S. NGOs are involved with. In addition, the question of food aid to North Korea has been politicized in ways that have raised past suspicions about the intent of food aid to North Korea. Karin Lee has suggested the possibility of a review of "the risks and rewards of small scale development assistance in the field of food security vs. food aid." Such a review might be a basis for examining whether the intent of U.S. laws governing nonhumanitarian assistance toward North Korea are truly achieving their objectives or are counterproductive to the objective of promoting North Korea's opening to the outside world.[12]

A second constraint accompanying the current political environment is that whereas one of the most effective ways of promoting change inside North Korea is through the promotion of educational exchanges, particularly longer-term exchanges, the U.S. government has (through at least 2012) continued to place political barriers in the way of such efforts. The U.S. government should be more active in establishing a transparent and predictable environment enabling NGO-led exchanges that bring North Koreans to the outside world, both through the regularization of visa policies that are consistent and not subject to political considerations and through the active promotion of long-term educational opportunities for North Korean specialists in the United

States without regard to political considerations. The promotion of such exchanges would presumably provide U.S. NGOs with greater opportunities for access and development of relationships and projects in new sectors in North Korea, thus contributing to the further integration and exposure of North Korean society to the outside world.

U.S. NGOs should attempt to deepen their engagement with North Korean counterparts through greater technical exchange. The door to such exchanges should be opened much wider and should be shielded from political interference, in contrast to the current environment, in which the political context directly affects the way in which North Korean visa applications are scrutinized. NGO capacity to promote long-term educational exchange should be greatly strengthened so that North Korean specialists have opportunities for long-term training in specialized areas in nontechnological and nonpolitical fields of inquiry.

Achieving this environment will require the U.S. government to commit in advance to a more transparent and consistent policy of actively encouraging North Korean educational opportunities in selected fields of study. U.S. government sanctions on long-term North Korean educational opportunities in the United States should be waived and a path toward enhanced North Korean exchanges opened and actively supported, both as a symbol of U.S. willingness to engage and to support the transformation necessary for North Korea to become a successful and integrated member of the international community.

On the North Korean side, the challenges are more difficult. The North Koreans need to move away from an approach to foreign NGOs that sometimes seems to focus on the hardware of resource extraction at the expense of the opportunity to learn from international experience and adapt more efficient approaches to specific technical problems. In addition, there needs to be greater space for technical learning in a nonpolitical environment and greater autonomy for NGO operations on the ground in North Korea, as Edward Reed has called for. Even if long-term exchange opportunities are offered under current circumstances, there is little guarantee that qualified North Koreans would be able to take advantage of such opportunities. The current focus on internal political reconsolidation in North Korea's domestic politics may not appear to bode well for the changes that would enhance opportunities for U.S. NGOs in the near future.

NOTES

1. Edward P. Reed, "Unlikely Partners: Humanitarian Aid Agencies and North Korea," in *A New International Framework for North Korea? Contending Perspectives*, ed. Choong-young Ahn, Nicholas Eberstadt, and Young-sun Lee, 199–229 (Washington, DC: Korea Economic Institute of America, 2004).
2. U.S. Library of Congress, Congressional Research Service, *Foreign Assistance to North Korea*, by Mark E. Manyin and Mary Beth Nikitin, R40095, March 12, 2010.
3. World Vision, "Statement of NGO Partners on Cessation of Food Aid Program in the Democratic People's Republic of Korea (DPRK)," March 19, 2009, http://www.worldvision.org/content.nsf/about/20090319-korea-foodaid-statement?OpenDocument (accessed July 6, 2010).
4. Karin J. Lee, "Humanitarian Programming in the DPRK, 1996 to 2009: The U.S. Administration and Congress," *Asian Perspective* 34, no. 2 (2010): 141–171.
5. U.S. Congress, House Committee on International Relations, *North Korea: Human Rights, Refugees, and Humanitarian Challenges: Joint Hearing before the Subcommittee on Asia and the Pacific and the Subcommittee on International Terrorism, Nonproliferation and Human Rights of the Committee on International Relations, House of Representatives*, 108th Cong., 2nd sess., April 28, 2004, Committee Print 108-94, 10.
6. L. Gordon Flake and Scott Snyder, eds., *Paved with Good Intentions: The NGO Experience in North Korea* (Westport, CT: Praeger, 2003).
7. Lee, "Humanitarian Programming in the DPRK."
8. Nancy Lindborg, president, Mercy Corps, statement before the U.S. Senate Foreign Relations Committee, June 11, 2009, http://www.foreign.senate.gov/imo/media/doc/LindborgTestimony090611p1.pdf.
9. World Vision, "Statement of NGO Partners."
10. Edward P. Reed, "The Role of International Aid Organizations in the Development of North Korea: Experience and Prospects," *Asian Perspective* 29, no. 3 (2005): 51–72.
11. Peter Beck and Nicholas Reader, "Facilitating Reform in North Korea: The Role of Regional Actors and NGOs," *Asian Perspective* 29, no. 3 (2005): 31–49.
12. Lee, "Humanitarian Programming in the DPRK."

CHAPTER 10

Toward the Enhancement of Non-Traditional Security in North Korea

BRENDAN HOWE

Prussian General Carl von Clausewitz, the great military strategist, famously referred to war as "a mere continuation of policy by other means." However, his preceding concept that "war is an act of violence intended to compel our opponent to fulfill our will" is equally important to this study.[1] When combined they present vital implications for our analysis of traditional and non-traditional security: namely, that in dealing with North Korea we are asked to consider strategic relationships, meaning (1) interaction with, and attempts to alter the rational payoffs of our opponent and (2) the relationships between the military and wider society. Strategic relationships occur at the areas where political, economic, psychological, and military factors overlap, thus our analysis of them must consider interdisciplinary and interdependent factors.

The foundation of traditional strategic analysis is the assumption of rational behavior based upon calculating decision making by unitary actors. These actors (states or statesmen acting on their behalf) rank potential outcomes in accordance with a preferential hierarchy and coldly assess the costs and benefits associated with different courses of action independently of "emotional tensions, sentimentality, crowd behavior, or other irrational motivation."[2] This representation of security decision making has been variously referred to as the rational calculation model, or, more commonly, the rational actor model, or simply RAM.[3]

The rational actor model has dominated foreign and security policy decision making and analysis since the collapse of the liberal internationalist paradigm during the interwar "twenty-years' crisis."[4]

A generation of analysts share the core RAM assumptions of a unitary state as principal rational actor and believe that survival is the rational actor's most important objective, that states seek to dominate one another, and that states are inherently selfish and self-regarding in the pursuit of survival and security, unwilling to depend on other states for their vital interests or to compromise in their own security to enhance the security or well-being of others.[5] The state is considered to be, if not the only legitimate actor, at the very least the most influential, and with the capacity to coerce the behavior of the other actors. In addition, the state is often used as a convenient unit of analysis. In a world where it is impossible to consider all variables, it is important to have a modeling process that will select those variables that are to be considered. It is also for this reason the state is often considered to be a unitary actor, since it is only with this degree of simplification that we can possibly generate a useful analytical tool. Hans Morgenthau has postulated that such a model

> provides for rational discipline in action and creates that outstanding continuity in foreign policy which makes American, British, or Russian foreign policy appear as an intelligible, rational continuum . . . regardless of the different motives, preferences, and intellectual and moral qualities of successive statesmen.[6]

This concluding chapter, and indeed the volume as a whole, challenges the traditional belief that diplomats should ignore the internal affairs of states in order to preserve international stability and posits that the lack of internal justice may actually increase international disorder. Regarding states as unitary rational actors misses alternative explanations for the behavior of statesmen, leads to the adoption of self-fulfilling worst-case-scenario planning, is inherently confrontational, and contributes to the likelihood of the emergence of a traditional security dilemma whereby an increase in one state's military capabilities is automatically considered a threat to the security of its neighbors.

Indeed, although to a great extent internal policy decisions in Pyongyang are responsible for the current malaise in the country, with a faltering state economic and political apparatus and military prioritization perhaps doing most to undermine development and threaten the human security of ordinary North Koreans, to glory in the fall of the adversary, to seek to promote it, or even to follow policies that are designed to give as little succor as possible to a despicable regime may nevertheless prove counterproductive since it is North Korean weakness rather than strength that most threatens international peace and security in the region.

Whereas the hostility of neighbors previously victims of North Korean aggression or that have previously been forced to address aggressive statements and actions emanating from Pyongyang may be understandable, taking a hard line in response may contribute toward a vicious cycle whereby the Democratic People's Republic of Korea (DPRK) either perceives a dangerous external security environment as necessitating further internal sacrifices and military prioritization or uses the environment as justification for such measures. These measures are likely to further increase the non-traditional security threats posed by North Korea to surrounding countries in terms of hastening regime collapse or the traditional security threats in terms of diversionary acts of aggression to divert internal constituencies from the problems generated at home by Pyongyang's policies. Thus, unpalatable as it may seem, some process of engagement with North Korea might mitigate Pyongyang's security concerns and also help the internal situation by removing both justifications and motivations for dangerous policy prioritization in the DPRK.

North Korea certainly poses a traditional security threat to its neighbors. There has been, however, considerable exaggeration of the degree of traditional threat posed by North Korean military prioritization, weapons systems, and aggression. At the same time, North Korean insecurity poses a greater threat, one that has often been underestimated. Although the country has pursued a political and economic strategy that is enormously destructive for human security internally, in part this has been exacerbated by actions, policies, and at times inactions or sanctions of components of the international community. Consequently, if the strategic negotiating partners and opponents of the

DPRK truly wish to reduce the threat posed by the rogue regime, it is essential that all aspects of the security spectrum be considered: traditional and non-traditional, state-centric and human security, and internal constituencies and external operating environments. This chapter provides an overview of the relationships between traditional, non-traditional or new, comprehensive, and human security studies and expands the discussion on narrow and broad approaches to human security in relation to North Korea.

ON SECURITY

The concept of security in international affairs was originally developed to deal with conflict between states. It is conventionally defined as the protection of the territorial integrity of sovereign states through a focus on "foreign and defense mechanisms to avoid, prevent, and if need be win interstate military disputes."[7] This so-called traditional notion of security is related more to states than to people and is often used interchangeably with "national security," which is defined as the promotion of "rights ascribed to nations rather than to individuals, sub-national groups or mankind as a whole, and which subordinates other interests to those of the nation."[8] The United Nations defines the concept of national security as the safeguarding of territorial integrity and national independence from any external threat, thereby showing much resemblance to the traditional definition of security.[9]

In general the field relates to the investigation of the causes of and the reduction in frequency and effect of major wars. Conflict is seen as inevitable, but cooperation (however limited) is always a possibility. Indeed, conflict need not always be seen as negative—it is one of the paths to maturity in both individuals and societies; it is often necessary for social change. It is the worst manifestation of conflict, major interstate wars, that preoccupies the thinking of traditional security theorists and practitioners. The major concerns have revolved around the concepts of military capabilities (both offensive and defensive), the distribution and balance of power in the international system in terms of polarity and concentration in the hands of the dominant states, and policy prescription in terms of the strategic implications of these considerations, including offensive (power projection), defensive, and deterrent spending.

Security itself is, however, an essentially contested concept. Definitions range from the traditional state-centric one of a relative freedom from war, coupled with a relatively high expectation that defeat will not be a consequence of any war that should occur, to the systemic, implying both coercive means to check an aggressor and the prospect of mutually shared benefits transforming hostility into cooperation. The contradiction between state and systemic security is exposed by the concept of relative certainty of victory if one goes to war in the former and the collective security principle and rationale of relative certainty of defeat of an aggressor in the latter.

New thinking on security has gradually come to the fore in the field, with input from academics and also from practitioners in international organizations and states (in particular Japan, Canada, and Norway). Critical and postmodern perspectives have tended to conceive of security as emancipation or the freedom to make choices. The constructivists of the Copenhagen school introduced the concept of securitization, examining how certain issues are transformed into a matter of national security by those acting on behalf of a state. In the early 1980s Japan adopted a "comprehensive security" (*sōgō anzen hoshō*) policy under the direction of Prime Minister Zenko Suzuki. Comprehensive security not only looked beyond the traditional security elements of individual self-defense by focusing on regional and global security arrangements but also stressed the need to take into account other aspects vital to national stability such as food, energy, the environment, communication, and social security.[10] It was an explicitly inclusive approach that emphasized multilateralism, and the concept as such can be traced to Japanese thinking on security as far back as the 1950s.

Non-traditional security agendas are now in vogue in other parts of the world and are often termed new security challenges. The characteristics of such challenges include some or all of the following: a focus on nonmilitary rather than military threats, transnational rather than national threats, and multilateral or collective rather than self-help security solutions.[11] It may be that as other countries adopt elements of new or comprehensive security agendas (and there is evidence of Western commentators looking to what lessons can be learned from

Japan in this area) Japan's security policy will be seen as increasingly "normal."[12] But Japan has also been instrumental in pushing forward the next step in the evolution of security conceptualization, providing many of the policy initiatives and much of the impetus for the development of the human-security discourse and acting as the largest contributor to the human security–related practices and institutions of the United Nations.

The concept of human security is in fact rooted in the ideals of the United Nations, which was founded on the principle that it would always give equal weight to all territories and people. In 1945, the U.S. secretary of state, Edward Stettinius Jr., reported to his government the conclusions from the San Francisco meeting that led to the establishment of the United Nations:

> The battle of peace has to be fought on two fronts. The first is the security front where victory spells freedom from fear. The second is the economic and social front where victory means freedom from want. Only victory on both fronts can assure the world of an enduring peace. . . . No provisions that can be written into the Charter will enable the Security Council to make the world secure from war if men and women have no security in their homes and their jobs.[13]

Stettinius suggested that there were two major components of human security, freedom from fear and freedom from want, arguing that both should be given equal weight.[14] During the great bipolar conflict between the United States and the Soviet Union, with the looming shadow of mutually assured destruction, perhaps not surprisingly the focus was more on the freedom from fear rather than freedom from want. Yet as intrastate conflicts or conflicts involving nonstate actors have sharply increased since the end of the Cold War, the international community has struggled to respond effectively. The complexity of the many perils threatening people's daily lives has tended to involve transnational dimensions and reach beyond national security. Such threats encompass poverty, unemployment, drugs, terrorism, environmental degradation, and social disintegration.[15] In response to these recent threats, the concepts of security and poverty have changed. The former began to address security threats that are not at the national level, and the latter began to look seriously at how security directly affects poverty.

The changing understanding of security was also driven by many developing countries that were sensitive to any threats to their already fragile national identity after their recent independence.[16] In some cases, protection of national identity came at the expense of ignoring the concerns of citizens seeking security in their daily lives. For these common citizens, security meant "protection from the threat of disease, hunger, unemployment, crime, social conflict, political repression and environmental hazards," the very things that would grant their daily survival.[17] The international community also began to see security threats not only *between* but also *within* states and focus on people in addition to states.[18] This posed a challenge to the existing concept of security, which was exclusively concerned with territorial integrity and national sovereignty. It is in this context that the term "human security" was devised to shed light on the significance of security at the level of individuals.

Although distinct in terms of focus and (when looking at elements of human security) referential objects, there remains a close relationship between traditional and non-traditional security approaches. National insecurity can divert resources from human development. It can constitute a severe drain on energy supplies—a particular concern in a state where energy security is already challenged and blackouts are a regular feature of public life. It can create a permissive political climate in which national security is privileged over human rights and the individual is sacrificed for the "national interest." Furthermore, it is likely to produce and perpetuate an operating environment within which the use of internal as well as external violence by the state becomes the norm. Meanwhile, desperate conditions among the disaffected youth of refugee camps or inner cities can produce fertile breeding grounds for religious extremism or terrorism. Mass cross-border migration patterns, whether in terms of refugees or economic migrants and whether legal or illegal, can contribute to an increase in interethnic tensions in the new host country and also in crime, whether petty or organized transnational. Thus human insecurity can itself become a source of insecurity for states.

A non-traditional security issue has the potential to become a traditional security threat, and issues of human security can morph into ones of pressing concern for the survival of states themselves or the peace and security of a region or even the globe. It may thus be in the enlightened self-interest of states and statesmen as well as the international community, however broadly defined, to pay attention to non-traditional and human-security concerns.

National, traditional, non-traditional, and human-security approaches are all interrelated and nonexclusionary. The following section addresses the relationship between human insecurity and underdevelopment, a key consideration for analysis of non-traditional security perspectives on North Korea.

HUMAN SECURITY

Human security is an emerging multidisciplinary paradigm for understanding global vulnerabilities at the level of individual human beings. It incorporates methodologies and analysis from a number of research fields, including strategic and security studies, development studies, human rights, international relations, and the study of international organizations. It exists at the point where these disciplines converge on the concept of protection. The Commission on Human Security, established under the chairmanship of Sadako Ogata, former UN high commissioner for refugees, and Amartya Sen, Nobel Economics Prize laureate, in its final report, *Human Security Now*, defines human security as follows:

> Protecting fundamental freedoms . . . that are the essence of life . . . protecting people from critical (severe) and pervasive (widespread) threats and situations. . . . Using processes that build on people's strengths and aspirations . . . creating political, social, environmental, economic, military and cultural systems that together give people the building blocks of survival, livelihood and dignity.[19]

Proponents of a "narrow" concept of human security (a freedom-from-fear emphasis that underpins both the UN responsibility to protect approach and that of the Human Security Report Project's *Human Security Report*) focus on violent threats to individuals while recognizing that these threats are strongly associated with poverty, lack of state capacity, and various forms of socioeconomic and political inequity. Proponents of the "broad" concept of human security such as that articulated in the United Nations Development Programme's 1994 *Human Development Report* and the Commission on Human Security's 2003 report *Human Security Now* argue that the threat agenda should be broadened to include hunger, disease, and natural disasters because these kill far more people than war, genocide, and terrorism combined.

All proponents of human security agree, however, that its primary goal is the protection of individuals. Whereas national security focuses on the defense of the state from external attack, human security is about protecting individuals and communities from *any* form of threat to their well-being or even their very existence. Although relatively new, the term is now widely used to describe the complex of interrelated threats to individual human well-being associated with interstate war, civil war, genocide, ethnic cleansing, the displacement of populations, natural disasters, and pandemics. Some of the broadest interpretations include aspects of security related to food, health, the environment, communities, politics, and human rights. In this volume, chapters 3 and 8 look at broader aspects of human security with regard to women and refugees, respectively.

The closest relationship between security and development in both theory and practice is that found between human security envisioned as the protection of persons and human development as the provision of basic human needs. Human security and human development are both people centered. They challenge the orthodox approach to security and development—that is, state security and liberal economic growth, respectively. Both human security and human development emphasize that people are to be seen as the ultimate ends but never as means and treat humans as agents who should be empowered to participate in the process of their own need satisfaction. Both perspectives are multidimensional and address people's dignity as well as their material and physical concerns. Both impose duties on the wider global community. Hence, in terms of a narrow focus, in December 2001 the International

Commission on Intervention and State Sovereignty released a report entitled *The Responsibility to Protect.*

In the intervening years this new paradigm has gained momentum and garnered international recognition. In response to this international normative shift, at the High-Level Plenary Meeting for the 2005 World Summit (September 14–16), the world's leaders agreed on a "responsibility to protect" (RtoP) that includes a "clear and unambiguous acceptance by all governments of the collective international responsibility to protect populations from genocide, war crimes, ethnic cleansing and crimes against humanity." Resolution 1674, adopted by the UN Security Council on April 28, 2006, "reaffirm[s] the provisions of paragraphs 138 and 139 of the 2005 World Summit Outcome Document regarding the responsibility to protect populations from genocide, war crimes, ethnic cleansing and crimes against humanity" and commits the Security Council to action to protect civilians in armed conflict.[20]

Nonviolent challenges and the inactions or incompetence of states may, however, actually pose a greater threat to human security, especially in terms of freedom from want, than that of violent actions in terms of freedom from fear. Whereas states clearly have a duty not to harm their citizens and the international community has a duty to come to the aid of victims of internal as well as external aggression, little has been said about the duty states owe to their citizens in terms of providing for their basic human needs or that owed by the international community when states fail to act. Freedom from want is becoming more important in both absolute and relative terms than freedom from fear. As mentioned and as is particularly relevant to the North Korean case, hunger, disease, and natural disasters all kill far more people than overt acts of violence. But also war-related deaths have been declining, and the international community is both more likely to be informed of internal acts of aggression and more likely to act against them than in previous decades.

Human security and development can be seen as mutually reinforcing. Hence in his January 2009 speech to the U.S. Institute of Peace, World Bank president Robert Zoellick pointed out the need for a stronger link between security, governance, and development. A peaceful environment frees individuals and governments to move from a focus on mere survival to a position where they can consider improvement of their situations. Likewise, as a society develops, it is able to afford more doctors, hospitals, welfare networks, internal security operations, schools, and mine-removal operations.

On the other hand, as former UN secretary-general Kofi Annan observed in his report *In Larger Freedom*, "we will not enjoy security without development, development without security, and neither without respect for human rights. Unless all these causes are advanced, none will succeed."[21] Conflict retards development and underdevelopment can lead to conflict. According to Dharam Ghai, as of 2003, of the forty-nine lesser-developed countries, twenty-one have experienced grave episodes of violence and instability in the past three decades.[22] Indeed, the prevalence of warfare around the globe has resulted in postconflict development "become[ing] the norm rather than the exception."[23] The negative reinforcement of insecurity and underdevelopment can continue long after the official cessation of hostilities. Postbellum threats to both life and well-being include the breakdown of law and order, the spread of disease as a result of refugee-camp overcrowding, poor nutrition, infrastructure collapse, scarcity of medical supplies (although ironically often a proliferation of illicit drugs), continued criminal attacks on civilian populations, unemployment, displacement, homelessness, disrupted economic activity, explosive remnants of war, and stagflation.

Some of the key non-traditional security challenges facing North Korea that are also likely to spill over into the traditional interstate security operating environment can be found in the preceding list. Poor governance combined with a number of exogenous forces and events have undermined the human security and development of North Korea. The next section addresses the mechanisms and processes through which North Korean internal insecurity transfers to the international operating environment and contributes to the traditional security dilemma.

TRADITIONAL AND NON-TRADITIONAL SECURITY DILEMMAS

North Korea has a long history of brinksmanship, using incendiary rhetoric often aimed at its target's deepest fears to improve Pyongyang's leverage.[24] In addition, ever since the terrorist attacks on September 11, 2001, and the infamous "axis of evil" speech, much has been written about U.S. aggressive unilateralism and the heightened possibility of war on the Korean Peninsula.[25] Events such as reports of the North Koreans restarting their nuclear program, the United States attacking the first member of the axis, and the sinking of a South Korean naval vessel may be seen to have brought such a conflict even closer.[26] As mentioned, in traditional security and strategic analysis, a security dilemma exists when the military capabilities of one state, even if they are perceived by that state as being for defensive purposes to deter others from aggression, are viewed by other states as a potential threat.[27] Thus, North Korean acquisition of enhanced military capabilities, particularly those with long-range force projection (such as missiles) or mass destruction potential (such as nuclear weapons), is seen as posing a threat to the security of other parties.

In the wake of a second, more successful North Korean nuclear weapon test on May 25, 2009, therefore, and the test-firing of more missiles the following day, South Korea and the United States upgraded the threat level and readiness of their forces to the second highest level.[28] South Korea announced it would join the Proliferation Security Initiative, leading to the prospect of South Korean personnel boarding North Korean vessels.[29] The Security Council issued statements of concern and criticism and on June 12 passed resolution 1874 (with the support of both China and Russia) condemning Pyongyang's actions, increasing existing sanctions, and adding some new provisions aimed at curtailing the regime's nuclear activities. Pyongyang responded to criticism from the United States and South Korea by announcing that it was abandoning the truce that ended the Korean War and, further, that it would consider any search or seizure of its vessels an act of war to which it would respond with a military strike.[30] In response to resolution 1874, the North Koreans asserted that "it has become an absolutely impossible option for North Korea to even think about giving up its nuclear weapons."[31] Indeed, spokespersons and commentators on both sides have described threats emanating from the other as constituting more than the usual saber rattling.[32]

Yet in examining the increased threat posed by an actor, it is important to assess the two components of threat individually: (1) an increased capability of the actor to inflict harm and (2) an increased desire or intent to do so. The importance of recent developments in Northeast Asia is not only that more successful nuclear and missile tests suggest increased North Korean capability but also that they, along with other bellicose statements, may be perceived as indicating more hostile intent. This, however, is subject to debate. Pyongyang has no incentive to restart the Korean War. Pyongyang has few friends, has many more powerful enemies, and has been the target of three hostile policy initiatives from Washington in recent years (labeled part of the "axis of evil," one of the "outposts of tyranny," and targeted by the North Korean Human Rights Act). Brutalized by Japanese occupation during the colonial period, Koreans north and south of the border have viewed Japanese moves to "normalize" (for which some read "militarize") Japan's foreign and security policy with trepidation, and Tokyo has likewise recently issued a number of anti-Pyongyang statements.[33] After two consecutive liberal administrations in Seoul, South Korea has turned away from the constructive engagement of the "Sunshine Policy," taking under President Lee Myung-bak a far more hard-line approach and linking any further aid to progress on human rights and security, to which Pyongyang has responded, "The group of traitors [in the South] has already reduced all the agreements reached between the North and the South in the past to dead documents."[34]

Pyongyang may thus feel that it needs to increase its capabilities to ward off attack from others, and the perceived threat posed by North Korea may be the result of a security dilemma whereby arming for self-protection nevertheless is seen as hostile and potentially dangerous by other parties. Furthermore, what friends North Korea does have may not be reliable in the future. According to Andrew Coe, "Pyongyang's ballistic missile and nuclear weapons programs had been initiated precisely because Kim Il-sung recognized that his patrons' commitments might be revised or even reversed."[35] The country may project the image of a strong, secure state: a one-million-strong army; nuclear weapons and missiles; and the military-first politics of Kim Jong Il, combined with risky provocations and harsh rhetoric such as threatening to turn Seoul into a "sea of fire." But such a projected image, which well serves Pyongyang's purpose of deterrence while giving it leverage at diplomatic negotiations, is misleading.

It is not in fact the increasing strength of North Korea that poses the threat to regional security but rather Pyongyang's increasing weakness—an "insecurity dilemma" rather than a security dilemma. For Georg Sørensen, an insecurity dilemma exists when inwardly weak but outwardly strong states pose an intervention dilemma for liberal states—they do not pose a threat to others but do pose a threat to their own people.[36] The term is used slightly differently here in that in addition to posing a threat to its own people, the insecure state's vulnerability is projected outward as a diversionary and unifying tactic, thereby causing international uncertainty and instability and even potential security threats to neighboring states and their allies, almost as a form of collateral damage.

Although considerably the architect of its own demise, North Korea has also been disadvantaged by developments in its international operating environment that have fostered a belief (even if erroneous) in the need for, or justification of, policies that have further undermined internal development and human security. During the Cold War period, North Korea had relied on the former Soviet Union and China for critical resources, such as petroleum, at a concessional rate. More recently, however, with the waning of support from its allies, Pyongyang has prioritized energy sovereignty in its strategy by privileging domestic sources and minimizing its reliance on trade. As pointed out in chapter 1 of this volume, the North has pursued an energy strategy emphasizing sovereignty because of its concerns about national security. The sense of insecurity at the national level has, in other words, led Pyongyang to adopt energy policies that contribute ultimately to the underproduction and inefficient use of energy. The exploration in chapter 2 of this volume of the causes and consequences of North Korean energy insecurity ends with the conclusion that "the impacts of energy insecurity in the DPRK affect every sector and profoundly affect industrial output, the availability of transport services, agricultural production, military posture, and, in many different ways, human welfare."

North Korea has emphasized sovereignty also in its food policies. The North's food strategy reflects its profound sense of insecurity in the face of larger, more affluent, and militarily stronger neighbors. Its dependence on any one, or combination, of them would make North

Korea vulnerable to the use or threat of use of their influence, potentially compromising Pyongyang's sovereign ability to provide for security. The insecure state therefore embraced food sovereignty with zeal. The policy has, however, proven disastrous for human security. Although it boosted agricultural productivity in the early decades, it began to show its limits in the 1980s when the growth rate of rice production began to slow. When hit by the combination of the natural disasters of the 1990s and the collapse of the Soviet bloc that cut off petroleum and other inputs essential for agricultural production, the limits of food sovereignty exploded into mass starvation and famine.[37] As chapter 5 in this volume highlights, despite limited reforms there is a continuing food crisis in North Korea, and indeed the impact of any reforms is constrained by lack of infrastructure and by price and market controls that reduce farmer incentives to increase production of staple grains and obstruct investment in farm equipment, maintenance, and supplies necessary for sustainable production. Chapter 6 in this volume addresses the challenges facing the international community of aiding North Korea with its food insecurity.

With regard to North Korean belligerence, from an external perspective, if the international community is overly concerned with what North Korea is projecting into the external operating environment, then less attention may be paid to meddling in the internal processes of power succession—certainly a consideration in the context of the North Korean Human Rights Act and the floating of balloons to the North carrying propaganda and currency by South Korean nongovernmental organizations (NGOs).[38] An additional external consideration is that if other states become sufficiently concerned about the deterioration of the systemic security of Northeast Asia, they may ultimately be willing to grant the comprehensive peace treaty for which North Korea has been pushing.[39] This is the interpretation placed on the sinking of the *Cheonan* by at least one former South Korean officer and current security commentator.[40]

From an internal perspective, the generation of an external threat has traditionally been used as a tool for uniting a divided country in time of crisis around the flag, the party, or perhaps the army. North Korea used the "hostile" international environment to justify domestic policy. As a result, "the 'military first policy' becomes a useful tool both domestically and internationally."[41] One explanation for the attack on the *Cheonan*, if indeed it was sunk by a North Korean torpedo, is that it was an attempt by the leadership to show solidarity with the armed forces and improve their morale through gaining revenge for the earlier 2009 naval clash and humiliating defeat.[42] O Kuk Ryol, a North Korean hard-liner and Kim Jong Il loyalist, was implicated by some in the *Cheonan* incident, but he was also deeply enmeshed in the succession politics, supporting the controversial candidacy of Kim Jong Eun, the young, third son of the former leader.[43] Thus the roots of the international military operation can be seen in domestic mass and elite politics.

CONCLUSION

Previous North Korean belligerence could well have been a smoke screen meant to distract from governance failure in Pyongyang and the internal problems of succession given the failing health of Kim Jong Il, the unsuitability of his sons, and a potential power struggle between the party, the army, and the Kim family and its supporters. In other words, the overly aggressive nature of Pyongyang's actions and statements came not from strength based on new capabilities but from weakness generated by internal crisis. These internal frailties have changed little with the succession, thus, not surprisingly, their outward projection in terms of brinksmanship has continued. North Korea poses a threat because of its inherent internal instability and its deliberate generation of external instability in order to distract from internal fault lines but not because of developing greater military capability or the intent to use such capability against its enemies.

The decline of North Korean capabilities rather than their augmentation is what truly threatens. Civil war or implosion could lead to an even greater exodus of refugees than has been caused by famine and political oppression in North Korea, and this time any criminals or desperados in their midst could be armed. Although chapter 4 of this volume finds that the current levels of North Korean criminal activities are probably lower than estimated by commentators or portrayed in the international media, it nonetheless registers concern about the consequences of a collapsing regime in the North. Regardless of the actual physical impact of increased North Korean criminal activity, regional and global perceptions and the securitization of the issue could further contribute to the international security dilemma. Of most concern, both military technology and weapons of mass destruction could diffuse to other undesirable state and nonstate actors.[44]

If North Korea collapses, the resulting power vacuum could lead to conflict between neighboring states that would rush to fill the void. As pointed out by Kei Koga, "without any coordination on contingency among them, it is highly likely that the other five states will face grave security risks, including flows of refugees and the proliferation of nuclear weapons and cruise missiles to such non-state actors."[45] Not surprisingly, then, Russia has already increased security on the short border shared with North Korea.[46] China has long-standing historical claims on much of the territory of North Korea and entered the Korean War when UN forces got too close to the Chinese border. South Korea would hope for support from the United States in unifying the peninsula, since both would fear the expansion of China to the border with the South.

The changing nature of the international normative environment may well have imposed upon us an obligation to protect the lives of North Koreans and even a duty to provide for their basic human needs. This chapter has also demonstrated, however, that it is in the narrow self-interest of the key actors in international affairs to address the insecurity dilemma facing the Pyongyang regime lest it contribute to an international security dilemma. Doing so requires thinking outside the box in terms of engagement and the promotion and protection of human security and development but also thinking inside the black box of foreign and security policy decision making, examining the various pushes and pulls acting on policy formation rather than viewing North Korea as a single, monolithic, unitary rational actor. This may well entail better strategic utilization of nonstate entities such as NGOs. Indeed, with the democratization of the media and the huge growth in the number and impact of NGOs, it has become harder for governments to perpetrate, cover up, or turn a blind eye to inhumane practices in their jurisdictions or in those of other states. What is certain is that traditional security perspectives appear to have done little either to deescalate crises in Northeast Asia or to provide for the non-traditional security of some of the world's most vulnerable people.

Nevertheless, alleviating North Korea's traditional security concerns may be a prerequisite to addressing the non-traditional security concerns of its people. Pyongyang has long craved a comprehensive peace treaty, and given the impracticalities of actually intervening in North Korea to put an end to both traditional and non-traditional threats, it may be time to consider granting that desire.[47] Indeed, to a certain extent the international community is responsible for dragging its heels on this issue and is thereby indirectly responsible for the human security consequences. Section 3 of the 1994 Agreed Framework between the United States and North Korea pledges both sides to work together for peace and security and for a nuclear-free Korean Peninsula.[48] Although Pyongyang clearly violated the second half of this clause, it could be argued that more could have been done by Washington regarding the first part. In fact, section 2 pledges that the two sides will move toward full normalization of political and economic relations, yet America and its allies have made little progress in this direction and refuse even to recognize the North Korean state while continuing to impose economic sanctions.

Human security is most noticeable in its absence, as in the case of North Korea. The country lags behind in terms of human development and clearly fares particularly poorly when it comes to respect for basic human rights and civil liberties. Misguided by its warped dual policies of *juche* (self-reliance) and *songun* (military first), the government itself is a major source of threat to its people. Economic mismanagement, failed governance, negligence, and state oppression have had grave consequences for ordinary citizens, and the country remains deep in distress despite recent, flawed attempts at reform and the inflow of international aid.

On the other hand, international aid efforts have failed to alleviate human security challenges in North Korea and their consequent spillover into traditional security considerations in Northeast Asia. Current distrust in both the North Korean government and in the international community hampers the effectiveness of aid and has contributed to donor fatigue. In the first ten years of the Consolidated Appeals by the World Food Programme (WFP), the Food and Agriculture Organization, the United Nations Development Programme, the United Nations Children's Fund, the World Health Organization, the Office for the Coordination of Humanitarian Affairs, the United Nations Population Fund, and various NGOs, total humanitarian assistance to North Korea amounted to $U.S.2.427 billion, and this does not include the bilateral and multilateral commitments made by the United States, China, Japan, and South Korea.[49] Donations had, however, started to dwindle by 2005, and yet another series of floods devastated the nation in 2006.

The WFP, which feeds nearly one-third of the population, spoke out in 2008 about the increasing difficulty of getting donations, and a senior UN official warned that the Pyongyang office risked closure if more funding was not forthcoming.[50] Unlike the food aid the WFP distributes to selected target groups such as flood victims and pregnant or nursing women, the aid that passes through local Public Distribution System warehouses before being distributed via schools, orphanages, and hospitals is subject to diversion, which exasperates donors.[51] At the same time, the North Korean government distrusts aid agencies and restricts their operation by demanding long notice periods before visits to rural areas and banning the use of translators not provided by the government.

If aid is to succeed as a policy for improving the non-traditional security of the North Korean people, there needs to be a more constructive relationship between recalcitrant North Korean agencies and the donor community. This in turn is most likely to be achieved through a shift in focus from traditional state-centric and monolithic engagement to one where nonthreatening international nongovernmental actors approach key stake holders in Pyongyang and the North Korean provinces over specific non-traditional security issues such as the disabled, education, and the environment. Substantial progress has already been made in these areas through unheralded and unreported "backdoor" and "side-door" negotiations from both North Korea and the international community.[52] The political sensitivity of such interactions for both sides may mean, however, that at least for the foreseeable future they remain not only non-traditional but also unacknowledged.

NOTES

1. See generally Carl von Clausewitz, *On War*, trans. J. J. Graham (London: Gutenberg, 1909).
2. Theodore Abel, 'The Element of Decision in the Pattern of War,' *American Sociological Review* 6 (December 1941): 59.
3. See Graham Allison and Philip Zelikow, *Essence of Decision: Explaining the Cuban Missile Crisis*, 2nd ed. (New York: Longman, 1999).
4. Edward H. Carr, *The Twenty Years' Crisis* (London: Macmillan, 1939).
5. Allison and Zelikow, *Essence of Decision*, 32.
6. Hans Morgenthau, *Politics among Nations: The Struggle for Power and Peace*, 6th ed. (New York: Knopf, 1985), 6.
7. Gary King and Christopher Murray, "Rethinking Human Security," *Political Science Quarterly* 116, no. 4 (2001): 588.
8. Arnold Wolfers, " 'National Security' as an Ambiguous Symbol," *Political Science Quarterly* 67, no. 4 (1952): 481.
9. Erica-Irene A. Daes, *Freedom of the Individual under Law: An Analysis of Article 29 of the Universal Declaration of Human Rights* (Geneva: United Nations Centre for Human Rights, 1990).
10. Tsuneo Akaha, "Japan's Comprehensive Security Policy: A New East Asian Environment," *Asian Survey* 31, no. 4 (April 1991): 324–340; Kurt W. Radtke and Raymond Feddema, *Comprehensive Security in Asia: Views from Asia and the West on a Changing Security Environment* (Boston: Brill, 2000).
11. Ole Wæver, "Securitization and Desecuritization," in *On Security*, ed. Ronnie D. Lipschutz, 46–86 (New York: Columbia University Press, 1995).
12. Alan Rix, *Japan's Aid Program: Quantity versus Quality* (Canberra: Australian Government Publishing Service, 1987); Edward A. Olsen, *Homeland Security: Learning from Japan*, November 18, 2004, Independent Institute, Oakland, CA, http://www.independent.org/publications/policy_reports/detail.asp?type=full&id=17 (accessed June 15, 2012).
13. UNDP, *Human Development Report 1994* (New York: Oxford University Press 1994), 24.
14. Ibid.
15. Ibid., 11.
16. Ibid., 22.
17. Ibid.
18. According to the *World Report on Violence and Health*, only seven out of one hundred ten conflicts recorded between 1989 and 2000 were between

states, and the rest were civil wars; see WHO, *World Report on Violence and Health* (Geneva: WHO, 2002), 218.

19. Commission on Human Security, *Human Security Now: Final Report* (New York: CHS, 2003), 4.
20. United Nations, *2005 World Summit Outcome*, September 14–16, 2005, http://www.un.org/summit2005/presskit/fact_sheet.pdf (accessed June 15, 2012); UN Security Council, Resolution 1674 (2006), 5,430th meeting, April 28, 2006, S/RES/1674 (2006), http://www.unrol.org/files/S-Res-1674%20on%20protection%20civilians%20in%20armed%20conflict%20(28Apr06).pdf (accessed June 15, 2012).
21. UN General Assembly, Fifty-ninth Session, *In Larger Freedom: Towards Development, Security and Human Rights for All*, March 21, 2005, A/59/2005, http://daccess-dds-ny.un.org/doc/UNDOC/GEN/N05/270/78/PDF/N0527078.pdf?OpenElement (accessed June 15, 2012).
22. Dharam Ghai, "Least Developed Countries," in *The Elgar Companion to Development Studies*, ed. David A. Clark, 333–336 (Cheltenham, UK: Edward Elgar, 2006).
23. Gerd Junne and Willemijn Verkoren, *Postconflict Development: Meeting New Challenges* (Boulder: Rienner, 2005), 318.
24. This section draws on material prepared for "North Korea's Insecurity Dilemma," *North Korean Review* 6, no. 10 (Fall 2010): 74–85.
25. Nicholas J. Wheeler, "To Put Oneself into the Other Fellow's Place: John Herz, the Security Dilemma and the Nuclear Age," *International Relations* 22, no. 4 (2008): 504.
26. Sheena Chestnut, "Illicit Activity and Proliferation: North Korean Smuggling Networks," *International Security* 32, no. 1 (Summer 2007): 80.
27. Wheeler, "To Put Oneself into the Other Fellow's Place," 494.
28. Blaine Harden, "S. Korean, U.S. Forces Raise Alert Level," *Washington Post*, May 29, 2009, http://www.washingtonpost.com/wp-dyn/content/article/2009/05/28/AR2009052800372.html (accessed June 15, 2012).
29. Ian Davis, "Containing Nuclear North Korea: Intercepting Shipping Imports to North Korea Will Not Bring the Nuclear Crisis to End, but It Could Buy Us Some Vital Time," *Guardian*, May 28, 2009, http://www.guardian.co.uk/commentisfree/2009/may/28/north-korea-shipping (accessed June 15, 2012).
30. "N Korea Threatens Military Action," *BBC News*, May 27, 2009, http://news.bbc.co.uk/2/hi/8069457.stm (accessed June 15, 2012).
31. Martin Fackler, "North Korea Vows to Produce Nuclear Weapons," *New York Times*, June 13, 2009, http://www.nytimes.com/2009/06/14/world/asia/14korea.html (accessed June 15, 2012).

32. "North Korea: Sanctions a Declaration of War," *CNN*, April 18, 2009, http://www.cnn.com/2009/WORLD/asiapcf/04/18/nkorea.threat/index.html (accessed June 15, 2012); "North Korea Accuses South of Declaring War," *Reuters*, January 24, 2010, http://www.reuters.com/article/idUSTRE60N06C20100124 (accessed June 15, 2012); "North Korea Threatens War as It Tears Up 50-Year Armistice," *Times*, May 28, 2009, http://www.timesonline.co.uk/tol/news/world/asia/article6369797.ece (accessed June 15, 2012).
33. Donald Kirk, "North Korea Plays on Tokyo's Mind," *Asia Times*, March 6, 2010.
34. Committee in charge of inter-Korean affairs in a statement carried by the state-run Korean Central News Agency, January 30, 2009.
35. Andrew J. Coe, "North Korea's New Cash Crop," *Washington Quarterly* 28, no. 3 (2005): 74.
36. Georg Sørensen, "After the Security Dilemma: The Challenges of Insecurity in Weak States and the Dilemma of Liberal Values," *Security Dialogue* 38, no. 3 (2007): 357–378.
37. Stephan Haggard and Marcus Noland, *Hunger and Human Rights: The Politics of Famine in North Korea* (Washington, DC: U.S. Committee for Human Rights in North Korea, 2005), 14.
38. Peter Schurmann, "Balloons—Not Missiles—Raise Tensions between North and South Korea," November 24, 2008, *New America Media*, http://news.newamericamedia.org/news/view_article.html?article_id=e4f8f7d23f80ad98e33090dac7a8b65f&from=rss (accessed June 15, 2012).
39. Peter Walker, "North Korea Calls for Peace Treaty with US," *Guardian*, January 11, 2010.
40. Interview with Sang-soo Lee, Korea National Defense University, April 9, 2010.
41. Kei Koga, "The Anatomy of North Korea's Foreign Policy Formulation," *North Korean Review* 5, no. 2 (Fall 2009): 29.
42. Sang-ho Song, "Military Spy Agency Believes Ship Attacked by N.K.: Sources," *Korea Herald*, April 23, 2010.
43. Kim So-hyun, "What Are the Motives behind the Cheonan Attack?" *Korea Herald*, May 27, 2010.
44. Sheena Chestnut, "Illicit Activity and Proliferation: North Korean Smuggling Networks," *International Security* 32, no. 1 (Summer 2007): 80–111.
45. Koga, "Anatomy of North Korea's Foreign Policy Formulation," 30.
46. Adrian Blomfield, "North Korea: Russia Takes Extra Security Measures in Case of Nuclear Conflict," *Telegraph*, May 27, 2009, http://www.telegraph.co.uk/news/worldnews/asia/northkorea/5394262/North-

Korea-Russia-takes-extra-security-measures-in-case-of-nuclear-conflict.html (accessed June 15, 2012).

47. Stephanie Hoo, "North Korea's Insistence on Nonaggression Treaty Could Hinder Talks, Says South Korean Official," Associated Press, January 31, 2003.
48. "Agreed Framework between the United States of America and the Democratic People's Republic of Korea," October 21, 1994, Geneva, http://www.kedo.org/pdfs/AgreedFramework.pdf (accessed June 15, 2012) [circulated by the Korean Peninsula Energy Development Organization].
49. Haggard and Noland, *Hunger and Human Rights*, appendix 2.1.
50. "Donor Fatigue Threatens Aid for North Korea," *Financial Times*, March 3, 2010.
51. Haggard and Noland, *Hunger and Human Rights*, 24.
52. Based on conversations held at the workshop "Towards a Human Security Framework for North Korea: Promoting Human Rights through Pragmatic Approaches," Chatham House, London, December 2–3, 2010. The "Chatham House Rule" allows no direct attribution of sources.

CONTRIBUTORS

Tsuneo Akaha is professor of international policy studies and director of the Center for East Asian Studies at the Monterey Institute of International Studies in Monterey, California. He received his Ph.D. in international relations from the University of Southern California. His most recent publication, *The U.S.-Japan Alliance: Balancing Hard and Soft Power in East Asia* (2010, coedited with David Arase), was given a Masayoshi Ohira Memorial Award Special Prize. Other recent publications include "Japon: Le difficile équilibre entre soft power et hard power," *Politique étrangère* 76, no. 1 (2011); "Human Movement across National Borders in East Asia: From a Human Security Perspective," in *Transcending: Prospects of Borderless Politics*, ed. Takashi Oshimura (2010, in Japanese); " 'China' in the Contemporary Nationalists' Reconstruction of 'Japan,' " in *Reconceptualising the Divide: Identity, Memory, and Nationalism in Sino-Japanese Relations*, ed. Gerrit Gong and Victor Teo (2010); "International Migration and Multicultural Coexistence in Japan: Resistance and Accommodation to Change," *Journal of Asiatic Studies* 53, no. 2 (2010); and "Human Security in East Asia: Embracing Global Norms through Regional Cooperation in Human Trafficking, Labor Migration, and HIV/AIDS," *Journal of Human Security* 5, no. 2 (2009).

Peter Hayes is executive director of the Nautilus Institute for Security and Sustainable Development, a nongovernmental policy-oriented research and advocacy group. He graduated with a degree in history from the University of Melbourne. He has a Ph.D. from the Energy and Resources Group at the University of California, Berkeley. Professionally active as an environment and energy consultant in developing countries (for the Asian Development Bank, Canadian International Development Research Council, United Nations Development Programme, United Nations Environment Programme, United States Agency for International Development, and the World Bank), he also writes widely about security affairs in the Asian-Pacific region. He was executive director of the Environment Liaison Centre in Nairobi, Kenya, 1974–1976. He was deputy director of the Commission for the Future (Australian government) from 1989 to 1991. He has visited North Korea seven times. He is a member of the Pacific Council on International Policy and the U.S. Committee of the Council for Security Cooperation in the Asia Pacific. He was awarded a MacArthur Fellowship in 2000.

Brendan Howe is associate professor of international relations and is currently serving as associate director of the Institute for Development and Human Security at Ewha Womans University. Trained at Oxford University (B.A. and M.A., modern history), the University of Kent at Canterbury (M.A., international conflict analysis), the University of Dublin, Trinity College (Ph.D., political science), Georgetown University (international law), and Harvard University (international negotiation), he has held visiting research fellow positions at the Centre for International Security Studies, Sydney University, and at the Research Institute for Strategic Studies, Korea National Defense University, as well as serving as the Posco Research Fellow in Politics, Governance, and Security at the East-West Center in Hawai'i. He has previously taught at Beijing Foreign Studies University, Universiti Malaysia Sarawak, and Merced College, California. Current research interests include security decision making, normative war fighting, and human security and development. He has published extensively on security decision making and East Asian security operating environments.

W. Randall Ireson has contributed to and directed a variety of rural development projects in Asia, including irrigation rehabilitation projects in Pakistan and Laos and integrated rural development projects in Laos. From 1998 to 2007 he directed the American Friends Service Committee (Quaker) agricultural assistance program in North Korea, making numerous trips to North Korea and leading more than a dozen study programs for North Korean agricultural scientists in the United States, China, and Vietnam. Previously he headed the Research and Evaluation unit of the Oregon Department of Corrections and was associate professor of sociology at Willamette University. He received his Ph.D. in development sociology from Cornell University.

David C. Kang is professor at the University of Southern California with appointments in both the School of International Relations and the Marshall School of Business. He is also director of the university's Korean Studies Institute. His most recent book is *East Asia Before the West: Five Centuries of Trade and Tribute* (2010). His other publications include *China Rising: Peace, Power, and Order in East Asia* (2007); *Crony Capitalism: Corruption and Development in South Korea and the Philippines* (2002); and *Nuclear North Korea: A Debate on Engagement Strategies* (2003, coauthored with Victor Cha). Kang has published numerous scholarly articles in journals such as *International Organization* and *International Security,* as well as opinion pieces in the *Financial Times, Los Angeles Times, New York Times, Washington Post,* and numerous Korean and Chinese newspapers. He is also a regular consultant for both multinational corporations and U.S. government agencies. He was previously professor of government and adjunct professor at the Tuck School of Business, Dartmouth College. He has been a visiting professor at Stanford University, Yale University, Seoul National University, Korea University, and the University of Geneva. He received an A.B. with honors from Stanford University and Ph.D. from the University of California, Berkeley.

Shin-wha Lee is professor in the Department of Political Science and International Relations at Korea University. She received her Ph.D. from the University of Maryland at College Park in 1994 and held a postdoctoral fellowship at Harvard University. She has held various positions at organizations such as the World Bank and the United Nations and visiting professorships at universities such as the Institute for Defense and Strategic Studies (Singapore), Princeton University, and Columbia University's School of International and Public Affairs. She received the Nakasone Yasuhiro Award of Excellence in 2008 and has served as an executive committee member and board member of the Academic

Council on the United Nations System and consultant to various South Korean government ministries, including the Ministry of Foreign Affairs and Trade, Ministry of Defense, Ministry of Reunification, Korean Navy, Korean National Police Agency, and Joint Chiefs of Staff. She has published numerous articles and books, including *South Korean Strategic Thought toward Asia* (2008) and *Promoting Human Security* (2004), which cover the fields of global security, including non-traditional security, international organization, and East Asian foreign policy and security cooperation.

Mark E. Manyin is a specialist in Asian affairs at the Congressional Research Service (CRS), a nonpartisan agency that provides information and analysis to members of the U.S. Congress and their staff. At the CRS, his general area of expertise is U.S. foreign economic policy toward East Asia, particularly Japan, the two Koreas, and Vietnam. He also tracks the evolution of Asia's regional architecture, terrorism in Southeast Asia, and the environmental causes of security tensions in Asia. From 2006 to 2008, he served as the head of the CRS's eleven-person Asia Section, overseeing the service's research on East, Southeast, and South Asia as well as Australasia and the Pacific Islands. Prior to joining the CRS in 1999, he completed his Ph.D. in Japanese trade policy and negotiating behavior at the Fletcher School of Law and Diplomacy. He has written academic articles on Vietnam and Korea, given numerous lectures on U.S.–East Asian relations, taught courses on East Asian international relations, and worked as a business consultant. From 2005 to 2010, he was a Term Member with the Council on Foreign Relations. He is a 2010–2011 Council on Foreign Relations Hitachi Fellow.

Kyung-Ae Park holds the Korea Foundation Chair at the Institute of Asian Research of the University of British Columbia. She is a former president of the Association of Korean Political Studies in North America. She is the author, coauthor, and editor of many scholarly publications on issues ranging from North Korean and South Korean politics and foreign relations to gender and development, including *North Korea in Transition* (2012), *New Challenges of North Korean Foreign Policy* (2010), *Korean Security Dynamics in Transition* (2001), and *China and North Korea: Politics of Integration and Modernization* (1990). She has also authored articles in a number of journals, including *Asian Survey, Comparative Politics, Journal of Asian Studies, Pacific Affairs,* and *Pacific Review.* Since the mid-1990s, she has made several trips to Pyongyang and hosted North Korean delegation visits to Canada, playing a key role in promoting track-two exchanges and diplomacy between Canada and North Korea. She recently set up the Canada-DPRK Knowledge Partnership Program at the University of British Columbia, which has been hosting North Korean professors as part of a long-term knowledge exchange and thus represents an unprecedented, groundbreaking program in North America.

Scott Snyder is director of the Center for U.S.-Korea Policy at the Asia Foundation, a senior associate with the Pacific Forum, Center for Strategic and International Studies, and an adjunct senior fellow for Korean studies at the Council on Foreign Relations. He is based in Washington, DC. He lived in Seoul, South Korea, as Korea Representative of the Asia Foundation during 2000–2004. Previously he served as a program officer in the Research and Studies Program of the United States Institute of Peace and as acting director of the Asia Society's Contemporary Affairs Program. His publications include *China's Rise and the Two Koreas: Politics, Economics, Security* (2008); *Paved with Good Intentions: The NGO Experience in North Korea* (2003, coedited with L. Gordon Flake); and *Negotiating on the Edge: North Korean Negotiating Behavior* (1999). He received his B.A. from Rice University and an M.A. from the Regional Studies East Asia Program at Harvard University. He was the recipient of a Pantech Visiting Fellowship at Stanford University's Shorenstein Asia-Pacific Research Center from 2005–2006, an Abe Fellowship, administered by the Social Sciences Research Council, in 1998–1999, and he was a Thomas G. Watson Fellow at Yonsei University in South Korea in 1987–1988.

Jae-Jung Suh is associate professor and director of the Korea Studies Program in the School of Advanced International Studies, Johns Hopkins University, and distinguished professor in the Graduate School of International Studies, Ewha Womans University. He has previously served as assistant professor in the Department of Government at Cornell University and on the Presidential Commission on Policy Planning

(Republic of Korea). An expert on U.S.-Korea relations, U.S. policy toward Asia, international relations of East Asia, international security, and international relations theory, he has authored and edited numerous journal articles and books, including *Truth and Reconciliation in the Republic of Korea: Between the Present and Future of the Korean Wars* (2012, editor); *Power, Interest and Identity in Military Alliances* (2007); "The Imbalance of Power, the Balance of Asymmetric Terror: Mutual Assured Destruction (MAD) in Korea," in *The Future of US-Korean Relations: The Imbalance of Power*, ed. John Feffer (2006); *Rethinking Security in East Asia: Identity, Power and Efficiency* (2004, coeditor); and "Changes in U.S. Military Strategy and the U.S.-Korea Alliance," *Ch'angjakkwa pip'yŏng*, no. 125 (2004, in Korean). He is the recipient of numerous grants and fellowships, including a Fulbright-Hays Faculty Research Abroad Fellowship, SSRC-MacArthur Foundation Fellowship for Peace and Security in a Changing World, Smith Richardson Foundation grant, and East-West Center fellowship. He has been visiting professor at Seoul National University, research professor at Yonsei University, visiting scholar at Massachusetts Institute of Technology, and visiting fellow at the University of California, Irvine. He holds a Ph.D. and M.A. in political science from the University of Pennsylvania and a B.A. in physics from the University of Chicago.

David von Hippel is based in Eugene, Oregon, and is a senior associate at the Nautilus Institute for Security and Sustainable Development. His work with Nautilus has centered on energy and environmental issues in Asia and particularly in Northeast Asia. He is currently involved in several Nautilus initiatives, including the multination Asia Energy Security Project, centered around energy-paths analysis, and the related East Asia Science and Security Network, which focuses on potential nuclear-materials issues in the region. These projects involve training and working with a group of Northeast Asian energy researchers to develop and evaluate the energy-security implications of different energy paths for their countries. Also for Nautilus, he has done extensive analyses of the patterns of fuels use and prospects for energy efficiency and energy-sector redevelopment in North Korea and is currently involved in preparing an update to Nautilus' DPRK Energy Sector Analysis and in the DPRK Building Energy Efficiency Training project, an engagement activity with a DPRK counterpart. In previous work with Nautilus and other groups he has worked on topics ranging from power-grid integration in Northeast Asia, "clean coal" technologies in China, to utility planning and energy efficiency in the Middle East and reducing greenhouse-gas emissions in several states and the Midwest region in the United States. He holds M.S. and Ph.D. degrees in energy and resources from the University of California, Berkeley, and M.A. and B.S. degrees from the University of Oregon.

INDEX

HAWAI'I

Production Notes for Park | *Non-Traditional Security Issues in North Korea*
Jacket design by Mardee Melton
Design and Composition by Publishers' Design and Production Services, Inc.
with display and text type in Warnock Pro
Printing and binding by Sheridan Books, Inc.
Printed on 60 lb. House White, 444 ppi